Empire of Ruin

EMPIRE OF RUIN

*Black Classicism and
American Imperial Culture*

━━◦◦◉◦◦━━

JOHN LEVI BARNARD

*To Larry —
With admiration
and gratitude.*

OXFORD
UNIVERSITY PRESS

OXFORD

UNIVERSITY PRESS

Oxford University Press is a department of the University of Oxford. It furthers the University's objective of excellence in research, scholarship, and education by publishing worldwide. Oxford is a registered trade mark of Oxford University Press in the UK and certain other countries.

Published in the United States of America by Oxford University Press
198 Madison Avenue, New York, NY 10016, United States of America.

CIP data is on file at the Library of Congress
ISBN 978-0-19-066359-9

1 3 5 7 9 8 6 4 2
Printed by Sheridan Books, Inc., United States of America

For my parents

Contents

Acknowledgments

THIS BOOK IS more than anything a work of collaboration. It began as a dissertation at Boston University, where I was fortunate enough to have what a friend and colleague once called a "dream team" of advisors. Susan Mizruchi has been unwavering in her belief in the project from the beginning, and while she has always been a tough and honest reader, she has at the same time been my fiercest advocate. Neither the completion of the project nor the trajectory of my career would have been possible without her guidance and support. In addition to being (as everyone knows) a brilliant scholar of nineteenth-century American literature, Maurice Lee is also the best editor I've ever had, and anything I know about crafting an argument I learned from him. Gene Jarrett was the first to identify the politics of classicism as the real thread that held the study together, and I remain deeply indebted to him for his intellectual mentorship and professional advice. Gene's book *Representing the Race: A New Political History of African American Literature* was the model I had always in mind as I struggled in this project to follow in his formidable footsteps. James Winn not only sparked my interest in seventeenth- and eighteenth-century classical translations—and in English poetry of the period more generally—but also provided a model of professionalism as a scholar-teacher to which I can only aspire. Beyond these close advisory relations, BU offered a rich and supportive community of learning. To name only a few, Hunt Howell was a generous reader of the dissertation, Kevin Van Anglen was both a valued teaching mentor and a much-needed guide through certain passages of Ovid, and Laura Korobkin's sharp writing and impassioned teaching inspired me to become an Americanist in the first place.

Harvard University, my working home for an amazing two years, provided unmatched institutional resources and a vibrant and inspiring intellectual community. The Committee on Degrees in History and Literature was a collegial and generative setting, encouraging creative and collaborative modes of teaching, and providing numerous opportunities—both formal and informal—to share and discuss work with brilliant scholars from across the disciplines. I'm especially grateful to Jeanne Follansbee, Mo Moulton, Eoin Cannon, Steve Biel, Molly Geidel, Amanda Claybaugh, and Rachel Anne Gillett for fostering that welcoming and congenial environment, as well as to the students—especially those in my first-year seminar African American Visions of American Empire—for keeping me focused on why we do this work.

Since leaving Harvard, I've found a supportive and congenial home at the College of Wooster. In addition to generously providing research leave, which allowed me to get the book finished and out into the world, the college also introduced me to another community of brilliant and engaged scholar-teachers who have helped to shape my own practice in both regards. I'm especially thankful for conversations and fellowship with my colleagues Leslie Wingard, Leah Mirakhor, Robert Maclean, Ali Salerno, Joe Aguilar, Bryan Alkemeyer, Deb Shostak, Tom and Terry Prendergast, Seth and Jill Kelly, Michael Forbes, Jeff Roche, Tom Tierney, Phil Mellizo, and Shannon King, all of whom have contributed in various ways not only to the life of this project, but to making life good in Wooster, Ohio.

Beyond the walls of any particular institution, my larger network of friends and colleagues across the country and around the world has left me—to borrow a phrase from one of those friends—in "an embarrassment of debt." Jason Leddington—whom I've been consulting about such things since we read the *Odyssey* together in ninth-grade English—commented on early drafts of my articles, and I am much obliged to Jason and the Bucknell University Department of Philosophy for housing me during the summer of 2014, when a good portion the book manuscript was drafted. Arielle Zibrak—for years one of my closest friends and liveliest interlocutors—has been a generous and incisive reader of many a draft of this material. Chris Love—with whom I've been discussing classical matters ever since our lunchtime Plato reading group in San Francisco, so long ago it seems like ancient history—gave extremely helpful feedback on the introduction. Emily Donaldson Field and Aaron Shapiro have offered invaluable advice and more valuable friendship over the years. The book would be a shadow of itself without my friend Benjamin Fagan, who not only turned me on to antebellum black newspapers, but taught me how to read them. It was also Ben who first invited me to present a portion of this work at the Civil War Caucus at the Midwest MLA in 2012. Over the next few years, the project in many ways grew up at the Caucus, and I am deeply indebted to Kathleen Diffley for putting together this collegial group of scholars. At the Caucus and elsewhere, I have benefited greatly from scholarly and social discussions with Julia Stern, Elizabeth Duquette, Coleman Hutchison, Christopher Hanlon, Jeffrey Insko, Nathan Grant, Gregory Laski, Derrick Spires, Andrew Kopec, Ian Finseth, Timothy Sweet, Christopher Hager, Cody Marrs, and Barbara McCaskill.

Portions of chapters 3 and 4 appeared in different forms in *PMLA* and *American Literature*, and I thank the MLA and Duke University Press for permission to reprint that material here. The anonymous reviewers for these journals provided indispensable feedback, as did the readers for Oxford University Press. All of these readers helped to shape the project in ways I never could have conceived on my own, and I can only hope to pay forward the extended time and remarkable care they dedicated to helping to improve my work. Scott Briscoe at Sikkema Jenkins Gallery and Emily Smock at the Ohio State University library provided generous assistance with acquiring images. Finally, many thanks are due to my editors Brendan O'Neill and Sarah Pirovitz at Oxford University Press, as well as to Sasirekka Gopalakrishnan for shepherding the book through production.

Neither the project nor any aspect of my career would have been possible without my family. My parents, Helen and Russ, encouraged me from early on to pursue my literary and scholarly endeavors, even when those endeavors did not look so promising. The late Gretel Neal was also unshakeable in her faith, and I will be forever grateful for her love and generosity. Chris and Esther Pullman have been perpetual and enthusiastic supporters, including providing something of a "residential fellowship" in their Cambridge home as I finished the dissertation. My brother Chris and his partner Lauren Anderson, both professors in different fields, have been inexhaustible in their love and good counsel. And from farther afield, my aunt Ardis, my sister Anne and her husband Thanassis Cambanis, and my very classical nephew and niece—Odysseas and Athina—have all been sources of wisdom, encouragement, and joy.

All that being said, my greatest debt is to Justine Murison, who was generous enough to allow me to join a panel she had arranged at the Midwest MLA in Dearborn, Michigan, and kind enough to allow me to stick around ever since. She has read more drafts than anyone should ever have to, but her care and insight have made the book—and its author—far better than they ever otherwise would have been. Reading and writing together with you has been quite something, by the shine of which—as one of our favorite poets says—we come to "see ourselves whole, see in whole perspective."

Introduction

ON A PROMINENT interior wall of the National September 11 Memorial Museum in New York City, visitors encounter an inscription drawn from book 9 of Virgil's *Aeneid*. "No day shall erase you from the memory of time," the quotation reads, conveying the solemn promise of commemoration to the thousands of victims of the terrorist attacks at the site in 2001. Uncoupled from its context, the sentiment expressed here could have come from anywhere and is entirely uncontroversial. But, returned to its context, the quotation becomes, as the classicist Caroline Alexander pointed out well in advance of the museum's opening, more than a little problematic.[1] The "you" to whom the passage refers are Nisus and Euryalus, a pair of Trojan soldiers who have ambushed their sleeping enemies, slaughtering them in what David Dunlap, writing about the choice of the quotation in the *New York Times*, aptly described as "an orgy of violence."[2] Before the two soldiers can escape, they are discovered and killed by a returning patrol of opposition forces. Taken in context, then, the inscription works against its own purpose, conflating civilian victims of a terrorist attack with combatants deliberately killing their enemies as they sleep.

The committee tasked with selecting a commemorative passage from literature obviously assumed a strict separation of the text from its context, and chose the line, as Alexander has suggested, as merely some "high-sounding, stand-alone phrase."[3] But while the meaning of the quotation is clearly not intended to be informed by its context within the larger epic, which would lead us to a nonsensical blurring of the distinction between innocent victims and violent aggressors, that does not mean, as Alexander concludes, that the selection was "never intended to lead visitors to any more profound thoughts or emotions."[4] Leaving the immediate context aside—which seems reasonable given the generic content of the quotation—the choice of Virgil as the source is in itself significant, and likely to lead visitors to a rather specific array of thoughts and emotions.

Even for those unfamiliar with the particulars of the *Aeneid*, that text and its author may well be understood as "classic" or "classical," and the reference here performs the function the idea of "the classics" has always performed. As Seth Schein has observed, the classical is and always has been ideological, deriving its force not purely "from its relation to a real or imagined past," but in large part "from its relation to current social, political, and moral values that it helps to legitimate."[5] As my focus throughout will be on this ideological dimension of the classical, I will frequently link the term "classicism" to the distinct yet related notion of monumentalism, an aesthetic and historiographical practice—most obviously manifested in the construction of actual buildings and monuments—that "supports the work of nation-building," as Dana Luciano has observed, "by creating, through the manipulation of a mythical past, a feeling of national belonging."[6] Throughout US history, classicism and monumental culture have performed precisely the kinds of work Schein and Luciano have described: contributing to the ideological underpinnings of the Revolutionary War and the nation's founding, providing sites at which to cultivate a collective national identity through historical commemoration, and legitimating and authorizing an expansive imperial project by matching the millennial religiosity of Manifest Destiny with a sense of secular purpose. Through identification with the precedents of Greece and especially Rome, American writers, artists, and political leaders could figure the United States as the inheritor of the best traditions of classical antiquity—whether as a "New Republic" or what Thomas Jefferson would call an "empire for liberty"—and thus as the standard bearer for the idea of civilization itself.[7] While the 9/11 memorial did not intend to alter the victims' status as innocents—whether through direct identification with Nisus and Euryalus or a more general association with the *Aeneid* as the epic of empire—by drawing on Virgil to commemorate them the memorial does enlist the dead in a long and ongoing tradition of appropriating classical history and literature to the narrative of the exceptional progress and the Manifest Destiny of the American nation.

In the pages that follow, I trace the development of a critical practice within African American literature, art, and activism that challenges this appropriation of classical tradition to an American imperial culture. Where dominant narratives—articulated through political speeches and editorials, poetry and the visual arts, and the monumental architecture of Washington, DC—have envisioned the political project of the United States as modeled on ancient Rome yet destined to surpass it in the unfolding of an exceptional history, the writers, artists, and activists I canvass here have connected modern America to the ancient world through the institution of slavery and the geopolitics of empire.[8] The book tracks this critique over more than two centuries, from Phillis Wheatley's poetry in the era of revolution, through the antislavery writings of David Walker, William Wells Brown, and the black newspapers of the antebellum period, to the works of Charles Chesnutt, Toni Morrison, and other twentieth-century writers, before concluding with the monumental sculpture of the contemporary artist Kara Walker.

Such critical engagements with the politics of American classicism began in the revolutionary period and continued across the long nineteenth century, during which the precedent of ancient Rome was central to discourses of US nation building and national identity. A tract entitled *A Sermon, on the Present Situation of the Affairs of America and Great-Britain*, printed in 1782 but dated by the author September 1781, exemplifies the function of the Roman precedent in the context of the American Revolution, as it asserts a typological relationship between Roman republicans opposing the rise of Caesar and American patriots resisting the tyranny of the British Crown. Noting the triumph of superior virtue and valor over superior numbers, the sermon's author argues that "notwithstanding all their boastings," the British "have been fought with bravery equal to that of Romans, by the raw and undisciplined Americans."[9] These Americans, the sermon suggests, should take pride in their steadfast resistance to tyranny, and should look to the heroic figures of republican Rome as justification for the violence of revolution: "Let me once use the language of Semphronius, when he said 'Rise and revenge your slaughtered citizens or share their fate.' "[10]

This call to "rise and revenge" is drawn from Joseph Addison's 1713 play *Cato: A Tragedy*, a text that was foundational for both of the primary strains of classicism I identify within the dominant American culture: first, the libertarian strain, which animated the rhetoric of the Revolution; and, second, the imperial strain, which would inform the ideology of Manifest Destiny as well as its representation in literature, architecture, and other aesthetic forms.[11] While the action of the play largely supports the libertarian strain, a new epilogue to the play, written by the poet Jonathan Sewall for a 1778 performance in Portsmouth, New Hampshire—and later appended to numerous printed editions—makes explicit the imperial mode. Effectively reconciling

the libertarian sentiment of the play with an imperial vision that was coalesc-
ing around the prospect of victory in the war, Sewall's epilogue analogized
George Washington to Cato, while at the same time figuring him as the
future leader of a continental empire. Unlike Cato, who had been trapped
and forced into suicide in his home province of Utica, for Washington and
America, the epilogue declares, "No pent-up Utica contracts your pow'rs, /
But the whole boundless continent is yours."[12]

This openly imperial ambition is equally explicit in the 1782 sermon, which
imagines an expansive future for a postrevolutionary "America": "An empire
which," the author imagines, "will be one of the greatest in the world!"[13] Both
the appeal to Cato and the vision of empire in the sermon are completely
conventional and could have been written or uttered by any number of recognizable contributors to the revolutionary cause. What makes them worth
noting here is that, as the full title of the sermon announces, this particular
iteration was "Written by a Black" from South Carolina. Since the rhetoric of
revolution, influenced by the language of Cato, framed the conflict ideolog-
ically as one between slavery and freedom, it obviously held a certain appeal
for both enslaved and free blacks in the colonies. If the classical tradition, as
Schein argues, has generally served to legitimate existing structures of social
and political power, in the setting of the American Revolution this tradition
became, in fact, potentially revolutionary—not only for the white patriots
who originally invoked it to authorize violent resistance to political slavery,
but for enslaved people seeking a rhetoric through which to argue their own
case for liberation.

Many enslaved people were, for good reason, skeptical of this rhetoric's
applicability to their own situation, and therefore took full advantage of
Lord Dunmore's proclamation of 7 November 1775, which offered liberty
as an incentive to desert and rebel against rebellious slaveholders. Thomas
Jefferson alluded to this policy in the Declaration of Independence, listing
among colonial grievances that the king had "excited domestic insurrection
among us."[14] The sermon by the black southerner—who self-identifies in a
prefatory note as "A Black Whig"—similarly accuses the British of arming
"domestics to fight against their masters," a violation "contrary to the laws
of civilized nations."[15] But if the Revolution had offered two potential paths
to freedom for enslaved people—the one through "domestic insurrection"
and alliance with the British, the other through identification with the
Revolution itself—by the time the Black Whig penned his sermon, open affiliation with the soon-to-be victorious Americans would have been an increasingly pragmatic position to announce. But even Phillis Wheatley—the most

prominent black writer in the colonies at the time—who had chosen from the outset to align herself with the revolutionary cause, announced her affiliation in similar terms, appealing to the principle of freedom and the idea of empire as well as the classical sources from which they were derived. By aligning with the American cause through identification with the historical ideal of Roman liberty, writers like Wheatley in Boston and the Black Whig in South Carolina hoped to link the revolutionary struggle against political slavery to the plight of enslaved people in America. After invoking the valor of the Romans, the Whig makes the connection between political and chattel slavery explicit in a direct appeal to his "fellow citizens": "after you have rid yourselves of the British yoke," he urges, it would be not only consistent but also "virtuous" to "emancipate those who have been all their life time subject to bondage."[16]

My argument here is that we should understand the Whig's sermon not as transparent admiration for either an "American" cause or a "white" cultural tradition but as an example of calculated political rhetoric, crafted from the point of view of enslavement at a moment when emancipation appeared within reach. This rhetoric recognized the two predominant strains of thinking associated with American classicism—the libertarian and the imperial—and appealed to them both as a means of fostering identification of whites and blacks as "fellow citizens," mutually invested in the construction of something like Jefferson's "empire for liberty." Faith in this rhetoric and its underlying assumptions—that the beneficiaries of white supremacist structures of power could be convinced to alter or abandon those structures in the name of ethical consistency and egalitarian democracy—proved to be misplaced, and the "new-born *Rome*" that Wheatley would envision emerging from the Revolutionary War not only adopted a republican form of government and the forms of Roman architecture for its public buildings, but also retained slavery as its economic engine and empire as its geopolitical design.[17] Throughout the nineteenth century, from Jefferson's inauguration to ceremonies of rededication to national unity and expansion after the Civil War, the classics in general and the precedent of Rome in particular would provide legitimation for empire and slavery—as in the nationalist editorials of John L. O'Sullivan, or the proslavery arguments of John C. Calhoun and George Fitzhugh—as well as for the aesthetic and ideological foundations of public historiography and monumental culture. Through this culture, the violence of slavery and empire were assimilated to the narrative of American exceptionalism, and the ideas of American progress and the progress of civilization were rendered one and the same.

Classics and the Language of Power

While "black classicism" as I have thus far described it can be understood as a critical orientation toward a hegemonic classical tradition, the term also refers to what has become in recent years a vibrant field of scholarly research, and this book draws on but also departs from that body of work in various ways.[18] Much of the recent work in black classicism has developed in response—both affirmative and contentious—to the 1987 publication of Martin Bernal's *Black Athena*, which, as its subtitle suggests, advanced a theory of the "Afroasiatic Roots of Classical Civilization."[19] Bernal challenged foundational assumptions in classical studies in two distinct yet related ways: first, by arguing that Greek culture was not "essentially European or Aryan" in its origins, but was instead indebted to the influences of Egyptians and Phoenicians who had colonized the region; and, second, by suggesting that the dominant view, according to which Greece "was seen not merely as the epitome of Europe but also as its pure childhood," was in fact a rather recent development, the product of a white supremacist historiography linked to the larger imperial projects of eighteenth- and nineteenth-century European nations. Bernal thus argues that his own claims are not original, but merely serve to recover what he calls the "Ancient Model" of Greek history, which not only had traction in Europe prior to the eighteenth century, but also had been the "conventional view" among ancient Greeks themselves, who openly acknowledged their cultural indebtedness to Egypt and the Levant.[20]

While Bernal's book may have provided a point of origin for a burgeoning field of scholarly work, his "account," as Daniel Orrells, Gurminder Bhambra, and Tessa Roynon have noted, "of a fabricated intellectual history that had erased interactions between Europe and Africa from the dawn of time was certainly not the first revisionist intervention into the self-serving meta-narratives of the Western world."[21] Indeed, since at least the late eighteenth century, intellectuals of the black diaspora have routinely contested European and American "constructions of the past, present, and future."[22] In this regard, Bernal's argument—that prevailing understandings of Greek history, and thus of the history of the West more generally, were shaped in large part by the ideology of white supremacy and the agenda of empire— is supported by the texts and authors this study will survey. From the antebellum period onward, African American writers and artists have appealed to biblical and classical sources both to challenge exclusive Euro-American claims to a Greco-Roman heritage and to advance the notion of African and Asian civilizational precedence. Henry Highland Garnet, for example, cites

Herodotus in an 1848 address as evidence for the Egyptian origins of the "arts and sciences ... law, poetry, and history," while Pauline Hopkins reiterates this conventional Afrocentrism in her 1903 novel *Of One Blood*, in which a white European professor draws on biblical and classical sources to trace the roots of civilization back through Egypt to an earlier origin in Ethiopia.[23]

In the introduction to his pathbreaking work *Ulysses in Black*, Patrice Rankine has noted that, whatever the merits of *Black Athena*'s revisionary reconstruction of European cultural origins, Bernal's project "at least ... alerted us to the undeniable role of race-thinking in the creation of the discipline of Classical Studies," which emerged concomitantly with the expansion of New World slavery and empire.[24] As Toni Morrison has observed in one of her own key contributions to the field, what was striking about *Black Athena* was not only its account of "the *process* of the fabrication of Ancient Greece," but also its attention to "the *motives* for the fabrication."[25] As Bernal contends, for "18th- and 19th-century Romantics and racists it was simply intolerable for Greece," which they had figured as the point of origin for their own culture, "to have been the result of the mixture of native Europeans and colonizing Africans and Semites." Confronted with this intolerable version of history, white supremacist historiographers determined that "the Ancient Model had to be overthrown and replaced by something more acceptable."[26] This overthrow resulted in two mutually constitutive developments: the whitening of the classical past, and the use of that past as authorizing precedent for the imperial extension of white "civilization" in the present.[27] To put this another way, *Black Athena* identifies the operation of power within a supposedly disinterested philological field, and black classicism as a scholarly endeavor—whether primarily concerned with the literary and cultural history of the United States or that of the broader African diaspora—has focused on the relation between this particular field of knowledge and the exercise of oppressive power.[28]

In the US context, a number of major studies of black classicism have appeared in recent years. This scholarship has tended to focus on either the ways African American writers have appropriated aspects of classical tradition that have been useful in the construction of identity and the articulation of experience, or how certain African American figures aimed to combat racist charges of black intellectual inferiority by succeeding within the fields of academic and literary classicism. Examples of the former would include William Cook and James Tatum's readings of Frederick Douglass's oratorical techniques and Ishmael Reed's affiliation with the genre of Menippean satire, as well as Rankine's exploration of the "Ulysses theme" in the works of Ralph

Ellison and Toni Morrison, and Tracey Walters's analysis of classical appropriation and revision in African American women's writing from Phillis Wheatley to Rita Dove. Michele Valerie Ronnick's recuperation of the lives and works of a number of African American classical scholars—most notably that of William Sanders Scarborough—exemplifies the latter line of inquiry.[29] Eric Ashley Hairston's 2013 monograph, *The Ebony Column: Classics, Civilization, and the African American Reclamation of the West*, combines both approaches, offering comprehensive accounts of the formal and informal classical training of major figures such as Wheatley, Douglass, and Anna Julia Cooper as a basis for a fuller understanding of their literary and political work.[30]

Hairston's work—like that of Cook and Tatum, and even, in different ways, that of Rankine and Walters—aims to elaborate a certain type of affirmative appropriative relationship between black writers and classical tradition, through which "the classics" provided African Americans "a transforming set of ideals that could produce or develop an African-American *cultus* (culture) and *civitas* (citizenship), and enable a black counter-transmission of a virtuous, intelligent, resilient humanity."[31] While my own project acknowledges this type of affirmative relation, in what follows here I diverge from these other scholars in pursuing a specific and pointedly critical strain within black classicism, one that is less about selective appropriation and subversion—and less about the "value" of or "values" to be found within classical tradition—than it is about illuminating the ways certain African American writers and artists have understood the intricate relations between classical tradition and structures of power in the United States. What I draw out of black classicism as a critical practice is less its acknowledgment that "the classics" might be useful to authors writing from the perspective of the oppressed and the enslaved, than an apprehension among its practitioners that classicism is itself central to the cultural hegemony that underlies and authorizes the regime of oppression and enslavement.

Much of the scholarly work on black classicism in the United States tends to read the practice as what Kenneth Warren terms either "instrumental" or "indexical." Warren argues that African American literature—as he identifies it—has generally either contributed instrumentally "to the arsenal of arguments, achievements, and propositions needed to attack" the white supremacist social and political order, or provided "an index of racial progress, integrity, or ability."[32] Ronnick, for example, has done much to develop an intellectual history of black classicism as an index of achievement within white supremacist pedagogical and literary cultures, while Walters, Tatum and Cook, and Hairston demonstrate how African American writers have drawn on classical history, literature, and rhetorical techniques to develop arguments against both slavery and white supremacy.[33] While these prior studies have tended to assimilate African American engagements with classical tradition to one or the other (or both) of Warren's categories, the critical practice I aim to delineate here can be understood as neither instrumental in the sense of providing form or content for arguments in favor of emancipation or racial equality, nor as an "indexical" measure of black intellectual achievement, but rather as a direct and dialectical opposition to the foundations of white American culture in general and the exceptionalist conception of the nation's imperial "mission" in particular.

While I focus on this oppositional stance with respect to the dominant culture of classicism in the United States, this is by no means to say that the writers and artists I consider here have held a monolithic or unambivalent attitude toward the classical tradition itself. Wheatley, Chesnutt, Morrison, Ellison, and others have in various contexts expressed high regard and great admiration for classical works of history and literature, and they all have incorporated a wide range of classical tropes, themes, and allusions in their own literary writings. But this admiration and appropriation is inseparable from a critical understanding of the ways classical tradition has been widely deployed by the dominant culture to assert and maintain its dominance. While I am attentive to the significant intertextual relations between African American literary works and classical precedents, my primary aim is to historicize black classicism more thoroughly by tracing its development in relation to the role of classicism in the dominant culture and situating its various practices within and against the discourses of national identity and mission that have served to reinforce racialized structures of power.[34]

By employing such a dialectical framework, my project aligns most closely with Tessa Roynon's approach to black classicism in *Toni Morrison and the Classical Tradition: Transforming American Culture.* As I will do with a number of figures across a longer African American literary history, Roynon argues "that Morrison's classicism is fundamental to the critique of American culture that her work effects."[35] Roynon's book is an "*oeuvre*-wide" study of "the ways in which classical myth, literature, history, social practice, and religious ritual make their presence felt" in Morrison's novels. But whereas other studies of Morrison's classicism have focused on her adaptation of classical mythology, tragedy, and epic to the project of African American narrative, Roynon attends not only to Morrison's use of classical tradition in the literary reconstruction of African American history and identity within the white supremacist landscape of the United States, but also to her metacritique of the ways that tradition has informed the construction of "white" identity and "American culture as a whole."[36] To develop this reading of Morrison's critique and "transformation" of American culture and historiography, Roynon arranges her book chronologically not with respect to Morrison's literary production, but with respect to American history. Organizing her chapters around consecutive periods—from early conquest and North American settlement to the Great Migration and the civil rights movement—Roynon's readings of Morrison's novels reveal the author's "profound concern" with both the history of American white supremacist violence and the "uses to which dominant narratives of American history and identity have put the classical tradition." Whether "justifying colonization" or "bolstering notions of exceptionalism," such narratives have enabled and—as with the monumental constructions and national celebrations I will discuss in the following chapters—even celebrated that history of violence.[37] My project shares Roynon's focus on a dialectical engagement with "dominant American culture's strategic uses of the Egyptian, Greek, and Roman past," but whereas Roynon's study places a single contemporary author in relation to a number of historical contexts, mine observes this dialectical relation unfolding over the long course of American history, placing texts and contexts into mutually illuminating relations within a sequence of historical periods.

While this study—like those of Walters, Rankine, Cook and Tatum, and Hairston—focuses on a literary and cultural tradition specific to the United States, the project is most closely aligned theoretically with a body of work on transnational black classicism that has been developing at the intersections of classical receptions and postcolonial studies.[38] Most importantly to my own reading of African American responses to and interventions within a hegemonic culture of classicism, postcolonial approaches have emphasized the ways classical tradition can be deployed, as Susan Stephens and Phiroze Vasunia have put it in the introduction to the collection *Classics and National Cultures*, "as a language of power." This language can operate pedagogically, insofar as classical education "has been instrumental in the shaping of elites for nearly two centuries, both among the colonizers and the colonized," but it also operates symbolically, through the appropriation of classical political and aesthetic forms as a means of asserting national identity or imperial authority.[39] In both cases, classical tradition becomes closely associated with the project of empire.

Scholars taking a postcolonial approach to classical reception have done much to illuminate this association. In her introduction to the collection *Classics and Colonialism*, Barbara Goff has detailed the ways "possession of . . . classical heritage" becomes "a metonym for other kinds of possession," and how more generally classical tradition has informed for "European elites" a "vision of the imperial role."[40] In a more recent, book-length study of contemporary drama of the African diaspora, Goff and her collaborator Michael Simpson argue that diasporic writers have engaged Greek culture as "part of the apparatus of colonialism," while Emily Greenwood has noted the ways that "Roman culture has been repeatedly appropriated by colonial powers as a way of shoring up their authority through deceptive recourse to alleged classical precedents."[41] As Goff and Simpson contend, classical antiquity has been effectively "annexed by European culture" as part of a larger claim to the origin point of the idea of "civilization." Such claims provided the ideological authorization for Europeans and Euro-Americans as they "both vaunted the practice of their own cultures and asserted that only they possess the capability and authority to define what culture is; to control the definition of culture," and "to determine who has it and who does not."[42] And such assertions of cultural authority in turn provided authorization for the supposedly "civilizing mission" of empire.

Monuments, Ruins, and the Wreckage of History

This study brings together postcolonial insights on classical tradition as a mechanism of imperial power, while aligning with Roynon's essentially dialectical reading of African American cultural production in relation to dominant American cultures of classical monumentalism and public historiography. As I track this dialectic over the course of US history, I anchor the study in some of the most readily apparent manifestations of the dominant mode of American classicism. From the US Capitol to the Lincoln Memorial and the 9/11 museum, national buildings and monuments have appealed to classical antiquity—and to the precedent of Rome in particular—to commemorate a glorious past and anticipate the exceptional future of the United States. By contrast, the critical tradition I delineate in the following chapters has apprehended this proliferation of classical monumentalism as evidence of national hypocrisy and imperial hubris. Whereas Thomas Jefferson could imagine the neo-Roman edifice of the US Capitol as a fitting home for a democratic government enduring to "the thousandth and thousandth generation," for the abolitionists David Walker, Henry Highland Garnet, and William Wells Brown before the Civil War, and writers like Charles Chesnutt and Toni Morrison in the twentieth century and beyond, such grandiose constructions have signaled the fundamental unsustainability of the American imperial enterprise.[43]

These writers have articulated this sense of the unsustainability of US empire through a practice of contrasting such monumental manifestations of American imperial culture with historical imagery of the ruins of empires. The contemplation of ruins was a popular cultural practice in the late eighteenth century and even more so among nineteenth-century Romantics. Perhaps most famously, Byron's Childe Harold declared himself "A ruin amidst ruins; there to track / Fall'n states and buried greatness," but for African American writers ruins took on a special significance in relation to the burgeoning American empire and its classical style of self-representation. As the United States pursued the course of empire, justified in the popular imagination through the rhetoric of Sewall's epilogue to *Cato*, and commemorated in the classical architecture of its public buildings and national monuments, the writers that I consider in what follows here—from anonymous essayists in the antebellum black press to the first African American Nobel laureate in the field of literature—repeatedly conjure images of ruins in order to draw together the fates of empires past and present.

Refiguring the affirmative association of the dominant culture with classical antiquity—an association that has underpinned theories of American imperial mission from the Revolutionary War to the "War on Terror"—these writers, editors, orators, and artists have transformed classical precedents from powerful signs of American ascendancy to ominous foreshadowings of an American empire in ruins.[44] In both the dominant and the resistant modes of classical historical appropriation, the most prominent analogy was to Rome: white literary and political writers openly claimed the Roman republic as an authorizing classical antecedent for American political and aesthetic forms, while black writers and other abolitionists tended to identify Rome as the locus classicus of slavery and empire. Throughout the antebellum period, such writers constructed analogies between ancient Rome and modern America in order to emphasize the archaic forms of tyranny and slavery operating within a modern nation ostensibly dedicated to democracy and freedom, and to prophesy a grim future for the American nation itself.

From the antebellum period onward, images of Rome in ruins have conveyed not only a sense of the fundamental similarities between ancient Roman and modern American slavery and empire, but also a historical sensibility on the part of African American writers, artists, and activists that runs counter to the predominant understanding of history as linear and progressive. The dominant mode of white American classicism established a typological relation to the classical past, rendering it a prophetic early stage of a progress narrative for which Jefferson's empire for liberty would constitute the culminating fulfillment. This typological relation rests on an understanding of the present—to borrow the terms of Walter Benjamin's historical materialism—as a moment of "transition" within "a chain of events" conceived as a linear progression.[45] In the American context, the present is the moment of transition between the nation's prophetic prehistories—located in the stories of the building and rebuilding of the Temple at Jerusalem and the founding of Rome by the exiled Trojan Aeneas, exodus narratives translated to the New World in the voyages of the *Mayflower* and Columbus—and the providential fulfillment of its Manifest Destiny. By contrast with the easy linearity of this dominant narrative of American progress, for the authors and artists considered in the following pages the present is not what Benjamin would call a mere moment of "transition," but rather a site at which conventionally linear "time" potentially "come[s] to a stop," and from which it becomes possible "to blast open the continuum of history."[46]

Benjamin's materialist "philosophy of history" provides a useful theoretical framework for considering the disruptive temporality this study will identify as an effect of certain African American engagements with the classical past. Henry Highland Garnet conjures a near perfect image of this alternative temporality in the 1848 address "The Past and the Present Condition, and the Destiny, of the Colored Race," an address that aimed—in a moment of maximum tension between the revolutionary energies unleashed by a series of European democratic uprisings and the apparent achievement of American imperial ascendancy at the conclusion of the Mexican War—"to articulate the past" in precisely the manner Benjamin would describe in the context of the rise of German fascism, taking hold of "that image of the past which unexpectedly appears to man singled out by history at a moment of danger."[47] Speaking in 1848, a moment of danger in which the questions of empire and slavery would reach a fever pitch in light of the US conquest of Mexico, Garnet opens by inviting his audience "to travel" a "path of thought" which had not "been pursued heretofore to any considerable extent." This path begins with "The Present," which for Garnet is less a "time" of "transition" than a spatiotemporal coordinate. Garnet asks listeners and readers to join him, to "ascend" the "sublime eminence" of the present, "that we may view the vast empire of ruin that is scarcely discernible through the mists of former ages."[48] This present perspective ruptures "the continuum" of the historiography of progress by spatializing the temporal, making it possible to survey the "vast" sweep of history all at once. From the perspective of the African American historian—whether before the Civil War or after it—the long history of the West appears quite the same as it does to Benjamin's historical materialist, as "wreckage upon wreckage," an accumulation of ruin fit to the scale of an empire.[49]

African American Literature and the Present Past

Garnet's vision of the empire of ruin is emblematic of a historical conscious-ness he shares with the various writers and artists I consider in the following chapters, one largely constituted by a tangible sense of the presence of the past. This apprehension of the past as present allowed antebellum writers like Garnet, Walker, and Brown to connect the freedom struggle of blacks in the nineteenth-century United States to a long history of slavery and empire traceable to both classical and biblical antiquity, while for writers and artists after the Civil War it has informed an ongoing project of representing what Saidiya Hartman has called the "afterlife of slavery."[50]

By contrast, in his provocative 2011 book, *What Was African American Literature?*, Kenneth Warren argues forcefully against what he takes to be a counterproductive fixation in African American literary studies with this idea of the present past. Warren instead makes the case for a more "mundane" conception of history, one that would allow us "to put the past behind us" so that we might finally "understand both past and present."[51] From the premise of this mundane sense of history, Warren proceeds to argue for a periodiza-tion of African American literature that would make it, definitively, a thing of the past. Warren's answer to his own question about African American literature is that it "was" a phenomenon limited to the period between the 1896 Supreme Court decision in *Plessy v. Ferguson* and the passing of the Civil Rights Act and Voting Rights Act in 1964 and 1965, consisting of a cohesive set of instrumental and indexical challenges to the sociopolitical order of Jim Crow and the theories of white supremacy that supported it.

Warren's argument has prompted a number of objections and critiques—as well as a number of concurrences—most notably in a *PMLA* forum dedi-cated to taking up the question his title poses in terms of both periodization and the question of what constitutes "a literature."[52] On the issue of periodiza-tion, scholars have reacted to Warren with arguments that African American literature existed as a coherent entity well before the Civil War, and that it clearly extends beyond the Jim Crow era and remains a salient category today.[53] And the question of what constitutes a literature is inseparable from the problem of historical periods. In this regard, as R. Baxter Miller points out, it is no small thing that Warren's definition of African American litera-ture "cannot account for the writing by the former slave Frederick Douglass, who from 1845 to 1883 helped distinguish a literary tradition," the latter part of which was largely focused on the task of illuminating the real political and "symbolic recurrences in American history."[54] Douglass's late work is the subject of an entire chapter in Gene Andrew Jarrett's 2011 monograph *Representing the Race: A New Political History of African American Literature*. This chapter on postbellum Douglass immediately follows one titled "The Politics of Early African American Literature," and together these chapters establish precisely the kind of continuities across distinct eras—in terms of both political conditions and cultural production—that Warren's strict periodization aims to reject. Jarrett also accounts for what, at least in Miller's view, Warren's argument occludes: the antebellum tradition of African American antislavery writing and the ongoing relevance of this tradition to the literature of the Jim Crow era and beyond.

Though it is not my primary objective, this book does offer a critical response to Warren's historical periodization—one that highlights continuities and reverberations between the present and both the recent and the deeper past—while at the same time illuminating new dimensions of *what* African American literature *has been* from the early 1770s through today. To this end, I begin with the premise that cultural production—whether in the service of power or in resistance to it—is a form of political action, and the writers I consider have consistently perceived white American classicism and monumentalism as evidence of what Toni Morrison has called the entanglement of "knowledge" with "the apparatus of control."[55] By illuminating this entanglement, these writers reveal historical representation as a field of contention, and their own work as part of a struggle for the means of production of history.[56]

To understand what is at stake in this struggle we might return to Benjamin, whose opposition between what he calls "historicism" and "historical materialism" is almost perfectly analogous to the dominant and resistant approaches to US history this study examines. Historicism, Benjamin argues, which aims at "universal history," is the historiographical method of the "the victor," and "whoever has emerged victorious participates to this day in the triumphal procession in which the present rulers step over those who are lying prostrate." The construction of a victor's history involves not only the celebration of past achievements, but the transmission of a cultural lineage. This lineage consists of "the spoils," though these spoils more often go by the name of "cultural treasures." Of these treasures, Benjamin has famously asserted that there "is no document of civilization which is not at the same time a document of barbarism," and "barbarism taints" not only the document or artifact itself, but "also the manner in which it was transmitted from one owner to another."[57] Benjamin describes here what the hegemonic culture of classicism would know as the linked processes of *translatio imperii et studii*, the transmission of both power and knowledge that constitutes the "course of empire."[58] And it is therefore unsurprising that this transmission should be an object of critical attention for those writing from the perspective of colonization and enslavement. As Goff and Simpson have observed, "the preoccupation with how cultural artefacts move is a feature of much of the literature and theatre of the African diaspora," and the physical expropriation of ancient artifacts and the construction of monuments modeled on ancient examples are indeed preoccupations of many of the figures I consider here.[59] While the dominant classical tradition in the United States has been prominently expressed in a rhetoric of a national mission and the construction of national treasures in the triumphal style of Rome, the African American countertradition I explore in this study constitutes an incisive and persistent critique of both the "barbarism" inherent to the mission and the ways this barbarism is obscured and elided in the aesthetic forms of public memory.

Classicism and the Politics of Culture

If these forms of public memory are political insofar as they authorize an existing structure of power, the forms of black classicism I delineate in this book are political in their attempts to undermine that authorization. In this regard, this project follows Ivy Wilson's call for scholars of African American literature and culture to attend more closely to "the politics of cultural forms," especially to the ways "cultural projects . . . have come to constitute the political for African Americans." Wilson makes an important distinction between "formal politics" and what he calls "political aesthetics," a domain that was "especially important in the antebellum United States when most black Americans were denied access to the traditional domains of formal politics." In the realm of "culture," as Wilson argues, "African Americans had varying levels of agency," and it is possible—indeed, necessary—to read African American cultural productions as political acts. I would only extend this to point out that we should at the same time understand white American cultural productions as equally political, and recognize that African American writers and artists across the centuries have understood the role of what Antonio Gramsci would define as cultural hegemony—or the role of culture in upholding structures of power—and have taken the realm of culture to be a theater of contestation equally important to that in which "institutional practices such as electoral processes and policy making" play themselves out.[60]

To this end, the opening chapter considers Phillis Wheatley as an expressly political actor within the context of revolutionary-era Boston, and her political poetry as representative of the genre eighteenth-century readers would have known as the poem on the affairs of state. Within this larger category I identify two distinct yet related literary modes in Wheatley's work. The first, which I call her neoclassical poetics of political identification, is similar to what we have seen in the Black Whig's sermon at the end of the American Revolution. Through this poetics of identification, Wheatley engages with the revolutionary rhetoric of freedom as a means of linking the struggle of American revolutionaries with that of enslaved people in America. While this poetics of identification is rooted in a sense of optimism linked to the ethos of revolution, Wheatley simultaneously develops a poetics of opposition, which registers a lingering skepticism as to the likelihood of liberation for enslaved and free blacks in postrevolutionary America. This skeptical vision finds its most powerful expression in Wheatley's revision of the myth of Icarus as a parable of black liberation thwarted by white economic and military power. In a poem that merges Virgil's *Aeneid* with George Shelvocke's *Voyage around the World by the Way of the Great South Sea*—the text that would later provide the source for Coleridge's *Rime of the Ancient Mariner*—Wheatley imagines Icarus escaping in flight over the Atlantic, only to be shot down, as much like an albatross as a fugitive slave, from the deck of an American ship. Whereas Wheatley's poetics of identification appeals to the republican or libertarian strain of American classicism, the poetics of opposition—exemplified by her version of Icarus—casts a critical eye on the imperial strain, through which poets, historians, and political leaders appealed to ancient precedents to envision an American empire emerging from the Revolution.

The subsequent chapters examine the dialectical unfolding of a critical counternarrative to the authoritative conceptions of the American past and future that exceptionalist historiography and monumental culture have consistently advanced.[61] As an example of this monumental culture, the US Capitol building figures prominently in the second chapter, both as an evolving work of nationalist art, embodying and projecting a narrative of exceptionalism and American progress, and as a prominent symbol of a very different kind within the discourse of abolitionism. While the Capitol's classical features were meant to evoke the ancient origins of American democratic freedom, my second chapter shows how an array of antebellum African American writing—from the work of anonymous editorialists in the black

press to the fiction and memoir of William Wells Brown—routinely reconfigured the building's symbolic meaning. By juxtaposing the neo-Roman
Capitol with the notorious Washington slave pens, and drawing analogies between the slave economy of the United States and that of its ancient
Roman predecessor, these writers transformed what many considered a "temple of liberty" into a symbol of slavery and a national memento mori, evoking
the fates of ancient empires in order to construct a prophetic vision of an
American empire in ruins. The chapter concludes with a survey of William
Wells Brown's wide-ranging body of work, culminating in a reading of his
novel *Clotel* as the text in which both critical practices—the juxtaposition of
the architecture of democracy with the institution of slavery; the transformation of that triumphal architecture into a vision of ruin—converge in the
image of the mixed-race daughter of an American president choosing death
over slavery by leaping into the Potomac, against the backdrop of Washington
and "within plain sight" of the Capitol itself.

Chapters 3 and 4 connect the antebellum rhetoric of imperial ruin to later
iterations of black classicism in the post-Reconstruction African American
literary tradition. This section's symbolic beginning is Charles Chesnutt's
1879 visit to Washington, DC, where he encountered for himself the historical distortions and elisions—most notably the absence of images of slavery
and civil war—that characterize the architecture and interior design of the
Capitol. During the Civil War, renovation and adornment of the Capitol
intensified, transforming the building into the physical symbol of the national
reunification that was the Union's primary aim. As his early career developed,
Chesnutt's understanding of the racial exclusion that constituted not only
the nationalist aesthetic at the Capitol, but the very idea of reconciliation it
was meant to convey, would inform his criticism of both literary representations of slavery and monumental celebrations of national unity. Most notably,
the centennial celebration of George Washington's inauguration in 1889, for
which the Roman triumphal arch in New York's Washington Square Park was
constructed, provided the occasion for two of Chesnutt's most incisive early
satires. The third chapter reads Chesnutt's responses to the Washington centennial as critical of the "plantation genre" of fiction and the classical monumentalism embodied in the triumphal arch, both of which functioned to
elide the history of slavery in the past and the experience of slavery's "afterlife"
in the present.

If the Washington centennial marks the opening, then the dedication
of the Lincoln Memorial in 1922 provides a symbolic closing bookend to
Chesnutt's career. The classicism of the memorial's design and the segregation

of its dedication ceremony reaffirmed not only Chesnutt's apprehension of the racially exclusive nationalism embedded within American monumental culture, but also the widespread view among African Americans that in many respects little had changed since the era of legal slavery. The memorial, with its deliberately Greco-Roman grandeur, provided a perfect image through which to contemplate, as Chesnutt does in his late story "The Marked Tree," the ways antebellum slavery seemed to have survived emancipation, much as classical slavery had been reborn on the plantations of the New World. In this story, which is the focal point of my fourth chapter, Chesnutt analogizes the ruins of an American plantation to the ruins of ancient empires by drawing on the rhetoric of imperial decline that had been prevalent in antebellum abolitionist discourse. In conjuring a vision of the ancient world to prophesy a dark future for the United States, Chesnutt's late fiction resonates not only with the antebellum past, but also with the work of younger contemporaries such as Langston Hughes and Claude McKay, whose poems similarly invite readers to view monuments such as the Lincoln Memorial not as temples of American freedom, but as reminders of the ongoing presence of slavery and empire, containing within them the germs of their future existence as ruins.

The final chapter explores the tension between the association of the Lincoln Memorial with the civil rights movement and the continued prevalence—during and after the movement itself—of the rhetoric of imperial decline and ruination in African American political discourse and cultural production. The chapter considers the role of this rhetoric in the writings of Amiri Baraka, Nikki Giovanni, and Martin Luther King Jr. before turning to Kara Walker's art installation *A Subtlety*, which opened in Brooklyn almost simultaneously with the September 11 museum across the river in Manhattan. The centerpiece of the installation—a sculpture of an African American woman, molded out of refined white sugar in the shape of an Egyptian sphinx—was arguably the most prominent public monument ever constructed to enslaved people in the United States; but it also—in its form and in its location, within the husk of the soon to be demolished Domino Sugar factory in Brooklyn—aligned with the long tradition I have delineated here, through which African American writers and artists have refigured Thomas Jefferson's exceptional "empire for liberty" as merely another iteration of what Garnet identified as a transnational and transhistorical "empire of slavery," inexorably devolving into an "empire of ruin."[62]

Like the September 11 museum, Walker's installation was situated at a site of ruin, and both museum and installation incorporated these ruins into the monumental projects developed on the sites. Similar to the way the slurry

FIGURE I.I Kara Walker, *A Subtlety, or The Marvelous Sugar Baby, an Homage to the unpaid and overworked Artisans who have refined our Sweet tastes from the cane fields to the Kitchens of the New World on the Occasion of the demolition of the Domino Sugar Refining Plant*, 2014. Polystyrene foam, sugar. Approximately 426 × 312 × 906 inches (1,082 × 792.5 × 2,301.2 cm). Artwork Copyright Kara Walker, courtesy Sikkema Jenkins & Co., New York.

wall of the North Tower of the World Trade Center—a wall designed to hold back any potential flooding of the building's foundation from the Hudson River—stands exposed to visitors as part of the exhibit, Walker positioned her sugar sphinx between the load-bearing columns of a building long since abandoned to the weathering of time (figs. I.1 and I.2). And like the museum, Walker's installation announced its intention to commemorate the victims of a crime. The 9/11 museum chose the quotation from Virgil's *Aeneid* to do this. As I have suggested above, the reference here was not intentional but reflexive, indicating a deeply ingrained and nearly unconscious affinity for classicism as the idiom of commemoration. And the need for both the sentiment of perpetual remembrance and the authorization of classical precedent was strong enough, at any rate, to override any objections about the troubling connotations that arise when we read the passage in its literary context. The passage from Virgil articulates the memorial's intention not simply to remember the dead but to master history itself, to render this commemoration

FIGURE I.2 National September 11 Memorial and Museum. Photo by the author.

indelible and exempt from the vicissitudes of time. It announces not only the permanence of memory but of the monument and the people for whom that monument holds a powerful national meaning.[63] Through the reference to the *Aeneid*, the foremost epic of nation building in the Western tradition, the 9/11 memorial becomes definitively a national monument, just as the victims themselves—for the most part ordinary citizens murdered by a band of stateless criminals—become martyrs to a national idea.

Yet the context for the passage, despite the museum's desire to will away or repress its significance, inevitably haunts the text itself. At the very least, that troubling context generates an unsettling ambiguity about the memorial's meaning. By contrast, for all the inscrutability of its appearance and the blankness of its gaze, there is no such ambiguity concerning those whom Walker's monument is meant to remember. The work was, as the inscription beside the entrance made explicit, "an homage to the unpaid and overworked Artisans who have refined our Sweet tastes from the cane fields to the Kitchens of the New World." Just as the proliferating meanings of the Virgil quotation were unintentional, the simultaneous openings of the museum and the installation were no more than a coincidence. But I have nevertheless drawn them together here as a striking illustration of the story this study hopes to tell, in which narrative and counternarrative unfold across US history in an ongoing contest, and which ultimately reveals black classicism as a force so significant that classical history and literature can never be deployed in public discourse without at the same time conjuring their own dialectical undoing.

Phillis Wheatley
and the Affairs of State

IN A SEQUENCE entitled "Séance," published in *Callaloo* in 2001, the poet Yusef Komunyakaa conjures up historical figures from across vast stretches of space and time, from the ancient sages Imhotep and Herodotus to the nineteenth-century sculptor Edmonia Lewis and the jazz musician Louis Armstrong. At the center of the sequence is Phillis Wheatley, to whom the speaker initially refers as "one of my first loves." After recalling the way he "fell for" the "portrait of composure" that adorned the "oval frontispiece" of her 1773 volume *Poems on Various Subjects*, the speaker goes on to flesh out the historical contours of Wheatley's life: from her experience of the middle passage, "in the hull of a ship / of stormy midnights / . . . / where she crouched inside / seven years of African / memory," to her passage through the streets of Cambridge, Massachusetts, where "a faint perfume of England / nestles in Puritan cloth / when she shakes the hand / of George Washington." And between these bookends of the dramatic sweep of Wheatley's life—her capture in Senegambia at the age of seven, her correspondence with Washington in 1775—Komunyakaa adds an intensely mythic twist to a scene that has been central to what we might call the myth of origins of African American literature. Referring to Wheatley's appearance before a "tribunal" of white men assembled to test her knowledge of classical tradition—and thereby to determine the veracity of her claims to authorship of the poems she aimed to publish—Komunyakaa's speaker wonders "if the tongues / of that tribunal of good men / quizzing her turned to dust / in pure Latin & Greek."[1]

Komunyakaa draws the scene of this tribunal from a story that Henry Louis Gates Jr. has sketched out in a number of contexts, in which African American literary history begins with a qualifying exam in the classics.

According to Gates, Wheatley, an enslaved poet in the city of Boston, appeared sometime in 1772 before a panel of that city's most prominent citizens for what was surely "one of the oddest oral examinations on record."[2] These examiners supposedly had been convened to determine the extent of Wheatley's knowledge of the classics, and ultimately to attest that she was indeed the author of her own work. Though Gates has offered versions of this story—what he calls "the primal scene of African-American letters"— everywhere from the "General Introduction" to the *Norton Anthology of African American Literature* to his 2002 Jefferson Lecture in the Humanities, no evidence of such a tribunal actually exists, and a number of scholars have offered increasingly compelling and well-documented arguments that it never occurred at all.[3] As David Waldstreicher has suggested, such a qualifying exam would have been both unlikely and unnecessary, since most of the citizens who supposedly conducted it already knew the poet and were well aware of her considerable talents and the extent of her education.[4] The authenticating document in the front matter to Wheatley's *Poems on Various Subjects* was evidence neither of the occurrence of the exam nor of her qualifications in the field of classics; it was, Waldstreicher concludes, "more like a petition, or a subscription list—a common testimonial device prefacing eighteenth-century books."[5] Wheatley was well known and well connected in Boston, and most if not all of the signatories knew her personally. As Joanna Brooks has argued, Wheatley most likely secured the signatures for this authenticating document not by any theatrical demonstration of classical learning, but by walking right into a specific political meeting, which had been called to confront the crisis over the Crown's intervention in the colonial courts, and asking for them directly.[6] Brooks's scenario, while more likely than the "trial" Gates has imagined, lacks the compelling framework of a David confronting a Goliath, and the character at its center bears little resemblance to the "demure, soft-spoken, and frightened" girl of Gates's description.[7] In her place we see a confident woman who not only knew her way around the Boston political scene, but was well enough known by that scene's prominent figures to secure their signatures on the spot—during the breaks, it would seem, from the heated business of politics.

While Gates has justified his "tissue of conjecture" by claiming that the "details" are "lost to history," the growing body of historical scholarship now makes this claim more difficult to defend.[8] My aim here is not to join the chorus of critics taking issue with Gates's version of the story, but to reconcile to some extent the import of his story with the historical facts that have emerged; for while it seems clear from the evidence provided more recently by literary and historical scholars that the actual examination did not take place, the larger significance of Gates's central claim is nonetheless critical to understanding the relation between Wheatley's poetry and her politics. Trial or no trial, knowledge of the classics was certainly a form of intellectual and political currency in Wheatley's world. The history and literature of classical antiquity were central not only to the seventeenth- and eighteenth-century literary traditions that informed Wheatley's development as a poet, but also to the political rhetoric of incipient American nationalism.[9] So while there may not have been an actual "qualifying exam" in the classics, Wheatley was "already asserting" a form of "political authority" through the poetry she was writing, the politics of which were largely conveyed through the language of classicism.[10]

Both classicists and literary scholars have acknowledged the centrality of classical material to Wheatley's poetry.[11] This work has tended to evaluate Wheatley's classical appropriation for its subversive potential, discovering the ways her revisions of Greco-Roman mythology challenge both the slavery and the white supremacy for which classical tradition had typically provided authorization. Tracey Walters, for example, has noted that Wheatley's revision to the Niobe myth "emphasizes Niobe's victimization," while Jennifer Thorn had earlier observed that the tragic flaw of Wheatley's Niobe is not her hubris but her failure "to gauge accurately the power of profoundly unjust gods."[12] More generally, John Shields has argued that Wheatley employed a "subversive mode" of classicism throughout her oeuvre, especially in her use of "pastoral" and "short epic" forms.[13] While I attend to this subversive political dimension of her allusive practice, in what follows in this chapter I am less concerned with the specifics of her revisions of canonical texts than I am with her overall engagement with two intellectual historical contexts: the classically inflected political discourse of revolutionary America; and the literary tradition of public political poetry, traceable to Virgil but reinvigorated within the Anglo-American context of the long eighteenth century.[14] As I suggested in the introduction, throughout this project I read cultural production—whether in the service of power or in resistance to it—as distinctly political, and my reading of Wheatley aligns with Waldstreicher, Brooks, and others who have worked to establish the poet as "as an actor in, rather than a reactor to" the political drama of her moment.[15]

As I will elaborate in the following pages, Wheatley's political action takes the form of two distinct yet related literary modes. The first, which I call her neoclassical poetics of political identification, aligns with the revolutionary rhetoric of freedom—which drew inspiration and justification for colonial rebellion from the example of Cato's resistance to the tyranny of Caesar—as a means of linking the struggle of American revolutionaries against "political slavery" with the plight of enslaved people in America. While this poetics of identification is rooted in a sense of optimism fueled by the revolutionary spirit of the age, Wheatley simultaneously develops a poetics of opposition that conveys her skepticism as to the actual prospects of postrevolutionary emancipation. Wheatley develops this skeptical vision most powerfully in a poem called "Ocean," which refigures the myth of Icarus as a parable of the failure to achieve full emancipation in America. Written at the time of her own return from England to an uncertain future in Massachusetts, the poem describes Icarus escaping in flight over the Atlantic, only to be shot down by the captain of an American merchant vessel. This revision presciently imagines the sacrificial logic of both the constitutional convention and the slave economy it would sanction as the engine of national development.

In the following sections, I will briefly elaborate upon the libertarian and imperial modes of American classicism, before turning to an analysis of the ways Wheatley's poetry works with and against these modes toward two separate yet related ends: first, to challenge her New England readership to acknowledge the equal claims of enslaved people and political revolutionaries to both the rhetoric and the promise of freedom; and, second, to comment upon the entrenched structures and open brutality of settler colonialism, chattel slavery, and expanding commercial capitalism that she seemed to suspect, even at the height of her success, would prevent these questions from being settled in accordance with the ideals that revolutionaries outwardly professed.

Classica Americana

Though classicism was a central part of the Anglo-American literary and historical landscape from the time of the earliest Puritan settlements, it rose to the forefront of a *national* consciousness at the revolutionary moment, when classical sources provided the models for both the politics and the comportment of the nation's founders.[16] The rhetoric of the revolutionary movement frequently appealed to a binary logic, according to which a tyrannical monarch on the model of Caesar threatened the people's liberty. This logic was deeply rooted in the classical conditioning of the movement's leaders. As the historian Carl Richard has observed, this was a generation "steeped in a [classical] literature whose perpetual theme was the steady encroachment of tyranny upon liberty." Through reading "the political horror stories of the ancient historians," this generation came to understand the threat to its own liberty in classical terms.[17]

Joseph Warren, a leader of the Revolution in Boston, provides a perfect example of classicism's sway over the incipient "American" imagination. Three years before he fell as a martyr to the cause of freedom at Bunker Hill, Warren delivered the second annual address to commemorate the Boston Massacre. In this oration he made the Roman connection explicit, arguing that Rome's greatness had derived from its commitment "to a free constitution," and that the waning of this commitment had "plunged her from that summit, into the black gulf of infamy and slavery."[18] Likening British colonial policy to Roman imperial tyranny, he claimed the virtues of republican Rome for the "Americans." As the rhetoric of Warren and others would attest, these new republicans aimed to reconstruct an idealized version of ancient Rome in America.[19]

Warren's oration exemplifies revolutionary rhetoric not only in its insistent framing of the contest with the Crown as a struggle between liberty and slavery, but also in its reading of contemporary events as typologically related to the history of Rome. The most prevalent Roman analog was Cato of Utica, who provided revolutionary leaders like Warren with a model of both stirring oratory in defense of republican virtue and principled self-sacrifice in the name of country. Cato's patriotic rhetoric was matched only by his deeds, the last of which was to take his own life rather than submit to the victorious tyrant Caesar. Warren was likewise renowned for both his oratorical power and his courage under fire, and when he was killed by British forces at Bunker Hill he was immediately hailed as a martyr, with eulogies throughout the colonies likening him to Cato.[20]

Cato was a nearly ubiquitous figure in revolutionary discourse, which demonstrates the general pervasiveness of classical knowledge, and more specifically the widespread understanding of American history as typological with respect to the Roman republic. While Plutarch's *Lives* was the primary classical source for Cato's heroic, self-sacrificial defense of freedom, his popularity in America was due in large part to English adaptations of classical material. In 1720, John Trenchard and Thomas Gordon published a series of polemical essays under the pseudonym "Cato."[21] Following their initial publication in serial form in the *London Journal*, the essays were widely reprinted in colonial newspapers and ultimately appeared in book form under the title *Cato's Letters*. While the *Letters* were popular among libertarian readers on both sides of the Atlantic throughout the eighteenth-century, they took on a special significance for colonials as tensions with England began to rise. As

the historian Bernard Bailyn has observed, along with "the colonists' selec-
tively Whiggish reading of the Roman historians," *Cato's Letters* contributed
"to what might be called a 'Catonic' image, central to the political theory of
the time."[22]

The text that was most influential, however, on both the image and the
theory was Joseph Addison's *Cato: A Tragedy*. First performed in 1713, for a
time Addison's play appealed to the full spectrum of English political views,
as Whigs and Tories alike could lay claim to its nationalist and libertarian
message. Until the 1760s, in both England and the American colonies, the
play was received as a celebration of British liberty and an exhortation to a
general state of civic virtue, not an endorsement of any political faction.[23]
By the 1770s, however, contemporary history and the mythic past had converged. As antagonism with London increased, Addison's *Cato* seemed to
America's revolutionary generation the very manifestation of its struggle, and
the play was quickly transformed into a rallying cry for revolutionaries from
Virginia to New England.[24]

As Julie Ellison has demonstrated, the figure of Cato, understood primarily through Addison's text, was for Anglo-American audiences both
"the signature of the oppositional citizen" and the model for sacrifice in
the name of a national cause.[25] In the years leading up to the Revolution,
the idea of Cato loomed large in the patriot imagination, and Addison's
play provided a validating precedent for resistance to British imperial
power. The play also "entered deeply," as Ellison has suggested, "into iconic
self-dramatizations" of prominent revolutionary figures.[26] Patrick Henry
adapted his famous demand—"Give me liberty or give me death"—from
Addison's play, and the patriotic martyr Nathan Hale likewise drew on
it for his own last words—"I only regret that I have but one life to lose
for my country"—before his execution for espionage and treason in 1776.
A new epilogue, written in 1778 by Jonathan Sewall and included in subsequent American editions, explicitly identified George Washington with
Cato, and the play itself was Washington's personal favorite. Washington
admired and identified with its hero, referred to it in his letters, and even
had it staged in an effort to raise morale during the difficult winter at Valley
Forge. Sensationally popular—nine American editions were printed before
1800—Addison's *Cato* was instrumental in framing the American struggle
for political independence as an irresolvable conflict between virtuous liberty and sinister tyranny.[27]

Cato is the iconic figure, and Addison's play the central text, for the republican or libertarian strain of American classicism. While this strain of classical

thinking provided an authorizing precedent for resistance to what seemed the creeping autocracy of British rule, the idea that such resistance would *succeed* had to come from somewhere else. After all, Cato was a martyr to a just but losing cause, and the Roman republic had fallen into the tyranny of empire. To overcome this inconvenient historical truth, Americans looked to the theory of history known as *translatio imperii*, which held that the seat of empire was moving ever westward: from the Near East on to Greece, then Rome, and most recently to London, with each empire surpassing the last one in its achievements. The philosopher-poet George Berkeley put the idea to conventional Augustan meter in a series of memorable lines that have had a powerful resonance for Americans ever since: "Westward the course of empire takes its way; / The first four acts already past, / A fifth shall close the drama of the day; / Time's noblest offspring is the last."[28] Berkeley referred, of course, to the consummation of the *British* Empire in the New World, but American revolutionaries would come to see it rather differently. Given what would eventually transpire, a young John Adams appears prescient in a letter to Nathan Webb just prior to the outbreak of the Seven Years' War. Just as global supremacy had preceded the downfall of "Immortal Rome," so too could England—already in Adams's view "the greatest Nation upon the globe"—find itself in rapid decline, which would "transfer the great seat of Empire into America."[29]

   In the ensuing decades, colonial writers and orators increasingly highlighted what they discerned in British politics as the decadence and corruption of an empire in decline. Once a legitimate heir to the libertarian principles of Addison's *Cato*, England had become tyrannical, violently suppressing values it had formerly advanced. And as a sense of British imperial corruption increased, so too did the sense that the seat of empire might be on the verge of transference to America. Philip Freneau, who would come to be known as the "Poet of the American Revolution," echoed Adams's earlier vision of *translatio imperii* in his 1772 "The Rising Glory of America," in which one of the poem's speakers offers this prophecy of power transferred to the "New World": "I see / Freedom's established reign ... / And empires rising where the sun descends!" New "Nations shall grow, and states not less in fame / Than Greece and Rome of old!" (349–357).[30] And in the wake of the revolution's success, the poet and statesman Joel Barlow would open his own nationalistic epic, *The Columbiad*, with a Virgilian rendering of the *translatio*: "I sing the Mariner who first unfurl'd / An eastern banner o'er the western world, / And taught mankind where future empires lay / In these fair confines of descending day."[31]

The libertarian and the imperial strains came together most forcefully for the revolutionary generation in Sewall's 1778 epilogue to *Cato*, which both explicitly analogized Roman heroes to American patriots and linked the rallying cry of liberty to a burgeoning vision of national expansion. Sewall ends the epilogue with an exhortation to his countrymen not only to stand their ground for liberty, but to embrace the prospect of the transfer of empire:

> Rise then, my countrymen! for fight prepare,
> Gird on your swords, and fearless rush to war!
> For your griev'd country nobly dare to die,
> And empty all your veins for LIBERTY.
> No pent-up Utica contracts your pow'rs,
> But the whole boundless continent is yours![32]

Sewall's epilogue has all the intensity of wartime propaganda, but even as early as 1772, when Wheatley was assembling her manuscript and collecting signatures for the attestation page that would ostensibly validate the endeavor for a broader reading public, typological associations to classical antiquity were already contributing to a heady atmosphere of incipient nationalism and imperial ambition. The component parts of Jefferson's "empire for liberty" were certainly in the air, and many shared the vision of the American continent as the scene upon which the new Rome, rooted in the best republican traditions of the old one, but defended from its vices through the purifying force of Protestant virtue and an emergent notion of American exceptionalism, would play itself out.[33]

Over the fifteen years or so that constituted her career as a poet, Wheatley produced a body of work that engaged directly with this classically inflected political landscape, and so it is not surprising that when the colonials finally sealed the victory over their British "tyrants" with the Treaty of Paris in 1783, Wheatley marked the occasion with "Liberty and Peace," a poem in heroic couplets that celebrates the ascendancy of a new nation already imagining a grand future for itself:

> So Freedom comes array'd with Charms divine,
> And in her Train Commerce and Plenty shine.
> *Britannia* owns her Independent Reign,
> *Hibernia, Scotia,* and the Realms of *Spain*;
> And great *Germania's* ample Coast admires
> The generous Spirit that *Columbia* fires.

Auspicious Heaven shall fill with fav'ring Gales,
Where e'er *Columbia* spreads her swelling Sails:
To every Realm shall *Peace* her Charms display,
And Heavenly *Freedom* spread her golden Ray. (50–64)

Working the conventions of the neoclassical genre of the occasional poem on "affairs of state," Wheatley recasts John Winthrop's founding vision of a "city upon a hill" for the Age of Enlightenment, describing the birth of a nation upon which the eyes of the world will be fixed with anticipation. Whether this view would inspire admiration and envy or ridicule and contempt was an open question, but in its optative mood, the poem articulates a basic but powerful point that has animated American literature throughout its history: that the nation was—as Elizabeth Alexander would much later describe her own contemporary America in an inaugural poem for President Barack Obama—"On the brink, on the brim, on the cusp," positioned such that even the enslaved might believe that "anything [could] be made, any sentence begun."[34]

In the rest of this chapter I argue that, via the neoclassical poetics and classical typology that were central to the intellectual landscape of the age—and which clearly characterize "Liberty and Peace"—Wheatley engaged directly with the structure of white political power as a public poet addressing the affairs of the state. This engagement is driven by a measured optimism on Wheatley's part, born of a sense that the rising tide of revolution might indeed lift every boat, and that the arc of the emerging American narrative would indeed bend toward universal liberation. But I will also argue that beneath this public optimism concerning the American narrative of republican freedom there lies a profound skepticism about that narrative. This skepticism is rooted in a suspicion that the "avarice," as Wheatley called it in her 1774 letter to the Mohegan Reverend Samson Occom, that "impels" Anglo-Americans "to countenance and help forward the Calamities of their of their Fellow Creatures" was no accidental aberration, to be corrected through simple illumination of "the strange Absurdity of their Conduct," which was "diametrically opposite" to the "Cry of Liberty" that supposedly expressed the highest principle they shared as a people.[35] Beyond mere hypocritical disjunction between principle and practice, we can see in an alternate set of poems an apprehension of Anglo-American culture as fundamentally unprincipled and deeply committed, regardless of the moral expense, to the twin purposes of imperial expansion and economic growth. That she presents this incisive critique in the language of classicism, linking these aspects of the American enterprise to classical examples of brutality and conquest, underscores her understanding of the deep relations between culture and politics, the idea of tradition and the exercise and expression of power.

Founding Fathers

The libertarian mode of classicism draws together the ideas of "Cato" and "America" under the sign of "freedom"; and with "reference to *Cato*," as John Shields has argued, "what is *not* American is Caesar or any hint of a dictator or monarch."[36] In the language of both the play and the political rhetoric it inspired, to submit to any of these latter systems—tyranny, monarchy, autocracy—would amount to accepting a condition of *slavery*. In eighteenth-century Anglo-American thinking, the concept of freedom was largely understood in its opposition to slavery. According to the logic of this opposition, slavery was the "absolute political evil," as Bailyn has noted, and "it appears in every statement of political principle, in every discussion of constitutionalism or legal rights, in every exhortation to resistance."[37] Put another way, wherever freedom was invoked it carried with it the specter of its opposite. When Cato announces his determination to achieve "liberty or death," it is because he will not "live to swell the number / Of Caesar's slaves." This rhetoric of political slavery was generally not intended to apply to the population of chattel slaves in the American colonies, but in the end the "identification" of aggrieved colonials with enslaved people was "inescapable," as it was "built into the very language of politics."[38] This was the contradiction Wheatley identified in her letter to Occom, between "the Cry of Liberty, and the reverse Disposition for the Exercise of oppressive power over others," the egregiousness of which it did not "require the penetration of a philosopher to determine."[39] A year earlier, a group of four free black men in Boston had petitioned for emancipation on behalf of the entire enslaved population of Massachusetts, and their appeal had likewise focused on the contradiction between revolutionary rhetoric and American reality. In language that Wheatley would follow quite closely in her letter to Occom, the petitioners adopted what Nell Irvin Painter has called a decidedly "ironic tone."[40] Recent "efforts" by the citizens of Massachusetts "to free themselves from slavery" gave the petitioners "a high degree of satisfaction," and they would continue to "expect great things from men who have made such a noble stand against the designs of their fellow-men to enslave them." And like Wheatley after them, they noted the twin objectives of "civil and religious liberty," the worldly manifestations of the "divine spirit of freedom" that "seems to fire every humane breast on this continent."[41]

Both the petition and Wheatley's letter emphasize identification and agency: identification between white and black "Americans" through the notion of "enslavement"; and agency insofar as anyone willing and able to rebel against the overwhelming external force of British imperial power could surely choose to abandon their own internal regime of slavery. Though couched in the conventions of eighteenth-century verse, Wheatley's political poetry emphasizes these same points, and both the letter and the poems aim to bring her readers to a state of ethical consistency in which practice aligns with principle. If Wheatley's elegies, as Brooks has argued, aimed to cultivate a sympathetic community of white women readers by appealing to sentiment, Wheatley's more political poems targeted a specifically male readership by appealing to a notion of public and patriotic virtue characterized by this kind of ethical consistency and derived in large part from classical models.[42]

By appealing to this sense of virtue through classical allusion and neo-classical convention, Wheatley's political poetry fits the seventeenth- and eighteenth-century category of the poem of affairs of state. This was a broad category, and while satire was perhaps the predominant mode, it also included panegyrics to kings and other poems characterized by "gravity and patriotic fervor."[43] If the ironic tone of both the Boston petition and Wheatley's let-ter to Occom tend somewhat toward the satiric, Wheatley's poems on state affairs tend in the other direction, and her most pointed political statements appear in poems that adhere more or less to the conventions of panegyric.

While the ostensible function of the panegyric is celebration and "praise of Great Personages," as one late seventeenth-century dictionary described it, the political implications are often somewhat more complicated.[44] As Erasmus explained the politics of panegyric in the sixteenth century, the aim was to "exhort" the powerful "to virtue under the pretext of praise."[45] John Dryden, the most canonical practitioner of the form in English, would echo Erasmus on the purpose of the panegyric, while tracing its genealogy back to the ancient world. Figuring Virgil as a model for a poet such as himself, Dryden argued that the role of the public poet was "dext'rously" to manage "both the Prince and People, so as to displease neither, and to do good to both."[46] Three centuries after Dryden, in reflecting on the poem Robert Frost had composed for the occasion of his inauguration, John F. Kennedy expressed a similar view of the relation between "poetry and power." It was, Kennedy observed, "hardly an accident that Robert Frost coupled poetry and power. For he saw poetry as the means of saving power from itself. When power leads man toward arrogance, poetry reminds him of his limitations. When power narrows the areas of man's concern, poetry reminds him of the richness and diversity of his existence. When power corrupts, poetry cleanses." Kennedy concluded with a quintessentially American assessment of the role of the artist as the bearer of the jeremiad. Like Wheatley in her letter to Occom, which highlights the disjunctions between principle and practice, "great artists" criticize the nation "because their sensitivity and their concern for justice, which must motivate any true artist, make them aware that our nation falls short of its highest potential."[47]

It is also perhaps "hardly an accident" that Frost revived the panegyric form at the dawn of what we have come to accept as the "imperial presidency"—and for a president whose circle we call "Camelot"—since the panegyric has always been, as both Erasmus's and Kennedy's comments suggest, essentially a form of counsel to powerful individuals, if not autocrats then at least members of a governing elite. In this regard, Dryden's poems celebrating the Restoration of King Charles II to the English throne exemplify the pairing of praise and exhortation in addressing a man in power. The bulk of Dryden's "To His Sacred Majesty, A Panegyrick on His Coronation" is given over to the former.[48] The return of the king marks nothing less than the passing of the biblical flood. With the waters receding, the "kind beams" of the royal sun have "warm'd the ground and call'd the Damps away," and a new springtime breaks upon the world:

> Soft western winds waft o're the gaudy spring,
> And open'd Scenes of flow'rs and blossoms bring
> To grace this happy day, while you appear
> Not king of us alone but of the year.
> All eyes you draw, and with the eyes the heart,
> Of your own pomp your self the greatest part:
> Loud shouts the Nation's happiness proclaim,
> And Heav'n this day is feasted with your Name. (29–36)

Line after line increases the hyperbolic celebration of the monarch's return and the prospects it signals for the nation. Yet the poem concludes on a note of exhortation, emphasizing not the divine right of kings but their civic obligation to the people: "Your Subjects, while you weigh the Nation's fate, / Suspend to both their doubtful love or hate: / Choose only, (Sir,) that so they may possesse / With their own peace their Childrens happinesse" (133–136).

In the manner of Dryden, Wheatley dedicates the better part of "To the KING's Most Excellent Majesty" to singing the praises of George III. Like Dryden's Charles, Wheatley's George enjoys the love and approbation of both his subjects and the nations of the world. Writing from the perspective

of the colonies, Wheatley applauds the king's decision to repeal the Stamp
Act as a deed befitting his elevated status:

> May George, belov'd by all the nations round,
> Live with heav'ns choicest constant blessings crown'd!
> Great God, direct, and guard him from on high,
> And from his head let ev'ry evil fly!
> And may each clime with equal gladness see
> A monarch's smile can set his subjects free! (10–15)

In its effusive praise and its mild suggestion, the poem exemplifies Wheatley's
appropriation of the panegyric form. As in Dryden's concluding lines on
Charles's coronation, Wheatley emphasizes the relation between the monarch's agency and his moral obligation to his subjects. But Wheatley differs
from Dryden in the specific content of this obligation. While Dryden's
seventeenth-century poem appeals to the king to ensure the "happinesse" of
his people, Wheatley reminds the eighteenth-century king that the principal
attribute of the British "subject" is her "freedom." But while the notion of
freedom sets her apart, she follows Dryden and the panegyric tradition in
highlighting the monarch's power to *choose* to do the right thing with respect
to his subjects.

Though it was written in 1768 to applaud the Stamp Act's repeal in 1766,
the poem to King George was not made public (and therefore potentially
visible to the king himself) until the publication of *Poems on Various Subjects*
in 1773. By that time Wheatley had become something of a celebrity around
Boston, and she was thus in a position to apply the exhortative function of
panegyric more directly to the political questions of the moment. Wheatley's
most openly political poem prior to the Revolution and her own emancipation was in fact penned as something akin to a coronation poem, celebrating the appointment in 1772 of William Legge, Second Earl of Dartmouth,
to the position of Secretary of State for the North American colonies. The
poem was included the following year in *Poems on Various Subjects*, but it was
originally enclosed in a letter, addressed directly to the earl himself. In this
letter Wheatley again exhorts and praises, advocating freedom while apolo-
gizing for the freedom of her speech. She also explicitly—and significantly—
declares her identification with "America":

> The Joyful occasion which has given me this Confidence in addressing
> your Lordship in the enclos'd Piece will, I hope, Sufficiently apologize
> for this freedom from an African, who with the (now) happy America,

exults with equal transport, in the view of one of its greatest advocates
Presiding, with the Special tenderness of a Fatherly heart, over the
American department.[49]

The letter announces the intentions of the enclosed poem, which in its celebration and admonition, as well as its enfolding of the idea of political slavery
with the condition of enslaved people in the American colonies, exemplifies
Wheatley's particular panegyric mode.

The poem to Dartmouth resembles in many respects Dryden's poems on
the Restoration. It appeals to Dartmouth, as the enclosing letter had suggested it would, as a statesman and a father, who in both capacities is called to
serve the primary cause of freedom. While Dryden's other famous panegyric
on Charles's coronation, "Astraea Redux," celebrates the king as the figure for
"justice returned," Wheatley emphasizes the central trope of American political rhetoric both before and after the Revolution: the figure of *freedom* as the
nation's attendant deity. The emphasis on the principle of freedom, couched
in the broadly allusive fabric of Wheatley's neoclassical verse, would have
appealed quite strongly to a readership conditioned by the " 'Catonic' image"
that was so prevalent in prerevolutionary American discourse. Claiming the
legacy of Cato, patriotic rhetoric insisted that a new "golden age" was emerging in America, and that this age would be characterized by the triumph of
freedom.

Similar to Dryden's coronation poem, in which the rising sun of Charles's
restoration dries up the flood of civil war, Wheatley's poem to Dartmouth
associates the return of freedom with the morning sun.[50] Like the light of
justice returned, freedom, "smiling like the morn," rises sunlike, "New-
England to adorn." As if literally breaking through the dark clouds of tyranny,
the sun of freedom now "shines supreme," and the light of truth serves as a
purifying agent curing the disease of faction: "Soon as appear'd the Goddess
long desir'd, / Sick at the view, she languish'd and expir'd" (11–12).[51] Here
Wheatley, like Dryden and Virgil, adapts the Greco-Roman myth of origins
to contemporary politics. She traces the ages of man, which degenerate from
gold to silver, bronze, and finally iron, a devolution that concludes, in Ovid's
famous phrase from book 1 of the *Metamorphoses*, with "terras astraea reliq-
uit"—justice retiring from the land, hiding her head as if in shame, like the
sun behind the clouds.

In his poems on the return of the monarch, Dryden also employs imagery of the sun breaking through the clouds and justice returning from exile
to announce a new golden age. Both Dryden and Wheatley are recalling a

number of important classical sources for this material, but the most obvious is the opening to Virgil's Fourth Eclogue, from which Dryden had previously taken the epigraph for "Astraea Redux."[52] Dryden's own translation runs like this:

> The last great Age foretold by sacred Rhymes,
> Renews its finish'd Course, *Saturnian* times
> Rowl round again, and mighty years, begun
> From their first Orb, in radiant Circles run.
> The base degenerate iron-off-spring ends;
> A golden Progeny from Heav'n descends. (5–11)

As James Anderson Winn has observed, Dryden's publication of this translation, in the wake of the political tumult of the Exclusion Crisis, reflected a "widely held hope for civil peace."[53] "Astraea Redux" likewise expresses a desire for civil peace, which is reaffirmed through the choice of the epigraph. For the devoutly Christian Wheatley, the Fourth Eclogue was also of interest in that it was widely understood to be Virgil's proto-Christian prophecy, and thus seamlessly merged the Christian and the classical in a manner well suited to the American context.

Wheatley's appeal to both the Catonic principle of freedom and the vision of a new golden age reveals her understanding of the ruling elite's sense of itself as descended from classical civilization. The classical typology and neo-classical form were entirely conventional, and the allusions to various classical texts spoke directly to the standard self-conception of the political classes at this time.[54] By linking the language of classicism to contemporary politics, she played to well-established practice and subtly flattered her audience of politically powerful men. Public figures frequently spoke and wrote about themselves this way, as if they were replaying in the modern age the dramatic histories of ancient times. These same public men constituted the readership of her political poems, as well as the group of signatories that would testify to her authorial legitimacy in the front matter to *Poems on Various Subjects*. Moreover, and more importantly, these were also the men on the verge of reconstituting the government under which they lived. They were a group with the means and opportunity to put an end to human slavery and to establish a truly free republic.

Wheatley plays to this readership in two ways. The first, which draws upon their predilection for classical typology and uses classical history as a guide for advising public men on public morality, recalls the role of the poet as Dryden had described it through the example of Virgil. The second, which is more surprising, is her appeal to men of power as *domestic* men. Specifically, she addresses the Earl of Dartmouth as a father, encouraging him to consider both the "political slavery" of the colonists and, by extension, the chattel slavery in America, as institutions that destroy the family. If the earl should wonder, the poet says, "whence my love of Freedom sprung," he should look not only to the libertarian tradition exemplified by Addison's *Cato*, but also to Wheatley's experience of slavery and the effects of her enslavement on the father she left behind: "What pangs excruciating must molest, / What sorrows labour in my parent's breast? / Steel'd was that soul and by no misery mov'd / That from a father seiz'd his babe belov'd." Here she links her love of freedom and her understanding of the common good to her sympathetic identification with the feelings of a father who has lost his children to slavery. This stanza makes two distinct but related points: first, that pursuing the path of political oppression in the colonies is the moral equivalent of slavery, and therefore of stealing children from their parents; and, second, that failure to do justice to the colonies will implicate the British Crown in the loss of *its own* colonial children. She thus frames her plea for freedom—for both the political and the chattel slave—in language that appeals not only to the dignitary's moral sense that stealing children is a crime, but also to a father's fear of losing his own children. The poem suggests that all forms of slavery inevitably lead to this kind of loss, that slavery by its very nature threatens the children of enslaved and enslaver alike.[55]

Wheatley had already suggested as much in her long poem "NIOBE in Distress for her children slain by APOLLO." In a departure from both the classical source in Ovid and the various Renaissance commentaries she may have read, Wheatley makes Niobe a sympathetic figure by depicting her as a mother beset by the forces of slavery.[56] As Shields has noted, Wheatley generates sympathy for both mother and children by adding to the Ovidian source a full twenty-four lines of "glowing" description of Niobe's "Seven sprightly sons" and "Seven daughters beauteous as the op'ning morn."[57] With our attention drawn to both the mother's love and children's beauty, as well as to Niobe's condition as a figure for the contemporary woman enslaved, the bloody massacre of the children that follows prompts women to consider the political issue of slavery from the perspective of motherhood. And the poem to Dartmouth does the same for the class of the "Founding Fathers," situating them at a point of decision: given the power to choose, would they be the patriarchs of a system that sacrifices children, possibly their own?[58]

Though Wheatley describes her separation from her father and Africa as her "fate," the forces that have determined this fate are human and therefore contingent, and Wheatley's poem to Dartmouth works not only through appeal to sentiment but also through acknowledgment of the workings of power and the human costs of the economy of slavery. Even if, as some of her critics have argued, she did come to understand her own capture and enslavement as a sort of felix culpa, a fortunate fall from the "fancy'd happy seat" of Africa to the Christian "redemption" of the Anglo-American world, the poem to Dartmouth nonetheless emphasizes the price, exacted from her father, of this supposedly good fortune. And though it does include the language of felix culpa, the larger point of the stanza complicates the notion that her "redemption" in America is purely a matter of Providence. Unlike the earlier poem "On Being Brought from Africa to America," she is not "brought" but "snatch'd," and the whole procedure, from the initial kidnapping to the composition of the poem is still—felix culpa or no—an act of tyranny she hopes no one else will be forced to endure. In these poems Wheatley represents herself as neither purely the victim nor purely the beneficiary of anything so unambiguous as "cruel fate" or providential "mercy," but is rather variously affected—for better *and* for worse—by the self-interested actions of human agents within a political-economic system. For in reality it was neither "fate" nor "mercy" but *slave traders* who "snatch'd" Wheatley and "brought" her from Africa to America, just as it was a free citizen of Boston and subject of the Crown who purchased her upon her arrival.[59]

John and Susanna Wheatley's Anglo-American freedom allowed them to shop for slaves on the Boston docks one day in mid-July of 1761, to select from "A Number," as the advertisement ran in the *Boston Gazette*, "of prime young SLAVES" recently arrived "from the windward coast" aboard the slave ship *Phillis*.[60] Though a descendant of Mrs. Wheatley would later record the counterintuitive selection of a slight and rather unlikely seven-year-old girl from among a group of otherwise "robust, healthy females" as an act of both charity and good taste, contemporary records suggest otherwise.[61] In a letter of 4 September the same year, the owner of the *Phillis*, Timothy Fitch of Medford, Massachusetts, repeatedly admonished his captain, Peter Gwinn, to get better slaves. No more women and children, Fitch implored, and none so sickly and defective as the last "cargo" he had brought. "I had Rather you would be Two Months Longer on the Coast," wrote Fitch, "then to Bring off Such a Cargo as Your Last which were very small & the meanest Cargo I Ever had Come."[62]

In this and subsequent letters, Fitch insists that the value of a slave at the Boston market depends upon the quality of the slave as purchased on the

African shore, and though he also offers various suggestions for improving the conditions on board for the middle passage, he never considers that the condition of his "cargo" upon arrival might have anything to do with the passage they had all undergone—that is, with the actions and choices for which he was himself responsible.[63] I present all this not to comment on the merits of the slaving operations of Fitch and Gwinn, but simply to recall the material details of an economic system with which Wheatley was intimately familiar, a system in which, as the legal theorist Anthony Paul Farley has argued, "the black is the apogee of the commodity" and "humanity" is equated with "ownership."[64] Wheatley's experience with this economy, with slave traders and the middle passage, along with her sympathetic remembrance of the parents she left behind, generates in the poem to Dartmouth a critical challenge to the very idea of "fate." Though she writes, "such, such my fate" in describing her own experience, the story she actually tells emphasizes the role of human agency in both African slavery and American freedom.

While the poem highlights the obligations of government to the governed, it also reveals Wheatley's sense of obligation as an author of panegyric to exhort the ruling class to a state of virtue, even though this is the class responsible for what she has had to undergo.[65] This obligation does not produce a utopian vision, but leads Wheatley to articulate a pragmatic idealism. She speaks the truth to power, but in a language to which power—always eager to silence or assimilate opposition—cannot simply turn a deaf ear. Wheatley's poem serves as a reminder to her readers of the political class that they have the option to break with the practices of the past in a meaningful way, to counteract faction and build community. In the poem to Dartmouth, Wheatley concludes by reminding the secretary of this simple fact, that he should not merely rhetorically support but actually *do* justice to America: "Since [it is] in thy pow'r, as in thy will before, / To sooth the griefs, which thou dids't once deplore."

Wheatley goes on to suggest that for the man of power who heeds the poet's advice, right action of this kind reaps not only the mundane rewards of secular peace, but the transcendent blessing of sacred grace:

> May heav'nly grace the sacred sanction give
> To all thy works, and thou for ever live
> Not only on the wings of fleeting Fame,
> Though praise immortal crowns the patriot's name,
> But to conduct to heav'ns refulgent fane,
> May fiery coursers sweep th' ethereal plain,

And bear thee upwards to that blest abode,
Where, like the prophet, thou shalt find thy God. (36–43)

Here grace is clearly tied not to faith alone but to works, and the concluding lines couch the exhortation to virtue in the optative mood of a prayer. She prays that Dartmouth may act rightly and that he may reap the rewards of his right actions. And the right choice is to love freedom as she does, with the experience of one who has had it taken away. This is a love of freedom, as Elizabeth Alexander puts it so much later, that is "beyond marital, filial, / national, / love that casts a widening pool of light, / love with no need to pre-empt grievance." The need for both Wheatley's poem and Alexander's shows that the world neither was nor is yet free enough for this kind of love. These poems are themselves attempts to preempt grievance, examples of the sort of action they recommend.

Freedom and Obligation

If Dartmouth and England were free to choose freedom or enslavement with respect to the colonies, so too were the "patriots" who ultimately made them pay the price for their failure to choose wisely. Slave owners like Madison, Washington, Jefferson, and even the Bostonian John Hancock (who was a signatory to Wheatley's "attestation") were not only free to hold slaves, but free to make another choice; they could build a nominally free republic on a foundation of slavery, or they could enact universal emancipation.

As Eric Slauter has suggested, Wheatley may have downplayed the overtly political dimensions of her *Poems on Various Subjects* for the pragmatic purposes of securing publication and readership—and perhaps even as a means of hedging her bets in relation to the rising conflict between England and the American colonies.[66] But once the two fatal dice had been cast—Wheatley's decision to return from England to America after the publication of her book, and the American decision to commit to the Revolutionary War—Wheatley reversed course and specifically *played up* the political in the poems that followed. The most obvious example is the letter and poem "To His Excellency General Washington," a panegyric that links the general to a number of classical contexts and plays to the widespread sense of a typological relation to Roman history.[67] While Washington was widely regarded as analogous to Cato, as the subject of a panegyric he could also be linked to Augustus, and therefore to the idea that his ascension should coincide with the beginning of a new golden age. By linking Cato and Augustus in the figure of Washington,

Wheatley reveals the way the libertarian and the imperial strains of American classicism come together in the language of revolution.

Cato's struggle lingers in the background of Wheatley's poem to Washington, with its celebration of "freedom's cause" and the "valour" and "virtues" of "freedom's heaven-defended race." But so is the idea of an emergent American empire likewise modeled on the precedent of Rome. Like the poem to Dartmouth, "To His Excellency General Washington" works the conventions of the panegyric, singing the praises of both Washington and the cause of freedom. By adopting these conventions, Wheatley again connects with the tradition of Dryden; and by describing the conflict in epic terms, with special attention to the details and "the work of war," the poem looks back to Dryden's antecedent Virgil. Though Virgil wrote his epic on the occasion of Augustus's ascension to the seat of empire, the *Aeneid* carries us even further back, to the myth of the origins of Rome. The *Aeneid* already typologically linked first-century Rome to the nation's emergence from the wreckage of the Trojan War; and just as it made sense in Stuart England to associate Charles II with Augustus and therefore with Aeneas, it made the same kind of sense to appeal to these myths of origins in the context of revolutionary America, at a time when not only liberty but nationhood hung in the balance.

Wheatley further develops the dialectic between the libertarian and imperial strains of revolutionary thinking in the poem's concluding lines. Though she advises the "great chief" to "let the goddess" of liberty "guide" his "ev'ry action," she proposes, as a reward for his future triumph, the status and trappings of a monarch: "A crown, a mansion, and a throne that shine, / With gold unfading, WASHINGTON! be thine." In these lines we can hear echoes of Dryden's "Astraea Redux," which applies the theory of *translatio imperii* to the Restoration of Charles: "Oh, Happy Age! Oh times like those alone, / By Fate reserved for great *Augustus* throne! / When the joint growth of Arms and Arts foreshew / The World a Monarch, and that Monarch *You*" (320–24).[68] Dryden both celebrates the reunification of a divided nation under the sign of the monarch and prophesies a grand imperial future on the model of Augustan Rome. Likewise Wheatley envisions not only the triumph of liberty, but also the establishment of empire in America.

We may find the notion of a monarchical Washington linked with Augustus somewhat disconsonant with the widespread association of Washington with Cato. But this is emblematic of the dialectical relation between the ideas of liberty and empire that characterized early American classicism and nationalist thinking. Just as slavery itself proved assimilable to a national narrative of liberation, so too was the project of empire rendered consonant with the form of a republic. Moreover, typological conceptions of classical antiquity as a source of ideological principles and cultural forms informed a general sense of identification, through which colonial patriots came to understand that the struggle to establish a free America was an epic one, and that those who led this struggle were similar to the epic heroes of the past. This kind of broad identification with classical tradition allowed for the reconciliation of a Catonic image with an Augustan one, which would achieve its most memorable expression in Thomas Jefferson's vision of the new republic as also an "empire for liberty." But as with Jefferson's vision, in Wheatley's "Augustan" poems the idea of empire is always subordinate to the overriding principle of freedom; and the concept of freedom provides a center of gravity on which almost every classical reference can be grounded. The idea of establishing a land of their own based on the principle of freedom essentially elided the differences for American patriots between the triumph of Aeneas and the failure of Cato and the republicans, merging the two into an epic of freedom deferred and ultimately achieved.

If the poem to Washington leaned somewhat precariously toward a vision of American empire led by Washington as Augustus, Wheatley's poem on the death of General David Wooster definitively returned to the primary concerns of the poem to Dartmouth. Here again Wheatley links the causes of enslaved people and American revolutionaries, emphasizing the obligation of the latter to extend the circle of freedom to the former. Like the poems to Washington and Dartmouth, the Wooster poem is a panegyric, but if the poem to Washington is an example of patriotic propaganda, simultaneously a celebration of the martial virtues of Washington and a denunciation of the evils of Britain's "thirst of boundless power," Wheatley's elegy for General Wooster two years later provides a nearly perfect example of the poem of state as a form of counsel.

The first quarter of the poem is replete with panegyric and other neoclassical conventions. Following an invocation of the muse, Wheatley praises Wooster for joining "martial flames" to "Christian virtues" and offering up his life to "His Country's Cause." Blending the Christian and the classical to create the "American," Wheatley demonstrates the dialectic of national identity formation that Shields describes in *The American Aeneas*, which depicts the American character as constituted by a kind of classically martial valor, tempered and purified by the Christian virtues. The first ten lines are in these respects entirely conventional, but as with the poem to Dartmouth, there is a remarkable shift. In this case, rather than asking readers to draw the

connection between slaves and revolutionaries, Wheatley allows the hero in
his dying words to make the connection himself:

> Permit, great power while yet my fleeting breath
> And Spirits wander to the verge of Death—
> Permit me yet to paint fair freedom's charms
> For her the Continent shines bright in arms
> By thy high will, celestial prize she came—
> For her we combat on the feild [*sic*] of fame
> Without her presence vice maintains full sway
> And social love and virtue wing their way. (13–20)[69]

Here we can see war and poetry joined in the common cause of freedom.
Without freedom, "vice" reigns supreme, and "social love and virtue wing
their way," fleeing the scene like Ovid's Astraea from the age of iron. Thus the
poem prophesies again that, should freedom prevail, justice will return to the
world. But in order for Astraea to return, freedom must be general, not exclusive, extended across the lines of race. The dying general prays that God will
help the survivors through the "toils of war," that he will "conduct them and
defend / And bring the dreadful contest to an end" (22–24). But this victory
will be a pyrrhic one unless the victors attend to the principles for which the
war was supposedly fought. Wooster's prayer continues:

> For ever grateful let them live to thee
> And keep them ever virtuous, brave, and free—
> But how, presumptuous shall we hope to find
> Divine acceptance with th' Almighty mind—
> While yet (O deed ungenerous!) they disgrace
> And hold in bondage Afric's blameless race?
> Let virtue reign—And thou accord our prayers
> Be victory our's, and generous freedom theirs. (25–32)

Here Wheatley reiterates what she had suggested in the poem to
Dartmouth: divine approbation comes only to those who choose wisely;
grace rewards right action—and right action means the generous dispen-
sation of freedom. Wheatley has Wooster perform this generosity with his
dying words, and in doing so she links herself as public poet to this warrior
for American freedom, using the hero's voice to equate his objective with hers.
Here we see all the elements of a potential community working together to

bridge the gap of faction and erase the contradiction between principle and practice. The general does this through an act of generosity, relinquishing his exclusive membership in the American club by rendering it no longer exclusive. And as with the poem to Dartmouth, this secular move reaps rewards that transcend the political realm.

The poem concludes with lines addressed to Wooster's wife, which can only be read as the apotheosis of General Wooster:

> A little moment steals him from thy Sight
> He waits thy coming to the realms of light
> Freed from his labours in the ethereal Skies
> Where in Succession endless pleasures rise! (37–40)

We should note that Wheatley's promises—the transcendent rewards her martyrs are to expect—are generally nonspecific, described in abstract terms of "light" and "pleasure." It seems each is to discover her rewards for herself, like the Earl of Dartmouth, whom the poet had encouraged "like the prophet" to "find *thy* God." In an elegy for her minister, the Reverend Samuel Cooper, Wheatley similarly concluded that "to *his* fate reluctant we resign" him.[70] There are individual results for individual actors, the proper inheritance for the actions that they choose.

These emphases on identification between enslaved people and libertarian heroes, individual agency within historical contexts, and the transcendent rewards for worldly actions are all central to Wheatley's poetics of political identification. Freedom and slavery, from her perspective, are determined by the choices of human subjects, not some mysterious matrix of uncontrollable forces called "fate." And despite the idealism of the abolitionist message the elegy for Wooster proclaims, there is pragmatism in the mode and manner of its address. As both elegy and panegyric, steeped in Christian sentiment and classical allusion, this poem is the best example of Wheatley's simultaneous cultivation of female and male readers as a pluralist audience for her pluralist vision of the nascent state. She speaks deliberately to multiple readers through the same text, addressing them as individuals and part of the collective that would constitute the nation they were fighting to establish, and for which Wooster had died. That the poem was packaged with a request that Mrs. Wooster, who had been selling copies of Wheatley's *Poems on Various Subjects* in New Haven, return the unsold volumes to the author, that she might "dispose of [them] here [in Boston]" for a better price, neither diminishes the message nor suggests mere calculation on Wheatley's part. It only reinforces her understanding that in order to have an effect, one must first have an audience. And her survival as a professional poet was the primary means at her disposal to be useful to the cause of freedom.

Poems against the State

So far I have focused on Wheatley's neoclassical poetics of political identification, through which she appeals to both the Catonic (or libertarian) and the imperial strains of American classicism in order to link the colonial struggle against political slavery with the predicament of enslaved people throughout the North American colonies. In developing this poetics of identification, Wheatley allows for and even embraces the possible contradiction between a revolutionary rhetoric inspired by Cato and a nationalist vision of empire that aligns more closely with the historical agenda of Cato's opponents. Poems such as "To His Excellency General Washington" and "Liberty and Peace" demonstrate her willingness to adopt an essentially nationalist orientation and to conceptualize—with imperial Rome as a more or less explicit precedent—an American future in line with Jefferson's vision of empire.

"Liberty and Peace" is the culmination for Wheatley of this poetics of identification. It is also her most Virgilian work, as it announces not only the end of the war, but also the birth of both a nation and a national idea. What she describes is the institution of a Pax Americana, through which a "newborn *Rome*" would "give Britannia Law" and bless the world with "Freedom . . . array'd with Charms divine." The poem is a conventional celebration of such a peace, which restores order and points toward a future of "plenty." Dryden's "Astraea Redux," for example, performed essentially the same work for England at the time of the Restoration. Wheatley also echoes Dryden in her particular attention in "Liberty and Peace" to the relation between imperial power and transatlantic commerce. In "Astraea Redux," the poet assures the monarch that "Abroad your Empire shall no Limits know, / But like the Sea in boundless Circles flow" (298–299). With its ascendant naval power, Great Britain would rule the ocean and control its routes of trade: "Our Ocean in its depths all Seas shall drown. / Their wealthy Trade from Pyrate's Rapine free, / Our Merchants shall no more Advent'rers be" (303–305). Wheatley's poem likewise foresees a rise in global commerce as a result of victory in the war for independence. As "*Peace* resolves the din of War," the "Portals" of the new American nation are "open'd wide" to receive from "every Realm . . . the full commercial Tide"; and following freedom herself, with her "charms divine," is a "Train" in which "Commerce and Plenty shine." All of this suggests both Wheatley's ongoing commitment to the role of poet of state and her pragmatic willingness to work within the political economy of empire and a burgeoning global capitalism. And she expresses these commitments through the classical typology that provided that economy's cultural counterpart.

What I have not yet addressed—and what critics and scholars have been slower to apprehend—is the way classicism also provides Wheatley with a means to articulate a critique of the incipient ideology of American empire and its social and economic underpinnings. This ideology of empire, as we have seen, appeared throughout late eighteenth- and early nineteenth-century American literary and political rhetoric. Appropriating the historical theory of *translatio imperii*, many envisioned an empire in the traditional sense of outward expansion through conquest and colonization. As the historian Marc Egnal has argued, this was particularly true among political and economic elites, who stood to benefit from the establishment of an American empire in its own right.[71] Ample evidence for such an elite desire for empire can be gathered from the kind of poetry to which I have already referred—by the likes, for example, of Freneau and Barlow—and it was certainly evident in the prerevolutionary social circles in which Phillis Wheatley moved. Thomas Hutchinson, one of the signatories to the "Attestation" prefacing Wheatley's book, wrote extensively about the imperial rhetoric circulating among an increasingly ambitious American populace after the British victory in the Seven Years' War. With the French "removed" from North America, Hutchinson observed, "the prospect was greatly enlarged," with "nothing" left "to obstruct a gradual progress of settlements, through a vast continent, from the Atlantic to the Pacific Ocean." And this vision attended, much to Hutchinson's loyalist chagrin, "a higher sense of grandeur and importance of the colonies," and thus a greater tendency "to inquire . . . into the relation in which the colonies stood to the state from which they sprang."[72]

This growing sense of grandeur was characteristic of the group Egnal calls the "expansionists," which included John Hancock and James Bowdoin, two more of the signatories to Wheatley's authenticating note. And like their ideas about liberty, these expansionists derived their ideas of empire from classical antiquity.[73] As the historian William Appleman Williams has noted, the idea of empire "was common to the vocabulary of the Americans who made the revolution against Great Britain," and these revolutionaries had learned "the ideas" and the "language . . . of empire from their study of the classic literature about Greece and Rome; they used the word regularly in their talk about England; and they came increasingly to employ it in speaking of their own condition, policies, and aspirations." By the time the Revolution was won, the idea of empire had become for Americans "synonymous with the realization of their Dream."[74]

In addition to the visions of empire for which the precedent was Rome, a more conceptually wide-ranging and essentially modern notion of empire was also emerging in the late eighteenth-century American imagination. As Andy Doolen has argued, these early American ideas of empire were distinct from the conventional notion of power projected outward to conquered and colonized territories "from a single geographic place" like Rome or London. Early American imperialism, defined by what Doolen identifies as the "historical trinity" of "war, slavery, and territorial expansion," was less a traditional relation between a metropolitan center and "far-flung colonies" than it "was a vast network of power tied to the global economy, institutions of slavery . . . the forced dispossession of American Indians, and military power." All the elements of this network were in place prior to the Revolution, and together these elements "bridged the British empire and the new United States."[75]

This view of empire as a system of economic power and brutal exploitation lingers at the margins of Wheatley's appropriations of imperial poetic forms and cultural traditions. She surely acquired this sense in part as a savvy observer of current events and contemporary political culture, but to understand fully what I take to be a dark and prescient critique of the destructive— and self-destructive—energies of an emerging empire of American capitalism fueled by enslaved labor, we must take full account of Wheatley's experience of capture and transport through the middle passage. Beyond her reflections on her lost parents in the poem to Dartmouth, there is little in Wheatley's poetry that recalls her early life, and she wrote nothing about the details of her crossing from Africa to America. We do know, however, what the conditions of the middle passage were generally like for those who endured it. As Olaudah Equiano described it, the hold of the ship "was so crowded that each had scarcely room to turn himself," and "the closeness of the place, and the heat of the climate" led to "copious perspirations" and "loathsome smells" that made the air "unfit for respiration," and "brought on a sickness among the slaves, of which many died."[76] Death was a constant companion for enslaved people crossing the Atlantic, and on board the *Phillis* during Wheatley's passage, one in four would not survive. The dead were presumably thrown into the sea. In his biography of Wheatley, Vincent Carretta has suggested that the "sight of so much death around her" on the middle passage may "account for her subsequent attention to death in so many of her earliest poems."[77] But the middle passage, I would suggest, was more than a traumatic encounter with "death around her," but an introduction to the inner workings of the society and economy into which she had been violently "snatch'd." For all the "high culture" she would internalize, the packaging of human beings in the cargo hold, and the disposal of the bodies overboard like so much flotsam and jetsam, would surely have stuck in her mind as a striking counterpoint to Anglo-American claims to virtue and civilization.

Wheatley's apprehension of the brutality of slavery and the larger systems—social, economic, political—it supported and conditioned, appears most powerfully in "Niobe in Distress" and "Goliath of Gath," both of which seem to allegorize aspects of Wheatley's contemporary situation. As we have already seen, Wheatley's Niobe can be read as a sympathetic character whose "distress" is linked to the condition of mothers in slavery and those, like Wheatley's mother, who had their children stolen from their African homes and into bondage in the Americas. Viewed sympathetically as an enslaved woman oppressed by tyrannical powers, Niobe's insistence that her subjects no "longer off'rings to *Latona* pay" sounds like legitimate resistance, and certainly would resonate with prerevolutionary American readers concerned about taxes imposed by a distant and unaccountable government (84).[78] In the context of revolutionary discourse, Wheatley's figuration of Niobe as a distressed yet rebellious slave thus links her rhetorically with American patriots "crying," as she would put it in her letter to Occom, for freedom from political slavery.

As Eric Slauter has argued, the poem in this regard "allowed white colonial readers to see themselves within the context of their own rhetoric—as slaves to British tyranny," while at the same time "it may also have prompted them to reflect on their status as tyrants themselves."[79] Latona and Apollo are clearly rendered in the poem as tyrants quashing a rebellion. Niobe's resistance has filled "Each Theban bosom with rebellious fires," and in response Apollo openly embraces the imperative to "punish pride, and scourge the rebel mind" (96, 104). So while Wheatley does retain hubris as an aspect of Niobe's character, her refusal to submit to Latona is also figured as analogous to colonial resistance to the encroachments of an increasingly arbitrary and tyrannical British authority.

Wheatley's "Niobe" follows almost exactly the most widely read translation of Ovid—Samuel Garth's collaborative edition of 1717, with the Niobe story translated by Samuel Croxall—so what is important here is not originality per se, but the selection and selective adaptation of a text that would speak powerfully to the contemporary situation.[80] The Niobe story was already well suited to the moment in that it centers on a dramatic confrontation of power, but Wheatley alters the text in ways that render it more specifically analogous to the political conflict between colonies and Crown. Most important to this alignment of Niobe with American colonists is Wheatley's insistence, original to her version, that Niobe's refusal is an act of *rebellion* against arbitrary rule. But her alterations go further to announce not only the Latin poem's relevance to the struggle of enslaved people in America, but also the African American poet's skepticism as to that struggle's likely outcome.

The language of rights and payments with which Wheatley's Niobe harangues her people for submitting to the demands of Latona certainly draws on prerevolutionary rhetoric surrounding taxation and the status of colonials as British citizens. But one specific rhetorical question to her people—"Why vainly fancy your petitions heard?"—speaks pointedly to the concerns of enslaved people and free blacks in Massachusetts.[81] While the petition had long been a means for Englishmen to air "their grievances to crown and Parliament," in January and April 1773, enslaved African Americans first took up the form of the petition as a means to air grievances of their own.[82] Given that the Niobe poem was not included in Wheatley's 1772 proposal for her book, and that it claims to be based not only on Ovid's text but also on Richard Wilson's paintings of Niobe—which Wheatley probably saw in London during her trip in 1773—it is quite likely that Wheatley composed the poem after the petitions had appeared.[83] The second petition is particularly relevant, as it linked "civil and religious liberty" together as the "same grand object" pursued by both patriots and the enslaved, reminding the political class of Massachusetts that the "divine spirit of freedom seems to fire every humane breast on this continent." Wheatley reiterated this language almost verbatim in her letter to Occom of 1774, but the appearance of a petition in the poem on Niobe suggests that slave petitions were part of her thinking as she put together her volume of poems in 1773.

If the poem's rhetoric of legitimate rebellion invited white colonial readers to identify with enslaved people through the oppressed figure of Niobe, its reference to petitioning—and the implication that petitioning was an exercise in futility—forces these same readers into an identification with the oppressor. And to identify with this oppressor is to identify not merely with the reviled practice of arbitrary rule, but with an extreme level of brutality, a kind of violence out of all proportion to the apparent transgression of authority. What the Niobe story depicts above all is what Thomas Jefferson himself observed as characteristic of the enslaver class, namely the "the perpetual exercise of the most boisterous passions, the most unremitting despotism," a pattern of behavior marked by "the lineaments of wrath."[84]

As the opening lines of "Niobe in Distress" make plain, the poem's subject is precisely the unbridled violence of the despot's wrath. The lines follow Pope's translation of Homer's *Iliad*, substituting Apollo's wrath for that of Achilles. This wrath is "to man the dreadful spring / Of ills innum'rous," and Niobe is clearly figured in the opening as the victim of this violence: "The *Phrygian* queen, all beautiful in woe" (1–2, 10). This first stanza creates an opposition between gods and "men" in general and the "*Phrygian* queen" in particular. Niobe's status as Phrygian takes on a heightened significance in Wheatley's version. While Phrygia is primarily a geographical marker in Croxall's translation, Wheatley focuses on Niobe's "Phrygian garments of delightful hue." The phrase "Phrygian garments" would have suggested one garment in particular to readers concerned with the possibility of either American revolution or universal emancipation. The Phrygian cap was the hat given to emancipated slaves in ancient Rome to signify their freedom, and "the cap became," as Eran Shalev has observed, "a symbol of liberty from antiquity to revolutionary Boston."[85] Phrygian caps were part of the standard iconography of liberty during this period, notably appearing in Paul Revere's famous engraving of Samuel Adams (fig. 1.1), as well as on the masthead of the *Boston Gazette*. Given the widespread symbolic currency of the cap, Wheatley's readers may well have more strongly associated the idea of Phrygia with the idea of liberty than with any particular location in the maps of antiquity.

FIGURE 1.1 Paul Revere, *Samuel Adams*, 1774. Engraving. The figure on the left is "Liberty," holding a pole with the "Phrygian" or "Liberty Cap" at the top. She stands on a volume entitled "Laws to Enslave America." Image courtesy of Yale University Art Gallery.

In a second key revision to Croxall, whose Niobe declares that "Phrygia trembles at my pow'r," in Wheatley's version "*Phrygian* nations all revere my name" (72). Beyond suggesting that her power derives from the reverence rather than the fear of the governed, Wheatley's reference not to Phrygia alone but to multiple Phrygian nations may take on a larger adjectival function. Given the association of Phrygia with freedom through the icon of the cap, Niobe would be a figure revered by nations grounded in the principle of liberty. Following this logic, Phrygian nations would be free nations, and Apollo's wrath—which Wheatley has associated with the economy and culture of Anglo-American readership—is thus aligned against freedom and committed, as Wheatley would put it in her letter to Occom, to forwarding "the Calamities" of others.

The story of Niobe, then, provides a fitting analog for both white patriots and enslaved blacks struggling against their respective forms of oppression. But as with the problem of Cato, who failed in his fight for freedom, the poem is ultimately a parable of the triumph of power. Wheatley, as a middle-passage survivor, knew this kind of power from firsthand experience. And having been a commodity in the triangular trade, "snatch'd" from Africa and raised in America amid that trade's accumulated riches, it makes sense that she would come to conceive of slavery, as Katherine Clay Bassard has argued, as a "global system of captivity and forced labor," the violent underpinning of the larger and ever expanding economy of commercial capitalism.[86]

For Bassard, this apprehension of the global manifests itself in Wheatley's numerous poems on transatlantic crossings. In poems such as "Ode to Neptune" and "To a Lady on Her Coming to North America with her Son for the Recovery of Her Health," Wheatley "reinscribes the slave trade" by tracing the free movements of white people—for the purposes of leisure or "health"—along the routes marked out by the transatlantic economy of slavery. With this economy as backdrop, Bassard reads "A Farewel to America," which serves as a counterpart to "On Being Brought from Africa to America" and as the "provisional 'ending' to the volume" of *Poems on Various Subjects*, as a poem in which Wheatley "versifies her own reverse Middle Passage."[87] The key distinction Bassard draws between the two types of poems is that the former narrate the successful departures and returns of "white ladies" from and back to the places they call "home," while the latter describe the essentially homeless condition of the diasporic subject. The former indicate Wheatley's understanding of the linkage between economic power, whiteness, and freedom, while the latter signal her sense of the entrenched and impregnable nature of this relation, along with a burgeoning skepticism as to the prospects for the kind of universal freedom her poems of political identification would imagine.

This skepticism manifests itself most strikingly in the poem called "Ocean." Wheatley included "Ocean" in a proposal she drew up in 1779 for a second collection, but it remained unpublished in her lifetime and unknown to a broad public readership until a draft manuscript appeared at an auction in 1998. The poem, though roughly sketched in the version that we have, includes what may be the most striking use of classicism in all of Wheatley's work. And through this classical adaptation she articulates her most pointed critique of the twinned courses of commerce and empire.

The occasion of the poem is the last of Wheatley's three Atlantic crossings, following the middle passage she underwent as a child and the voyage to England to secure publication for her book. The crossing to England, as well as the return recounted in "Ocean," was aboard the *London Packet*, the ship through which John Wheatley conducted most of his international trade. Wheatley had written a poem on the prospect of this journey, which conveyed an apparent tension between her desire to complete the transatlantic circuit— like the "white ladies" of the earlier poems—and return to the "op'ning charms" of her American home, and a powerfully contrary "Temptation" to break the circuit and remain in England, where Lord Mansfield's decision in the Somerset Case of 1772 had essentially outlawed slavery.[88] The decision, which was widely reported in the Boston press, made it impossible, under British law, to compel any enslaved person who had arrived in England to return to the colonies. The decision presented Wheatley with an immediate opportunity for freedom, as opposed to an indeterminate future in America, and this opportunity is surely the root of the temptation Wheatley seems to lament in her poem.[89] In the end, after securing publication of her book and, most likely, a promise of manumission from Nathaniel Wheatley (John Wheatley's son who had accompanied her to London), Wheatley decided to return to America.[90] But "Ocean," written on board the *London Packet* during the westward passage back to Boston, would seem to reveal some misgiving about the decision to return, and a deep-seated suspicion of the "promises" of both white Americans and of America itself.

In the "Ode to Neptune" and "To a LADY on her coming to North America," Wheatley had figured the ocean as a realm in which white travelers were safe under the protection of the gods.[91] In the latter poem, the lady "on Neptune's wat'ry realm, reclin'd," while "from above the Goddess with her hand / Fans the soft breeze" (7, 5–6). And in the "Ode to Neptune" the speaker even secures the "promise" of the sea god himself to provide safe passage for

Susanna Wheatley on her voyage to England: "Thy promise, *Neptune* keep, record my pray'r, / Nor give my wishes to the open air" (17–18). The poet can thus communicate with and even make demands of the gods on behalf of her white mistress. In "Ocean," by contrast, her poetic invocations of the gods on her own behalf do little to protect her. The first forty lines are essentially an imitation of the opening of Dryden's translation of the *Aeneid*, modified for the context of Wheatley's journey home. Here Eolus has let loose the winds upon Neptune's sea, creating a tempest that recalls the primal chaos that reigned before the "divine Command" brought order to the universe. The tempest Wheatley's Eolus creates recalls the tempest that batters and displaces the Trojan fleet, knocking them from their fated course to Latium and their destiny to establish the seat of empire at Rome. Analogizing the Atlantic to the ancient Mediterranean, the poet links herself to Aeneas and by extension to the American destiny.[92]

Here again we see Wheatley identifying with the American cause and embracing the mythic structure of a burgeoning national identity. By the logic of this identification, the voyager should survive the trials of the ocean and fulfill the national prophecy, but in Wheatley's poem, as W. E. B. Du Bois would later say about the Reconstruction, "there was a mistake—somewhere," and the epic journey doesn't end as it should.[93] Instead, there is an abrupt shift, as a strange and incongruous figure enters the scene: "an Eagle young and gay," pursuing "his passage thro' the aierial way" (41–42)—a symbol of freedom that is abruptly and shockingly destroyed. The poem turns from the "Eagle" back to the ship, where "Calef"—the captain of the *London Packet*—"aim'd his piece" and "brought" the flying figure "to pluto's dreary shore" (43–44).[94]

Wheatley's poem precedes Coleridge's "Rime of the Ancient Mariner" by a quarter-century, but it is possible the two poets shared a single source. George Shelvocke's *Voyage around the World by the Way of the Great South Sea* includes a story of the ship's encounter with an albatross, but unlike the snow-white bird of Coleridge's poem, Shelvocke's albatross is ominous precisely because it is *black*. The black bird, as Shelvocke recounts, "accompanied us for several days, hovering about us as if he had lost himself." In its disconcerting blackness and its steady "disconsolate" presence the albatross apparently prompts an officer named Hatley, whom Shelvocke calls "my second Captain," to a spasm of violence. Suffering from "one of his melancholy fits," Hatley "imagin'd, from his colour," that the albatross "might be some ill omen," and he took it upon himself to shoot the ominous bird.[95]

The passage from Shelvocke certainly would have been suggestive to Wheatley in its figuration of the black bird as the sacrificial victim of white maritime affairs. Wheatley calls this bird "Iscarius," which clearly refers to Icarus, the winged boy who flew too close to the sun. The sun melted the wax that held his wings to his body, and the boy plummeted down into the sea.[96] In her adaptation of the classical myth to the context of eighteenth-century Atlantic crossings, Wheatley's Icarus, like Shelvocke's bird, flies not too close to the sun but to the shipping lanes of white commerce. While the classical Icarus pays the price for his own overreaching, Wheatley's is the collateral damage of the relentless course of capital and empire—and Wheatley aptly identifies with this victim. As a poet she would be quickly forgotten, abandoned by her supporters with the coming of the war, and left to be buried in an unmarked grave, much as American revolutionaries would silence the idea of universal emancipation and bury slavery in the mystifying text of Article 1 of the Constitution.

Perhaps the scene is borrowed from Shelvocke, or perhaps Wheatley actually witnessed Calef shooting a bird off the stern of the boat; but in any case the act of killing becomes powerfully symbolic for Wheatley at this moment of transit—literal and figurative—in her life. In the midst of an optimistic identification with the Aeneas narrative that was so central to visions of the American future, the poet's identification shifts to a tragic narrative of a failure to escape. Though the shift is surprising in its abruptness, Icarus is a fitting choice for Wheatley, as he and his father, Daedalus, are fugitive slaves in flight from their captivity to Minos on the island of Crete. The opening lines of the story in the 1717 collaborative translation of Ovid—the text Wheatley had revised in her rendering of Niobe—would also have been suggestive in her refiguration of Icarus for the Atlantic world:

> In tedious exile now too long detain'd,
> Daedalus languish'd for his native land:
> The sea foreclos'd his flight; yet thus he said:
> Tho' Earth and water in subjection laid,
> O cruel Minos, thy dominion be,
> We'll go thro' air, for sure the air is free. (8.283–88)

But the air is not free. It is rather the domain of those, like Calef, who express their freedom through the exertion of force.[97] In Ovid's version it is circumscribed by a prohibition on "thoughts," which "aspire / To loftier aims" and drive the "childish" Icarus to "ramble high'r" (337–338). By all accounts Wheatley's trip to England was a great success, and she was returning—perhaps with promise of manumission in hand—to a promising future of both freedom and fame. But "Ocean" suggests a lingering sense that such a future may have been already foreclosed.

Not only do the shipping lane and the air above it belong to Calef and his kind, but so too does the classical tradition that helped transform that lane into the "westward" route along which "the course of empire takes its way." So much so, it would seem, that the Roman god of the ocean himself is subordinated to the American will. Following the crash of Icarus into the sea, Neptune arrives too late to do anything but bear witness to the disaster. Hearing "the cries" of the wounded Icarus, Neptune emerges and demands to know the cause:

> Old Ocean heard his cries.
> He strokes his hoary tresses and replies:
> What mean these plaints so near our wat'ry throne,
> And what the Cause of this distressful moan?
> Confess, Iscarius, let thy words be true
> Not let me find a faithless Bird in you. (51–56)

To which Icarus truthfully replies:

> Saw you not, Sire, a tall and Gallant ship
> Which proudly skims the surface of the deep?
> With pompous form from Boston's port she came,
> She flies, and London her resounding name.
> O'er the rough surge the dauntless Chief prevails
> For partial Aura fills his swelling sails.
> His fatal musket shortens thus my day
> And thus the victor takes my life away. (59–66)

As in the poem on the death of Wooster, Wheatley allows the dying martyr to speak for himself. But unlike that poem, the purpose of which was to connect the struggles of enslaver and enslaved through the shared rhetoric of libertarian nationalism, in "Ocean" the two are opposed as victor and victim in a contest in which freedom is a zero-sum game. Where the panegyric elegy for Wooster drew them together under the sign of the Roman martyr Cato, "Ocean" breaks the alliance apart, with the enslaved linked to Icarus as a martyr to freedom, and Calef a symbol of the triumph of the kind of empire—"a vast network of power tied to the global economy"—that Andy Doolen has described.[98]

That Wheatley wrote most of the panegyrics we have considered—including the poems to Washington and Wooster—*after* she had written "Ocean" attests to her commitment to an "American" idea and to her faith in its possibility. But the skepticism of "Ocean," derived perhaps from Shelvocke or a specific observation on board the *London Packet*, but surely rooted in her larger experience as a middle-passage survivor, would prove to be the more prescient. And her use of classical tradition—as evident in "Niobe" as it is in "Ocean"—to emphasize the violence of slavery and empire only thinly veiled by the veneer of "civilization" would anticipate the critical mode of black classicism the following chapters survey, emerging as an integral part of African American literary and political writing of the nineteenth century and beyond.

2

In Plain Sight

SLAVERY AND THE ARCHITECTURE
OF DEMOCRACY

IF THE REVOLUTION had ended for white Americans in the triumph of "Liberty and Peace" that Wheatley had celebrated in 1784, for African Americans who had believed in its principles the Revolution may have symbolically ended—in this case in failure—with the hanging of the rebel Gabriel in the fall of the year 1800. Gabriel, a skilled and literate enslaved laborer from a plantation outside Richmond, Virginia, organized a wide-ranging conspiracy among enslaved and free blacks, as well as poor whites, to overthrow the enslaver class, march on the capitol at Richmond, take Governor James Monroe as a hostage, and demand universal liberation. This planned rebellion was resonant with the larger ethos of the revolutionary age, and Gabriel drew specifically on the ideas and rhetoric of the American Revolution. Gabriel even framed the rebellion as an act of patriotism, a fight to liberate not only enslaved African Americans but the country itself from the system of slavery. Making his identification with the American Revolution explicit, Gabriel announced "Death or Liberty" as the motto for the flag he intended for his forces to carry into battle.[1]

The historian Douglas Egerton has speculated that Gabriel's inversion of Patrick Henry's famous ultimatum mirrored the truly revolutionary nature of his intentions, as Gabriel's "vision of political change"—which included not only freedom for the enslaved but a radically egalitarian re-ordering of society—would have appeared to powerful elites in the early republic as nothing less than "the world turned upside down."[2] Whatever the reason for the inversion may actually have been, there is no question that Gabriel appropriated the fighting words of Henry—a Virginia slave-owner who was legal counsel and personal friend to Gabriel's owner, Thomas Prosser—for good reason. The flag would not only provide "a visible reminder that white Virginians once claimed to believe in liberty," but a forceful statement that Gabriel's coalition still did and was willing to kill and die for it.[3]

Though his revolution ended before it could even begin—the plot was betrayed, and Gabriel and many others were executed as a result—Gabriel nonetheless staked out a radical claim to freedom and thus to the ideological mantle of the Revolution that had been framed and motivated by classically inflected rhetoric such as Henry's. As I have elaborated in the previous chapter, Henry and others drew this rhetoric from historical accounts of Cato's resistance to Caesar as well as Joseph Addison's historical drama *Cato: A Tragedy*, which was widely performed in North America before, during, and after the Revolution. Henry took his famous phrase directly from Addison's *Cato*, and in doing so self-consciously adopted for himself what Bernard Bailyn has called the "Catonic image," a classical precedent authorizing American rebellion.[4] I open this chapter with Gabriel's appropriation of Henry's famous claim because it anticipates a critical orientation toward American classicism and monumental culture that would become conventional among black writers and public figures in the nineteenth-century United States.

For many black writers and editors within antebellum cultures of print and political activism, the figure of Cato, rather than emblematizing a nation dedicated to freedom, revealed white American hypocrisy and provided an authorizing precedent for resistance to slavery. In the critical tradition I sketch out in this chapter, the Catonic image provided a veneer of legitimacy to a national agenda of slavery and empire that was more accurately reflected through what I have been calling the imperial strain of American classicism, a strain that is most visible in the architecture of the nation's most prominent and symbolic buildings and monuments. In what follows here, I will elaborate on three primary elements of "black classicism" that African American writers, editors, and activists would develop in relation to these dominant libertarian and imperial modes: the appropriation of the "Catonic image" and the classically inflected rhetoric of revolutionary liberty to the cause of radical abolitionism; the critical juxtaposition of the neoclassical architecture of national buildings and monuments with images of the infrastructure of slavery; and the imaginative transformation of these buildings and monuments from icons of the ideals of democracy and the progress of civilization to symbols of imperial hubris and harbingers of the future ruination of the American empire. I trace these developments through the pages of black newspapers and abolitionist polemics by radical figures such as

David Walker and Henry Highland Garnet, but the chapter's primary figure is William Wells Brown, who draws together all the elements of antebellum black classicism in an array of writings across a number of genres, from memoir and travel narrative to moving panorama, antislavery lecture, and finally his novel *Clotel*. In *Clotel*, Brown not only crystallizes his critique of the monumental culture of an imperial American slave society, but also envisions an alternative memorializing practice for the enslaved. By stark contrast to the hubristic design of national buildings and monuments, the unmarked graves of rebels and fugitives appear as monuments of an appropriately human scale, memorials that indicate the freedom struggle's alignment, not with American exceptionalist narratives encoded in the monumental landscape of the "land of Washington," but rather with a notion of natural law embedded in the land itself.[5]

Liberty or Death

Gabriel was not alone in staking a claim to Patrick Henry's language in resistance to slavery. In the decades between the failure of Gabriel's rebellion and the outbreak of the Civil War, Henry's legacy figured prominently in African American literary and political writing. In 1843, for example, Garnet delivered his incendiary "Address to the Slaves of the United States of America," in which he recalled how the "sentiments of . . . revolutionary orators fell in burning eloquence upon their hearts, and with one voice they cried, Liberty or Death. . . . It ran from soul to soul like electric fire, and nerved the arm of thousands to fight in the holy cause of Freedom."[6] But had this dedication to freedom, Garnet rhetorically asked, led these revolutionaries, once "the power of Government returned to their hands," to "emancipate the slaves? No; they rather added new links to our chains."[7] As a result, Garnet went on to assert, the rightful ownership of that "electric" phrase was passed to the likes of Denmark Vesey and the "patriotic Nathaniel Turner," each of whom had "died a martyr to freedom."[8]

William Wells Brown likewise assigned Henry's legacy to Nat Turner, leader of the most successful slave rebellion in US history. As Brown wrote in an appendix to the 1849 edition of his *Narrative of William W. Brown, an American Slave*, Turner "knew it would be 'liberty or death' with his little band of patriots. . . . He commenced the struggle for liberty; he knew his cause was just, and he loved liberty more than he feared death."[9] A year earlier, Frederick Douglass's newspaper the *North Star* had published a notice comparing a runaway slave to Patrick Henry. Prefiguring the climactic scene of *Clotel*, the fugitive had thrown himself into a river and drowned, rather than face capture and re-enslavement. As the paper acknowledged, "Patrick Henry has been immortalized for giving utterance to that glorious sentiment, 'Liberty or death!' But here is a poor despised, sorrow-stricken man, who acts out the sentiment which the orator merely proclaimed; and yet how few will bestow a second thought upon the tragedy!"[10]

Douglass himself was also compared to Henry. In his preface to the first edition of *Narrative of the Life of Frederick Douglass, an American Slave*, William Lloyd Garrison attested that, upon first hearing Douglass speak at an antislavery convention, he felt sure that "Patrick Henry, of Revolutionary fame, never made a speech more eloquent in the cause of liberty." In the text of the *Narrative* itself, Douglass claimed that his small band of compatriots, who were planning their escape from slavery, "did more than Patrick Henry, when he resolved upon liberty or death"; and in *The Heroic Slave*, Douglass described Madison Washington, the hero of the novella's title, as "a man who loved liberty as well as did Patrick Henry."[11]

Given that all these appeals to Henry refer solely to what had become his signature phrase, they appeal by extension to the phrase's equally well-known source. Garnet's "Address" referred explicitly to both Henry and his model, paraphrasing Addison's *Cato* to encourage slaves to "let it no longer be a debatable question, whether it is better to choose Liberty or death."[12] More explicitly, in 1827 the nation's first black newspaper, *Freedom's Journal*, reprinted Lydia Sigourney's poem "Africa," in which Cato—who "like a God revered, / Indignant pierced his patriot breast"—stands alongside Hannibal and Moses as ancient African heroes and prophets of freedom.[13] In 1849, the *North Star* reprinted an editorial from the *Cleveland Plain Dealer* that appealed to Addison's *Cato* in closing its argument for the abolition of slavery in the District of Columbia. The authors specifically recalled the "impression made upon us in boyhood by that profound exclamation of Cato, that 'A day, an hour of virtuous liberty, / Is worth a whole eternity of bondage'"—lines that had only "worn deeper and deeper in the progress of years."[14] Though they had once served as a powerful inspiration to American revolutionaries, the lines now stood as a cutting reproach to the nation for its failure to live up to its own inspiring ideals.

Through his combination of oratorical virtuosity and willingness to *act* to secure and defend his own liberty, Douglass was perhaps the most obvious inheritor of the Catonic image. Though schoolchildren throughout the antebellum United States would have read excerpts from Addison's *Cato* in Caleb Bingham's *The Columbian Orator*, Douglass would emerge to history as that book's most famous reader. In their study of classicism in African American literature, William Cook and James Tatum have rightly suggested that Bingham's volume served Douglass as a textbook on the techniques of classical oratory, which he ultimately put to compelling use in his own speeches and writings.[15] But more important to Douglass, I would suggest, than the classical nature of the form was his engagement with the *content* of the Catonic rhetoric of freedom—rhetoric that once had served to advocate for a cause the nation had now betrayed.

While *The Columbian Orator* includes an actual speech from the historical Cato, the excerpt from Addison's *Cato*, both in its resonance with the rhetoric of the Revolution and in its sheer dramatic flair, would perhaps have been for many American readers the most compelling text in the volume. The passage excerpted from *Cato* consists of a rousing speech by the blustery Sempronius in which he marvels at "a Roman senate" that can "long debate, / Which of the two to choose, slav'ry or death!" along with the eponymous hero's most famous celebration of freedom: "in Cato's judgment, / A day, an hour of virtuous liberty, / Is worth a whole eternity in bondage."[16] As the historian François Furstenburg has observed, Catonic sentiments such as these pervade *The Columbian Orator*. Furstenberg notes in particular an exchange between a white settler and a Native American, in which the latter's words—declaring his preference for death "in honorable war" over life "in dishonorable peace"—are "almost an echo of Cato's"; but a Catonic defense of liberty similarly marks the "Dialogue between a Master and a Slave" that Douglass specifically mentions as a powerful influence on his own thinking.[17] The title page of *The Columbian Orator* also includes an epigraph from Charles Rollin's *Roman History*, which points to Cato as evidence of the political force of language, and therefore as the presiding historical spirit for the collection: "Cato cultivated Eloquence," the *Orator* suggested to its readers, "as a necessary means for defending the rights of the people." *The Columbian Orator*, as Douglass's biographer William McFeeley has described it, "was a book of liberties, of men exhorting mankind to a sense of higher callings." Perhaps most important, in its selection of texts *The Columbian Orator* "did not ignore that denial of liberty that was slavery." Through reading the *Orator*, "a Baltimore slave boy" could effectively become "Cato before the Roman senate."[18]

While Douglass was straightforwardly Catonic in his writings and his public persona, perhaps the most compelling example of the transfer of Cato's legacy from revolutionary Americans to American slaves is almost wholly ironic. In William Wells Brown's play *The Escape; or, A Leap for Freedom*, the central figure is a slave named Cato. This Cato is a complicated character.

Throughout much of the action he performs the role assigned to him by the culture of blackface minstrelsy.[19] He is foolish, submissive, collaborative with the master, and Brown would seem to have drawn him in stark contrast to the more "heroic" characters Glen and Melinda. But as Glenda Carpio has shown, there is a strong "contrast between how Cato is perceived"—both within the play and by readers—"and his true convictions." Cato most clearly expresses these convictions in his songs, which are directly addressed to the audience, and which, as Carpio argues, "anchor the play." Whereas for the most part "he outlandishly fulfills the stereotype of the contented house slave," in his songs he drops "the minstrel malaproprisms that pepper his speech elsewhere" to deliver an "indictment of slavery" in "straightforward language."[20] In one song he couches his criticism in the idiom of Christian and familial sentiment, railing against slave traders who "take our wives, insult and mock, / And sell our children on the block," and against "preachers, too, with whip and cord," who "Command obedience in the Lord."[21] And in another, he aligns himself with the tradition that includes Wheatley's letter to Occom and Douglass's 1852 oration "What to the Slave Is the Fourth of July?," decrying the hypocrisy of a slave society—nominally "free states" included—built on a professed commitment to liberty: "You loudly boast of liberty, an' say your State is free, / But ef I tarry in your midst, will you protect me?"[22] In his songs, Cato reveals that the opposition between his "buffoonish minstrel antics" and Glen's more traditional "heroism" is a false one: "submission," as Carpio observes, "may cloak resistance, and resistance may be delivered to the tune of submission."[23]

That Brown chose Cato for the name of a character he modeled to some extent on himself is also revealing of the ways black classicism critiques both American slavery and the ways classical tradition functions to enable and even to celebrate it. The naming of enslaved people after classical figures was common. While these names were almost always meant to disparage, they mostly did so in a general way, conjuring up through names such as Caesar, Pompey, Hannibal, or Titus a sense of dignity and nobility that the white supremacist culture claimed for itself and denied to enslaved people of African descent. But the name Cato had a particularly galling significance, since it was the name whites associated most strongly with the concept of freedom. While revolutionary writers and orators routinely identified with Cato as the model of a free individual, to name an enslaved person Cato was specifically to insist, through crude mockery, on the incapacity of blacks for freedom. Thus, the African American Cato's critique of American hypocrisy on the subject of "liberty" not only stakes a claim to the "Catonic" legacy; it also highlights the bankruptcy of the typological claims to a classical heritage

that white Americans made for themselves. As a broader critique, it illuminates a desire among American slave-owners to aggrandize their own culture
through an association with classical civilization—a desire in conflict with a
racist impulse so vulgar as to make a mockery of that culture itself.

The Boundless Continent

Given the significance of classical names within the culture of slavery, it is
worth noting that Brown's Cato, upon his arrival in the North, changes his
name from Cato to "Alexander Washington Napoleon Pompey Caesar."[24] For
Cato, as this grandiose sequence would suggest, to be "free" in the American
context is to be imperial. If his given name is associated with an ideal notion
of liberty, the names he assigns himself register the ways that ideal had historically become entangled with imperial projects emerging from revolutions
and civil wars, from Augustan Rome to Napoleonic France and antebellum
America. This change in names, then, is not merely minstrel buffoonery;
through the transformation of an enslaved Cato into a free Caesar, Brown
satirizes both the unfolding of the early Republic into a continental empire
and a concomitant shift in the ways classical tradition would figure in the
discourses of slavery, abolition, and imperialism in the United States. If Cato's
original name ironically indicates that the Catonic legacy of the Revolution
had been largely transferred to enslaved people fighting for freedom, his own
self-naming reflects the increasingly imperial nature of both the expanding
American nation and the hegemonic mode of classicism through which that
national expansion was enabled, justified, and celebrated.

The Catonic sensibility had been rooted in Patrick Henry's distillation of
the moral of Addison's tragedy, namely that death was preferable to slavery;
and within the revolutionary-era context of the play's rise to prominence—
wherein imperial power was understood to be encroaching upon colonial
self-determination—the ideas of slavery and empire were bound closely
together. In terms of the Roman history to which American patriots related
themselves typologically, Cato and freedom were linked to the Roman republic, while slavery and tyranny were linked to Caesar and empire. But while this
was the essential message American readers and audiences would have taken
from the dramatic action of Addison's *Cato*, with the rising fortunes of the
American cause, the imperial aspect of the play's epilogue became increasingly prominent.

The epilogue, written by the poet Jonathan Sewall for a performance
in 1778, and appended to later printed editions, was originally intended as

a rallying cry in the midst of the Revolutionary War. Sewall explicitly analogized Cato to George Washington, and likened the cause of the Roman
republic to that of American patriots:

> Did Cesar, drunk with power, and madly brave,
> Insatiate burn, his country to enslave?
> Did he for this, lead forth a servile host
> To spill the choicest blood that Rome could boast?
> The British Cesar too hath done the same,
> And doom'd this age to everlasting fame.
> Columbia's crimson'd fields still smoke with gore;
> Her bravest heroes cover all the shore:
> The flower of Britain, in full martial bloom,
> In this sad war, sent headlong to the tomb.
> Did Rome's brave senate nobly dare t'oppose
> The mighty torrent, stand confess'd their foes,
> And boldly arm the virtuous few, and dare
> The desp'rate horrors of unequal war?
> Our senate too the same bold deed have done,
> And for a Cato, arm'd a Washington.[25]

This was all part of a discourse that increasingly described the British Empire
as decadent and tyrannical in a particularly Roman fashion. Eran Shalev has
labeled this the rhetoric of "Nerofication," which connected the idea of empire
with the excesses and dissipation of the most notorious of the Roman emper-
ors.[26] Beyond providing terms of disparagement, such a linkage also offered a
prophecy of victory for the rebel forces, as it suggested that the British Empire
was destined, like its ancient predecessor, for a catastrophic fall. But if these
lines rallied patriots to confront the forces of empire arrayed against them, a
couplet toward the epilogue's conclusion would ultimately gain the greater
purchase for a new nation bent on an imperial project of its own. Unlike his
unfortunate typological predecessor, hemmed in and fated to die a martyr
in his home city of Utica, there were no bounds to the triumph Washington
and his people would ultimately achieve: "No pent-up Utica contracts your
pow'rs," the epilogue declared, "For the whole boundless continent is yours!"

Over the course of the nineteenth century, these lines were deployed
so often that they became something of a national motto. A speech by
Pennsylvania congressman Alexander Ramsey in 1846 is representative of
the way these lines contributed to the discourse of American exceptionalism.

Compared to England, with its "starving laborers" at the mercy of "aristocratic landlords and immense monopolists," the prospects of the United States were "boundless":

> We have no vast entailed estates upon which to found power. . . . Our country has none of the remnants of feudalism about it: we are all kings—all landlords, as desert and industry may crown or endow us. There is no danger while "the whole boundless continent is ours" of any monopoly of breadstuffs or the necessaries of life. The spirit of competition will keep down prices, and the national character for adventure will make us the factors for the world.

The "national character" matched with a "boundless continent" meant that, unlike the cramped and worn-out nations of the Old World, whose decline was considered inevitable, "Centuries must roll over our country ere such contingencies can be feared by us, and perhaps never will be under our present confederation."[27]

Ramsey's speech was consonant with the rhetoric of Manifest Destiny that John L. O'Sullivan had been developing since the late 1830s, and when O'Sullivan himself wanted to put a point on his advocacy for national expansion, he likewise turned to Sewall's epilogue. As editor of the *New York Morning News*, O'Sullivan wrote in 1845 that "more, more, more will be the unresting cry, till our national destiny is fulfilled and 'the whole boundless continent is ours.'"[28] But both O'Sullivan and Ramsey were only channeling a dream of continental empire that had been central to the American imagination since the days of the Revolution. Thomas Jefferson famously articulated his own vision of "extensive empire" in a letter to James Madison in 1809. Contemplating future annexations and conquests in war, Jefferson foresaw "an empire for liberty as she has never surveyed since the creation."[29] While in this letter Jefferson was in a sense passing the torch of the burgeoning empire to his successor in the presidency, in his own first inaugural address eight years earlier he had envisioned precisely the kind of unencumbered future O'Sullivan and Ramsey would reiterate on the brink of the Mexican War. Americans would never face the Old World problems of conflict, scarcity, and monopoly precisely because of the exceptional coincidence of the American character with a boundless continent that was theirs to possess. Americans were, as Jefferson observed, "kindly separated by nature and a wide ocean from the exterminating havoc" of Europe, and "too high minded to endure the degradations" endemic to the rest "of the globe." By contrast, through possession of "a chosen country" of apparently infinite extension, Americans had "room enough for our descendants to the thousandth and thousandth generation."[30]

Jefferson delivered his first inaugural address in the Senate chamber of the still unfinished Capitol building in Washington. It was fitting that Jefferson's inaugural should at the same time inaugurate the Capitol as the seat of the American government, since the design of both the Capitol and the capital city had been among Jefferson's primary responsibilities over the preceding decade or more, during which he had served as Secretary of State and Vice President, and both city and building had been designed to match the expansive vision of the man himself.[31] For Jefferson—who was himself an accomplished architect—the idea of an "empire for liberty," with its connotations of both democracy and grandeur, could only be expressed through the neoclassical style. Though the design for the Capitol was ultimately chosen from among the entrants to a government-sponsored competition, Jefferson sketched out a plan of his own, which was based on the Pantheon in Rome. Of all the iconic buildings of classical antiquity, the Pantheon was perhaps Jefferson's favorite.[32] It had served him previously as inspiration for aspects of his own home at Monticello, and the Pantheon-based sketch for the Capitol later provided the basis for the design of the rotunda of the University of Virginia.[33] Not surprisingly, William Thornton's winning design aligned with Jefferson's vision, most notably in the resemblance of the central section to the Pantheon.

While his favored architectural model was a Roman temple constructed under the reign of Augustus, Jefferson was nonetheless motivated by what James McGregor has described as "the pervasive American belief that neoclassicism was a fundamentally democratic building style."[34] And yet, as Lawrence J. Vale has argued in his definitive study *Architecture, Power, and National Identity*, "classical allusion" in public architecture within a democracy always faces the risk of conjuring the opposite of what it intends. The "intended recall of classical democracy" risks being "indistinguishably diffused into reminders of classical empire."[35] However much buildings such as the Capitol are intended to symbolize "national identity or national unity," they have a tendency to remain "closely tied to political forces that reinforce existing patterns of dominance and submission."[36]

Vale's arguments most likely would go without saying to the enslaved population of such a democracy, especially when its architectural monuments were constructed with enslaved labor.[37] Whereas white American elites like Jefferson could construct a typological connection to the Roman republic, embodied in neo-Roman structures such as the Capitol and authorizing the American enterprise as the realization of classical ideals of high culture and democratic government, many black writers took a sharply different view of these historical relations. Whereas the dominant view enabled Jefferson's notion of an American "empire for liberty," unbounded by geography or history, formerly enslaved narrators and lecturers, along with writers and editors in the black press, constructed an alternate typology that figured the United States, as Garnet would make explicit, as an "empire of slavery," linked to classical antecedents not through elevated conceptions of individual liberty or collective civilization, but through its commitments to human slavery and imperial conquest.[38] This alternate view of the meaning of classical tradition was most prominently advanced through the critical juxtaposition of the images of the architecture of American democracy with the infrastructure and ongoing operation of the economy of slavery in the United States, especially in the nation's capital.

The Architecture of Democracy

When the African American newspaper the *Weekly Advocate* first appeared in New York City in 1837, it dedicated two full pages across its first two issues to a "A Brief Description of the United States." The feature devoted a paragraph to each of the twenty-six states of the union, detailing the state's major crops, its mineral resources, and other geographical and political facts and figures. The prevailing attitude of the piece toward the country it describes is positive. The introduction applauds the United States for being "the most interesting and important division of the western continent," and praises in particular "the excellence" of the national government and "the intelligence, industry and enterprise of the inhabitants." Given the innate qualities of the country's land and its people, the democratic form of its government, and its fifty-year history of progress, it made sense for the *Advocate* to conclude its introduction on a note that echoes Jefferson's vision of a boundless American future: the American "political system has survived the tender period of infancy, and outlived the prophecies of its downfall. It has born the nation triumphantly through a period of domestic difficulties and external danger; it has been found serviceable in peace and in war; and may well claim from the nation it has saved and honored, the votive benediction of *esto perpetua*."[39]

In the second part of the "Description," the paper's editors echoed and reinforced this suggestive deployment of a Latin phrase to project the American future. While the initial installment had appeared on the back page of the first issue of the *Weekly Advocate*, the second was the cover story of the paper's second issue. While the text here merely continued the descriptions of individual states, it was accompanied by a striking illustration of the neo-classical facade of the US Capitol (fig. 2.1). If we follow Benjamin Fagan's suggestion that we read this entire "page as an image," we can see "the separate states" as "visually bound together by the federal government," which is itself "metonymically represented in the Capitol building." Through this arrange-ment of text and image, the page provides an "illustration of the theory of federalism," a system that "theoretically allowed disparate populations to live in harmony despite vast differences in geography, ideology, and culture, so long as they shared a commitment to republican ideals and institutions."[40]

This view would suggest that the *Advocate*'s use of the image of the Capitol affirms the dominant narratives encoded in the building—namely the linked progress narratives of "civilization" and the American nation—as well as its status as a symbol of both the classical heritage and the bound-less future of the United States. But if we extend Fagan's logic of reading beyond the page, to read the introduction to the "Description of the United States" in relation to the other pieces in the first two issues of the *Advocate*, a more complicated picture of the Capitol's significance emerges. The first installment of the "Description" included, for example, a chart providing demographic statistics, listing the overall population of each state and, where it was applicable, the number of its slaves. The "Description" conspicuously avoids any extensive discussion of slavery, but these figures provide a subtle yet unavoidable reminder of slavery's constitutive role in both the nation's economy and its representative form of government. If the image of the Capitol building, surrounded figuratively by the states, was meant to rep-resent this representative government, the presence of two million slaves—who not only were unrepresented per se, but who were also incorporated, by virtue of the "Three-Fifths Compromise," into the voting power of the enslaver population—most certainly would have problematized the analogy for the *Advocate*'s black readers.

Other articles in the second issue further complicate the apparently pos-itive outlook of the "Description" and the apparent embrace of the conven-tional symbolism of the Capitol building. On the second page, immediately adjacent to a short notice explaining the inclusion of the "beautiful engrav-ing" of the "View of the Capitol at Washington," is a story entitled "Slavery at Washington, D.C." While the front page depicted in "beautiful" images both the literal and figurative architecture of a supposedly free republic, this second-page article invites readers to consider how "bitter is the thought" of

Published every Saturday.] Conducted by a Committee of COLORED MEN. [For the Diffusion of Useful Knowledge.

$1,50 Per Annum—$1 in advance.   Advertisements conspicuously inserted.

WEEKLY ADVOCATE.

ESTABLISHED FOR, AND DEVOTED TO THE MORAL, MENTAL, and POLITICAL IMPROVEMENT OF THE PEOPLE OF COLOUR.

PHILIP A. BELL, Proprietor.   New-York, Saturday, January 14, 1837.   { VOLUME I. } No. 2.

A BRIEF DESCRIPTION OF THE UNITED STATES---Continued.

Useful Knowledge.

Written for the N. Y. Weekly Advocate. COMPILED BY ROBERT FLARR.

NEW JERSEY.

PENNSYLVANIA.

DELAWARE.

MARYLAND.

DESCRIPTION OF THE CAPITOL.

The Capitol is a white free stone, composed of a central edifice and two wings, and is of the following dimensions:

VIRGINIA.

WASHINGTON.

NORTH CAROLINA.

SOUTH CAROLINA.

ILLINOIS.

ARKANSAS.

GEORGIA.

KENTUCKY.

MICHIGAN.

MISSISSIPPI.

LOUISIANA.

TENNESSEE.

INDIANA.

OHIO.

slavery "in these United States—the land of the free, and the home of the brave!" More specifically, the paper asks its readers to consider the "inhuman and disgraceful" presence of "slaves in the District of Columbia," and "regular slave traders" who "reside at the seat of Government!"[41] The item concludes with a lengthy extract from the Scottish philosopher Thomas Hamilton's *Men and Manners in America*. Hamilton's book offers a rather scathing critique of its subject, but his comments on slavery were in line with the emerging American abolitionist discourse of the time, most notably in their attention to the problem of hypocrisy. "Washington," Hamilton observed, "the seat of government of a free people, is disgraced by slavery. . . . While the orators in Congress are rounding periods about liberty in one part of the city, proclaiming, *alto voce*, that all men are equal, and that 'resistance to tyrants is obedience to God,' the auctioneer is exposing human flesh for sale in another!" Reinforcing the point made earlier in the article, the excerpted text from Hamilton suggests that while slavery in America is already an embarrassing contradiction, its presence in the capital is something akin to desecration. Echoing what had been a commonplace idea in England by the time Lord Mansfield invoked it in the Somerset case of 1772—namely that the English air was "too pure for a slave to breathe in"—Hamilton suggested that the District of Columbia was ground "consecrated to Freedom," and "that even the foot-print of a slave" would "contaminate" that sacred soil. The District was a "shrine of the Goddess" of freedom, now "polluted by the presence of chains and fetters," which marked the city as the site of "the most extraordinary and monstrous anomaly to which human inconsistence—a prolific mother—has given birth."[42]

"Slavery at Washington, D.C." runs across two columns, and thus is situated not only adjacent to the notice about the engraving of the Capitol, but above it as well. Just below is another notice, under the imperative headline "READ THIS," warning readers to "Beware of Kidnappers" trolling the streets of New York and other northern cities. The article suggests that the widespread practice of kidnapping free blacks in the North has become nothing less than a "reign of terror." This kidnapping demonstrates the lawlessness of American society with respect to the lives and liberties of blacks, and prompts the writer to a series of damning rhetorical questions concerning that society's fundamental nature:

> What year of the world do we live in! And under what government has our lot been cast! . . . what opinion are we to form of the manner in which our laws are administered; and what language shall we adopt in

portraying the *manly* conduct of such characters as reside among us? And from whence have these MEN derived that strange kind of power, which ought to be honestly resisted by all. . ... We hazard nothing when we boldly assert, that there is no crime of greater magnitude—no enormity more foul, than that of making a Slave of a Freeman among us; and DEATH is too light a punishment for that wretch . . . who should violate all the laws both natural and civil.

In this short piece the *Weekly Advocate* further develops the tension between the celebratory view of the form and function of the government and the impression of that government from the perspective of the lived experience of African Americans. While the cover image of the Capitol and the accompanying descriptions of the states suggest an orderly arrangement of political and economic interests both limited and bound together by the rule of law, the second page describes a "foul" and lawless regime of parasitism and crime. While the former, as Fagan has suggested, celebrates the American government, the latter specifically demands to know what kind of government this is, under which "our lot" has "been cast." That the accounts of slavery's desecration of democracy literally surround, in terms of their layout, the notice of the engraving of the Capitol makes the second page an ironic mirror to the first one. If the first page suggested the Capitol as the center of gravity for a nation in balance, the second refigured the Capitol as besieged on all sides by the presence of slavery. In either of these cases, however, the Capitol retains its conventional status as a symbol of the American ideals of freedom and democracy. In the first instance, these are the ideals that carried "the nation triumphantly through . . . domestic difficulties and external danger"; in the second they are the principles the country has failed to live up to in its practice.

In making the latter argument through the juxtaposition of the image of the Capitol with the business of slavery conducted nearby, the *Weekly Advocate* was participating in an already well-established mode of abolitionist discourse. An 1831 piece in the *Liberator*, for example, asked its readers to consider the same juxtaposition of images of freedom and slavery: "What avails the show of liberty," the paper demanded, "when the reality is wanting?—What avails the spirit that glows in our bosoms at the bare mention of our nation's birthday, when the clank of chains is heard beneath the very walls of our capitol[?]"[43] Later the same year, the *Liberator* adopted an image for its masthead that illustrated the point (fig. 2.2). In the issue of 23 April, the editors presented "a new head for the Liberator":

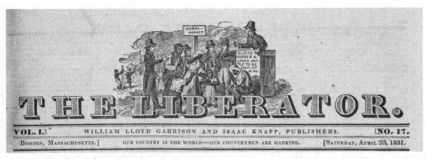

FIGURE 2.2 The masthead of the *Liberator*, 23 April 1831. The US Capitol is visible in the left background. *The Liberator*. Image courtesy of the American Antiquarian Society.

It is illustrative of a slave auction . . . appropriately located at the seat of the National Government. . . . On the right side of the vignette, stands the auctioneer with his hammer lifted up for a bid; at the side and in front of him are some southern speculators, with the family to be sold—a man and his wife, (whose attitudes express their grief,) and their two children, who are clinging to their mother. On the left side are seen in the distance, the Capitol of the United States with the American flag (on which is conspicuous the word LIBERTY) floating on the breeze.[44]

The *Liberator* also frequently reprinted the remarks of abolitionist speakers to the same effect. John Blain, a Baptist preacher from Pawtucket, Rhode Island, brought together the contrasting images of slavery and the Capitol in an address to the New England Anti-Slavery Convention in 1834. "The traveller may go," Blain suggested, "to the Capitol of this free republic, and see there the splendid pile, with its majestic dome, erected for the legislature of the country." And within that august neoclassical edifice, the same traveler could "hear the members" of Congress "discourse eloquently of liberty, and the inalienable rights of man; and within sight of that building over which waves the American eagle, he may see the flag that is put out to signify that human beings are to be sold to the highest bidder."[45]

Soon after beginning its run, the *Weekly Advocate* changed its name to the *Colored American*, and under that name it continued the practice of contrasting images of the Capitol and the Washington slave pen. In July of that year, the paper reprinted a speech by Salmon P. Chase (the paper recorded his name as "Solomon"), a young lawyer who would go on to become a US senator, governor of Ohio, Abraham Lincoln's secretary of the treasury, and Chief

Justice of the United States. The speech was part of his argument in the case of a fugitive slave named Matilda, on whose behalf he had filed a writ of habeas corpus. Since part of his case was to argue that the Fugitive Slave Act of 1793 was unconstitutional, it made sense that he would begin his appeal with the troubled imagery of the seat of the constitutionally established government itself. "You cannot but be aware," Chase argued, "that of the thirteen millions of human beings who tread our soil, more than two millions are slaves." Chase then followed the conventional pattern, moving from the general problem of slavery in the nation to the particular hypocrisy of its presence in the capital. Readers must also be aware, Chase asserted, that "in the District of Columbia . . . slavery and the traffic in human beings are tolerated—even in the very vicinity of the Capitol, where sit the representatives of a people who profess to hold freedom as the inalienable right of man."[46]

Solomon Northup, the most famous victim of the kind of kidnapping the *Weekly Advocate* had described in its pages, brought the practice of contrasting the Capitol with the business of slavery to the genre of the slave narrative. In *Twelve Years a Slave*, Northup noted the particular irony of Washington, DC, being the site of his capture. "Strange as it may seem," Northup wrote in his autobiography, "within plain sight" of the slave-trading house, "looking down from its commanding height upon it, was the Capitol. The voices of patriotic representatives boasting of freedom and equality, and the rattling of the poor slave's chains, almost commingled. A slave pen within the very shadow of the Capitol!"[47] The full title of the work—*Twelve Years a Slave: Narrative of Solomon Northup, A Citizen of New-York, Kidnapped in Washington City in 1841, and Rescued in 1853, from a Cotton Plantation Near the Red River, in Louisiana*—only emphasized the point. Northup significantly describes himself not only as a free black, but as a *citizen* of New York; and it is in the city of Washington—"within plain sight" of the Capitol—that his freedom and his citizenship are stolen.

Brown's Panorama and the Movement of History

William Wells Brown would similarly highlight the problem of slavery in the nation's capital in a number of contexts. In "The American Slave Trade," first published in the antislavery annual *The Liberty Bell* in 1848, and included in the appendices to the 1849 edition of his *Narrative*, Brown observed that among the most astonishing facts of American slavery was that "the greatest slave-market is to be found at the capital of the country! The American slave-trader marches by the capitol with his 'coffle-gang,'—the stars and stripes waving over their heads, and the constitution of the United States in his pocket!"[48] In a second appendix, the slave trader had moved the Constitution from his pocket to "his hat," but otherwise he continued marching through the capital city of "a country professing to be the freest nation in the world," parading "his gang of chained men and women under the very eaves of the nation's capitol."[49]

While the *Liberty Bell* essay indicates Brown's alignment with a conventional discourse about slavery and the Capitol, his pathbreaking moving panorama brought an entirely new dynamic to the practice of juxtaposition, one that not only highlighted American hypocrisy, but also unsettled the linearity of conventional notions of both American history and historical time. Brown presented his panorama as a performance piece while he was traveling and lecturing in the British Isles in 1850, and made the same point through the juxtaposition of visual images. Brown's stated purpose for the panorama was to counter prevailing conceptions of slavery as essentially benign, specifically "the very mild manner in which" John Banvard, a nationally famous practitioner of the form, had represented slavery in his moving panorama of the Mississippi River.[50] Brown went about this first of all by presenting images of the type that were included in his own published *Narrative*. These included depictions of whipping and harrowing scenes of slave catchers hunting slaves with packs of dogs—all of which clearly represented slavery as a regime of brutality. Brown intensified the critique inherent in these scenes of plantation slavery by contrasting them with images of the major monuments to American freedom that marked the landscape of Washington, DC. Four of the first six "views" in the panorama were set within the city and directed the viewer's attention specifically to the Capitol building, the White House, and the business of slavery being conducted nearby. In the text Brown used to accompany the images in the public performances of the panorama, he adheres to the pattern set forth by the other examples we have seen so far. Paraphrasing the English abolitionist Thomas Day, Brown observes that "'if there is anything truly ridiculous, it is for an American, with the Declaration of Independence in one hand, reading, "all men are created equal," and with the other brandishing a whip over the back of his trembling Slave.'" But even "more shamefully overwhelming" is the fact "that all the horrors of the African Slave-trade are perpetrated in the national domain, the capital of which is honoured with the cherished named of *Washington*."[51]

If the city of Washington and its buildings had provided important symbols of American freedom, they also figured prominently within a larger narrative of historical progress. As Jefferson had remarked of the Capitol, it served to embellish "with Athenian taste the course of a nation looking far beyond the range of Athenian destinies."[52] Here Jefferson doubly evokes the historical theory of *translatio imperii*, according to which imperial power—along with the cultural production that justifies and celebrates it—was understood to move progressively westward. Just as the ancient Romans had appropriated architectural and other cultural principles from the Greeks, after the "seat of empire" had moved westward to Rome, the United States now appropriated those principles from them both. Thus Jefferson could refer to the "Athenian" aspect of the nation's most emphatically "American" building, which had been modeled quite deliberately on the Pantheon in Rome. Just as Rome's "destinies" would extend "far beyond the range" of its Greek antecedents, so too would America's surpass those of Rome. Jefferson's idea was that classicism in nationalist art and architecture represented the ability to embrace the best attributes of the ancient civilizations—republican government, architectural symmetry, the idea of the national epic—as an inheritance, while shedding the inconvenient historical facts such as Rome's devolution from a free republic into a tyrannical empire, and from a mighty empire into a state of ruin. Indeed, the American narrative borrowed from the example of Rome but inverted the trajectory of its history. For the United States, the origin story of the Revolution replayed Cato's struggle against Caesar to a successful conclusion, with republican freedom triumphant over the imperial tyranny of the British Crown. This movement from tyranny to liberation was the essence of the American progress narrative.

If this movement characterized the predominant American historical narrative, through which the idea of human liberty attained its apogee in the United States, African American writers like Brown had good reason to view this story with a skeptical eye. By presenting the American landscape from the perspective of the fugitive slave, Brown's panorama revealed the dominant narrative to be a construction by reconstructing it before the eyes of a captive audience.[53] Brown's reconstruction manifested itself not only through the inclusion of images of slavery, but also through resistance to the conventional temporality of the panorama form. The panorama consisted of a long stretch of canvas, which moved across a stage from one roller to another, unfolding a series of painted scenes, while a showman narrator offered a running commentary on the images as they appeared. Most often, the moving panorama depicted a journey, and many of these journeys reflected the project of national expansion. The most famous and influential of the mid-century moving panoramas was John Banvard's *Panorama of the Mississippi River*. It inspired many imitators and competitors, as well as Brown's critical

response to its "mild manner" of portraying slavery.[54] Banvard's depiction was
apparently quite mild indeed. The accompanying pamphlet—using language
taken directly (and without attribution) from Timothy Flint's *History and
Geography of the Mississippi Valley*—describes "a plantation with all its busy
and cheerful accompaniments."[55] Though Brown announced Banvard as the
specific target of his critique, the appropriated text of the pamphlet shows us
that Banvard's attitude toward slavery was part of a well-established pattern
of representation of the Mississippi, which took a romantic view of the landscape, minimizing the problem of slavery and presenting the river, along with
the culture and commerce associated with it, as evidence of the inevitable
course of an American empire that was essentially benign.[56]

Banvard's panorama fit the imperial project in its sheer immensity (he
claimed his canvas was three miles long) and in its commitment to linear narrative. The idea was to replicate for viewers the experience of actual southward
travel down the Mississippi, and to demonstrate the progress of civilization
through westward national expansion. William Wells Brown's departures
from panoramic conventions thus generated a critique not only of the particulars of Banvard's depiction of slavery, but of those conventions themselves
for the way they contributed to a narrative of progress and the obscuration
of the retrograde institution of slavery. Brown did this through interrupting
linear narrative and providing his viewers something very different from a
smooth journey through a landscape; instead, Brown's panorama leapt from
one scene to another, juxtaposing images of plantation slavery with monuments to American freedom. Interspersed throughout the panorama are individual dramas of escape, recapture, and, finally, what Brown calls the "true
freedom" available only on British soil. But these stories of escape—narratives
of both literal and figurative progress for enslaved individuals—highlight by
contrast the prevailing historical stasis in America and the archaic nature of
what Brown calls—with echoes of Wheatley's letter to Samson Occom—the
"Republican Egypt."[57]

As the theater historian Sergio Costola has suggested, by properly "restoring slavery"—figured as a fundamentally premodern practice—to the contemporary national picture, and placing "slave bodies" in direct contrast to
the monumental images so central to the narrative of American progress,
Brown's performance creates "*dialectical images* that could bring present
and past into collision, thus advocating for other stories, other modernities
and trajectories."[58] That Brown conceived and performed his panorama in
England emphasizes the point. Like all fugitive slaves in the United States, in
order to secure freedom beyond the threat of recapture Brown had to travel

to a territory—whether Canada or England itself—under the governance and protection of the British Empire. From the perspective of the fugitive slave in England, American history was hardly a linear narrative of progressive liberation. Quite to the contrary, the practice of slavery prevailed in the United States, while freedom for the enslaved required a physical journey through space—eastward, and thus against the grain of history according to *translatio imperii*—and a figurative journey back in time, to the seat of the "tyranny" Americans claimed to have thrown off in their revolutionary break with both the "Old World" and the past itself.

A Vast Empire of Ruin

While the aim of the dialectical juxtaposition of idealized nationalist monuments with the very real presence of slavery was most commonly to highlight the disjuncture between the nation's principles and its practice, Brown's panorama—in its simultaneous unsettling of both the meaning of national monuments and the spatiotemporal linearity of exceptionalist historiography—performs another of the primary functions of antebellum black classicism, transforming those classical monuments from symbols of freedom and progress to embodiments of imperial hubris and harbingers of inevitable ruin. The dominant mode of American classicism—whether manifested in a play like Addison's *Cato*, a poem like Joel Barlow's *Columbiad*, or a neo-Roman edifice like the US Capitol—tended to reveal a desire to have it both ways with respect to classical precedents: on the one hand to stake a claim to a direct line of descent from Greco-Roman civilization to the "newborn Rome" of the United States, while on the other to advance a theory of historical exceptionalism. Thus John L. O'Sullivan could declare the United States "The Great Nation of Futurity," having "little connection with the past history of any" of the Western nations, "and still less with all antiquity," while at the same time drawing on the epilogue to *Cato* to express his vision of the empire that "futurity" would afford.[59] And thus could the buildings designed to embody and facilitate the national destiny to "the thousandth generation" be made to resemble the monuments of an ancient world that lay almost entirely in ruins.

Antebellum black writers and newspaper editors were as attuned to the ironies embedded in this dominant historical consciousness as they were to the related yet more conspicuous problem of slavery's persistence in "the freest nation in the world."[60] To highlight the irony, many of these writers and editors responded to this prevailing figuration of Rome as precedent for an ascendant America with prophetic visions of the ruins of ancient empires. The *Colored American*, for example, emphasized this darker typological association through a series of articles titled "Sacred Geography and Antiquities," which related the histories of ancient empires that figured prominently in scripture. As Fagan has argued, these articles resembled in form the earlier "Description of the United States," with descriptions of biblical empires anchored on the page by striking illustrations. As with the "Description of the United States," these sacred geographies ultimately focused on the capitals of the empires—Nineveh and Babylon—with special attention paid to the monumental architecture of these capital cities.[61] Fagan argues that the illustration of Nineveh in particular would have recalled for regular readers of the *Colored American* the image of the US Capitol, and, if one views the pages side by side, it is hard to miss the resemblance (fig. 2.3).[62] If we extend the logic of reading the "page as an image" to the entire run of the newspaper, we can read this image backward into the original picture of the Capitol, understanding the fate of ancient Nineveh as a possible future for the United States. The illustration accompanying the description of Babylon strengthens the case, as this image would have recalled for readers Thomas Cole's popular sequence of paintings entitled *The Course of Empire*. This series, which depicted across five paintings the rise and fall of an unnamed but definitively Greco-Roman empire, had shown in New York City in 1836, and had been

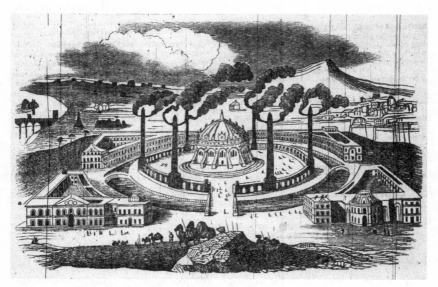

FIGURE 2.3 "Temple of the Sun at Nineveh," *Colored American*, 13 June 1840.

widely interpreted as an American allegory, somewhat ominously warning of the "destruction" and "desolation" that historically had followed the "consummation" of empires.[63]

By tapping into Cole's images as a widely shared American cultural reference, while also recalling the prominent image of the neo-Roman facade of the Capitol with which it had begun its run as a paper—and linking both to the oppressive empires of biblical history—the *Colored American* arranged these disparate spatiotemporal coordinates as "vital episodes," to borrow Fredric Jameson's phrasing, "in a single vast unfinished plot."[64] This arrangement reveals a historical consciousness that situated the struggles of enslaved people in the "New World" within the same collective story Marx and Engels were soon to describe: of "freeman and slave, patrician and plebeian, lord and serf . . . in a word, oppressor and oppressed," a conflict destined to culminate either in "a revolutionary reconstitution of society . . . or in the common ruin of the contending classes."[65] To illustrate the point, black writers of the antebellum period routinely drew on ancient models—with particular attention, because of its significance to mainstream nationalist historiography and political discourse, to the example of Rome—in order to suggest a direct causal relationship between the economics of slavery and the ruin of empires, and the historical continuities between ancient and American slavery.

This attention to the economic dimensions of slavery and empire anticipates the argument of the twentieth-century New Left historian William Appleman Williams that empire has been not only a geopolitical strategy but "a way of life" in America since its earliest days.[66] For Williams, the defining characteristic of empire is the ideology of limitlessness, which requires and justifies endless expansion and exploitation of both human and natural resources. The triad of empire, slavery, and ruin, which antebellum black writers used to great effect, provided a running critique of this ideology of limitlessness as unsustainable and ultimately self-defeating. From this critical perspective, empire as a way of life leads not to progress but to catastrophe, and the prophetic vision these writers developed—as the images from the *Colored American* make clear—is frequently catastrophic. By emphasizing the essential continuity between ancient Rome and nineteenth-century America in terms of a shared dependency on enslaved labor, black writers of the period were in ironic alignment with white southerners like John C. Calhoun, George Fitzhugh, and Thomas R. R. Cobb, who argued that slavery provided the essential foundations of both freedom and civilization. But where these proslavery advocates argued for slavery as "a positive good," African American writers and orators linked greed, corruption, empire, and slavery into a coherent theory of Western history as a pattern of unbridled accumulation resulting only in the proliferation of ruin.[67]

This coherent theory was forcefully advanced through the black press from its inception. *Freedom's Journal*, the country's first African American newspaper, appeared in New York City in March 1827, and by April of that year the paper had already published a lengthy essay in three parts on the theory of imperial decline. Entitled "The Mutability of Human Affairs," the essay begins with the author in the role of antiquary. With his "heart sickened" by "a recent visit" to one of the Egyptian mummies that were on frequent display in the antebellum United States, the author recounts having "pondered upon the picture my imagination had drawn," and like "Marius surveying the ruins of Carthage, I wept over the fallen state of my people."[68] This opening exemplifies what the historian Wilson Jeremiah Moses has identified as a "historiography of decline" that was prevalent within antebellum black writing. From this historical perspective, African Americans could identify with the ancient civilizations of Egypt and Ethiopia, which were, as the essay in *Freedom's Journal* would put it, "for more than a thousand years ... the most civilized and enlightened."[69] Afrocentrism of this kind served writers of the African diaspora much the same way as Greco-Roman classicism served Europeans and Americans: as a source of a narrative through which they could claim legitimacy as a people. Just as Greco-Roman classicism provided a repository of images and symbols suitable to both the American Revolution and the nation's expansion, so too could the descendants of Africa draw on the histories of that continent's ancient past to help shape the discourse of their own resistance. Looking back to Egypt and Ethiopia allowed African American writers to claim a history not only prior to enslavement, but prior even to the Greek and Roman civilizations white Americans claimed as their own legitimating antecedents. The historiography of decline also embraced a cyclical view of history's unfolding, as opposed to a linear or progressive one: ascendancy preceded decline, which was as true for Rome as it was for Egypt, and oppressed peoples—like native Britons under Roman occupation, or Africans under Anglo-American slavery—could expect eventually to triumph over their oppressors. This historical perspective thus helped explain the current status of Africans and Africa in relation to the ascendant empires of the West, while simultaneously suggesting the inevitable collapse of the American slavery regime.[70]

Perhaps the most influential Western text for this historiographical tradition was C. F. Volney's *The Ruins; Or, Meditation on the Revolutions of Empires*.[71] First published in 1791, and appearing in English translation in

1802, Volney's *Ruins* had a powerful impact on writers from Lord Byron and Mary Shelley to Herman Melville and Charles Chesnutt.[72] Though its overall outlook appealed to Romantics generally, Volney's *Ruins* held a special appeal for African Americans. First, it unambiguously acknowledged ancient black civilizations in Africa, attributing to these African societies "those civil and religious systems which still govern the universe"; and the decline of these civilizations, in the context of a "revolutionary" theory of history, implied the possibility of the re-emergence of both Africans and African Americans.[73] Second, in his chapter "The Causes of the Revolutions of Empires," Volney diagnoses the underlying economic cause of slavery: "Cupidity," according to Volney, had "excited among men a constant and universal conflict."[74] From this premise, he traces a "regular and connected series of causes and effects" by which empires "rose or fell": "agitated by their own passions . . . always greedy and improvident, passing from slavery to tyranny," men "have made themselves the perpetual instruments of their own misfortunes."[75] So while the historiography of decline apprehended the movement of history as cyclical, this was no more a natural law than was the theory of linear historical progress. History's grim repetitions were the result of human agency, driven by what Olaudah Equiano had described as the "improvident avarice" characteristic of the slave trader.[76] The ruins of empires impart these lessons, along with a proclamation that also appealed to African Americans for obvious reasons: "confounding the dust of the king with that of the meanest slave," the ruins announce "to man the sacred dogma of Equality!"[77]

Antebellum African American writers embraced this view of the course of empire—from human greed to slavery, tyranny, and ruin—in order to develop an alternative typology for the United States with respect to classical history. In its third installment in *Freedom's Journal*, the essay "The Mutability of Human Affairs" deployed this theory of history in a striking critique of New World slavery and empire, articulated by way of a sophisticated analogy to the ancient world. The beginning of the final decline of Egyptian civilization could be traced, the essay suggested, to "the time of the second Triumvirs [of Rome], when the disastrous battle of Actium . . . reduced it from its former splendor to a province of the Roman Empire." From the perspective of a people internally colonized within a Republic with imperial ambitions—and one that proudly self-identified with Rome—this was a suggestive historical claim, made more so by the fact that this encounter could be understood as the first in a chain of events that would prove ultimately disastrous to the ascendant Roman empire. "Time," the essay noted, "has not spared even imperial Rome." Though the empire once "comprehended the greater part of the civilized world," it had now "sunk comparatively into mere insignificance." Concluding with the irony most damning to the present American regime and its white supremacist ideology, the essay notes that while "the ancient mistress of the world" lies in ruins, "a new rival has arisen"—namely the British Empire—"whose name at the period to which we refer, was scarcely known; and her natives considered as a fierce and unconquerable body of barbarians."[78] By evoking the ancient Roman view of native Britons as savages, while at the same time recalling the ultimate fate of the Roman Empire, the essay casts an ironic eye on the ideology of white supremacy, and intimates the possibility of a historical reversal of fortune for an ascendant United States.

Ten years later, the *Colored American* published its own two-part meditation "On the Mutability of Human Things," which expressly likened the future of America to the history of Rome. "The Eternal City," the essayist observes, once stood a "haughty empress," receiving the "homage of the world." Rome was "filled with the wisdom of sages,—her dwellings were the abodes of heroes, orators, artists and poets, rendered immortal by their achievements. But where is Rome now?" the essay rhetorically asked, "Where her marvelous works?" What once had been the "spectacle of the world" had "fallen like a star from its place in the heavens," leaving nothing behind but "rubbish heaps" and "the crumbling ruins of temples." The essay then figures the Roman fall as a sign of the precariousness of American democracy: "If blind party spirit, led on by American Catilines and Syllas, be allowed to rear its hydra-head, and carry away, as in a whirlwind, the federal principles of our Union, then farewell, a long farewell to this Republic!"[79]

The "American Catiline" to whom the essay refers is John C. Calhoun, who had a month earlier delivered a speech on the Senate floor arguing that slavery, hardly a necessary evil, was in fact "a positive good."[80] Referring to the slaveholding societies of antiquity, Calhoun firmly asserted that slavery, far from the cause of decline, was the very basis of any civilization worthy of the name. This kind of classical argument in favor of slavery was common in the South. The prominent Georgia lawyer Thomas R. R. Cobb, for example, echoed Calhoun in a scholarly discussion of Roman slavery, noting its centrality to "every nation . . . worthy of record."[81] Cobb also adopted a common proslavery argument rooted in classical philosophy, citing both Plato (on the notion of hierarchy) and Aristotle (on the idea of natural slaves) as evidence that slavery was "an element essential in a true republic."[82] And the social theorist George Fitzhugh perhaps brought the classical defense of slavery to its apogee when he averred that "Calhoun and Washington," like "Scipio and

Aristides," were "the noble results of domestic slavery."[83] "The Mutability of Human Affairs" countered such proslavery assertions by arguing that the rise of any society organized around slavery was in fact the preliminary trajectory of its decline, because slavery inevitably led to ruin.

Thomas Jefferson, who knew Volney personally and contributed to the English translation of *The Ruins*, was inclined to both ways of thinking: that slavery could both underpin and undermine a free civilization.[84] In his *Notes on the State of Virginia*, after enumerating the ill effects of slavery on the character and capacities of slave owners, Jefferson even goes so far as to anticipate the black rhetoric of American decline in a declaration of his own apocalyptic fears: "I tremble for my country," he confesses, "when I reflect that God is just."[85] David Walker, perhaps the most radical voice of African American abolitionism, responded directly to Jefferson in his *Appeal to the Coloured Citizens of the World*. Walker's scathing polemic, which appeared in three editions in 1829 and 1830, attacked Jefferson's *Notes* for both its pseudoscientific argument for white supremacy and its historical conception of Roman civilization and its practice of slavery. While the "Mutability" essay in *Freedom's Journal* had developed a twofold analogy, which linked whiteness to pre-Roman British barbarism and Americanness to Roman imperialism, Walker tactically embraced American racial dualism and what Martin Bernal has called the "Aryan Model" of eighteenth- and nineteenth-century Euro-American classicism—which tied modern Western nations to ancient Greece and Rome through the concept of race—in order to link the ideas of empire and savagery under the sign of whiteness.[86] For Walker, there was nothing more savage than the history of white people:

> The whites have always been an unjust, jealous, unmerciful, avaricious and blood-thirsty set of beings, always seeking after power and authority.—We view them all over the confederacy of Greece, where they were first known to be any thing . . . we see them there, cutting each other's throats—trying to subject each other to wretchedness and misery—to effect which, they used all kinds of deceitful, unfair, and unmerciful means. We view them next in Rome, where the spirit of tyranny and deceit raged still higher. We view them in Gaul, Spain, and in Britain.—In fine, we view them all over Europe . . . and we see them acting more like devils than accountable men.[87]

From ancient Greece and Rome to imperial France, Spain, and England, Walker recasts *translatio imperii* as a story of "avaricious" upheaval and usurpation, resulting in the fall of one empire after another. Employing apophasis, the classical rhetorical device that Douglass would later put to "scorching" ironic use in "What to the Slave Is the Fourth of July?," Walker details the grim history of empires past:

> I will not here speak of the destructions which the Lord brought upon Egypt, in consequence of the oppression and consequent groans of the oppressed—of the hundreds and thousands of Egyptians whom God hurled into the Red Sea for afflicting his people in their land—of the Lord's suffering people in Sparta or Lacedemon, the land of the truly famous Lycurgus—nor have I time to comment upon the cause which produced the fierceness with which Sylla usurped the title, and absolutely acted as dictator of the Roman people—the conspiracy of Cataline—the conspiracy against, and murder of Caesar in the Senate house—the spirit with which Marc Antony made himself master of the commonwealth—his associating Octavius and Lipidus with himself in power—their dividing the provinces of Rome among themselves—their attack and defeat, on the plains of Phillippi, of the last defenders of their liberty, (Brutus and Cassius)—the tyranny of Tiberius, and from him to the final overthrow of Constantinople by the Turkish Sultan, Mahomed II. A. D. 1453. I say, I shall not take up time to speak of the causes which produced so much wretchedness and massacre among those heathen nations, for I am aware that you know too well, that God is just, as well as merciful![88]

With his closing reminder, that "God is just," Walker affirms the validity of Jefferson's fear and "trembling," while the passage as a whole draws together sacred and secular histories into a singular transnational history of unaccountable violence. If this violence consists primarily of white Western nations "cutting each other's throats," Walker unequivocally asserts that this violence can be attributed to divine retribution, that "they who believe that God is a God of justice will believe that SLAVERY *is the principal cause.*"[89] By recounting this history in the context of his argument against American slavery, he concedes "Aryan model" claims to a classical heritage as articulated by the likes of Calhoun and evinced by the aesthetics and historiography of Jefferson; but in reducing Western history to what he takes to be its primary characteristics—slavery and "wretchedness and massacre"—he undercuts the notion that this history provided a precedent for republican institutions and "civilized" culture. On the contrary, in Walker's view this history provides a precedent only for the slavery and violence endemic to the American enterprise, and a dark prophecy for nations that fail—or refuse—to learn that history's lessons.

As an intellectual descendant of Walker, Henry Highland Garnet took a similarly critical view of the long sweep of history. In an 1848 address, Garnet invited his readers to survey that sweep for themselves: "The Present," Garnet began, "is the midway between the Past and the Future. Let us ascend that sublime eminence, that we may view the vast empire of ruin that is scarcely discernable through the mists of former ages."[90] Where Walker had condensed millennia into a paragraph to illustrate the continuities—in terms of the constitutive violence of both—between ancient and modern "civilization," and thus to counter dominant American narratives of historical progress, Garnet imagines history as an expansive landscape to behold. This framing of history as landscape would have been especially significant given the timing of Garnet's address, which he delivered less than two weeks after the signing of the Treaty of Guadalupe Hidalgo in early February 1848—a moment when, as the *United States Magazine and Democratic Review* would describe it, the rest of the world could "behold with astonishment the flag of the United States waving in triumph over every considerable city, from the Rio Grande to California, and from the supposed impregnable Castle of San Juan de Ulloa to the halls of the Montezumas."[91] With Manifest Destiny apparently materializing before the nation's very eyes, Garnet pointedly appropriated the perspective of westward-moving conquest in order to reverse its imperial gaze. The spoils of the war would now allow the United States officially to declare that "the whole boundless continent" was finally "ours," and would afford Americans a view of the future such as Cortés had beheld, in John Keats's memorable imagining, as he "star'd at the Pacific" from his "peak in Darien."[92] In Keats's poem, the first glimpse of the new ocean inspires in Cortés and his men a sense of "wild surmise" as to the future prospects embodied in such a view, and the boundless continent now under a triumphantly waving flag inspired similarly heady notions about the American future.

The newly acquired territory, as the *Democratic Review* suggested, would "open a new field of enterprise to our ever-progressive population, and new channels of trade for the manufacturing and agricultural districts of the United States." Beyond these comparatively mundane and practical concerns, victory over Mexico signaled a major advancement in the "onward march of national greatness."[93] Garnet's historical perspective is more or less diametrically opposed. While the *Democratic Review* celebrates the "ever-progressive" nature of the American people, and considers victory over Mexico as the occasion to "boldly go forward," Garnet directs his audience's gaze to the long history of ruin that is the legacy of imperial victories. While the former view assimilates all manner of violence and catastrophe to its narrative of historical progress, the latter apprehends this progress itself as a catastrophe.[94]

Garnet would later turn explicitly to the example of Rome to apply his historical vision to the future of the United States. Referring specifically to the geopolitics surrounding the Mexican War and the possible extension of slavery to the new territories, Garnet suggested that the United States had "crossed its Rubicon" with respect to slavery, and thus had likely set in motion, at the moment of seeming victory, the process of catastrophic decline. If Garnet here ironically concedes, as Walker had before him, an ancient Roman precedent for the emerging American empire, he turns that typology even further to his advantage by appropriating the most popular classically inflected motto for Manifest Destiny to his own vision of an alternative future:

> At this moment when so much feigned hatred is manifested toward us, our blood is mixed with every tribe from Cape Horn to the Frozen Ocean. Skillful men have set themselves to work at analyzation, and yet in many cases they are perplexed in deciding where to draw the line between the Negro and the Anglo-Saxon. Whatever our colorless brethren say of themselves, so far do they proclaim our future position. Do they say in proud exultation,
> > "No pent up Utica contracts our powers,
> > The whole boundless continent is ours,"
> in this they bespeak our destiny.[95]

In this taut passage Garnet analogizes the United States to the Roman Empire, while articulating an incisive critique of racial essentialism and the racist nature of both slavery and American imperial expansion; and in doing so, he envisions not only the inevitable collapse of that American regime, but also an alternative destiny unbounded by the imperatives of American nationalism and white supremacy. In stark contrast to the *esto perpetua* of Jefferson's multigenerational vision of American empire, Garnet imagines a future beyond the linked empires of slavery and ruin—a future also visible from the "sublime eminence" of the present, where the "airy plains are radiant with prophetic brightness, and truth, love, and liberty are descending the heavens, bearing the charter of man's destiny to a waiting world."[96]

The Watchword of Revolt

Garnet's "The Past and the Present" was addressed to black audiences at a moment of global crisis, and, given the context, the tone is appropriately prophetic. Marked by the outbreak of democratic revolutions in Europe and the nearly simultaneous solidification of US empire across the North American continent at the end of the Mexican War, the early months of 1848 appeared to Garnet and other black writers as a moment of truth, at which either revolutionary energies would spread across the globe in a wave of universal emancipation, or the course of empire would continue to take its way.[97] These geopolitical upheavals provided the context not only for Garnet's address "The Past and the Present," but also for his republication of Walker's *Appeal*, which he packaged together with an updated version of his 1843 "Address to the Slaves of the United States of America," texts that together fully map out the transnational and transhistorical geography of what Garnet would explicitly name the "empire of slavery." Like Walker's *Appeal*, the "Address to the Slaves" was intended to inspire revolution, and Garnet employs the phrase "empire of slavery" to draw the planned uprising of Denmark Vesey into a history of anti-imperial resistance running from Moses to Toussaint. In drawing together these distant spatiotemporal coordinates, Garnet here aligns with Walker and the various writers we have encountered in the black press, who worked to situate current events within a sweeping historical drama of slavery, empire, and resistance.

Perhaps the most striking example of this type of constellation appears in William Wells Brown's *St. Domingo: Its Revolutions and Its Patriots*, a wide-ranging historical lecture—delivered in both England and the United States in 1854—that connects the Haitian Revolution not only to the French Revolution, but to the revolutionary uprising of the helots of ancient Sparta. Brown drew his account of the helot revolt largely from Edward Bulwer-Lytton's history of Athens, which describes Spartan society in a manner that easily invites critical comparison to the antebellum United States. According to Bulwer-Lytton, the "whole fabric of the Spartan character rested upon slavery," and since it was "beneath a Spartan to labour—to maintain himself—to cultivate land," indeed to do anything but "fight an enemy ... to live a hero in war—an aristocrat in peace,—it was clearly a supreme necessity to his very existence as a citizen, and even as a human being, that there should be a subordinate class of persons ... engaged in providing for the wants of this privileged citizen." Ultimately, Bulwer-Lytton concluded, "without Helots the Spartan was the most helpless of human beings," and were slavery to be

"taken from the Spartan state, the state would fall at once!"[98] In Brown's estimation, in "the gloomy history of human servitude, there are few chapters
more horrible than that which relates to the Helots"; and given the extent
of his subjugation within Spartan society, the helot appears as a near-perfect
figure for slavery itself, expressing "nearly everything that can be conceived of
the oppressed and degraded man."[99] The inevitable result of this prolonged
and brutal oppression was a fervent desire to rebel. Prompted to action by a
devastating earthquake, which had razed much of the city and decimated the
Spartans' fighting force, the helots rose up in rebellion.

While the allegorical meaning of this digression into ancient history would
have been clear enough to his audience in 1854, Brown nonetheless makes it
explicit: "What the Helots were to Sparta at the time of the earthquake, the
blacks were to St. Domingo at the time of the French revolution. And the
American slaves are only waiting the opportunity of wiping out their wrongs
in the blood of their oppressors."[100] By drawing the prospect of American slave
rebellion back through the Haitian Revolution to the ancient world, Brown
sketches out his own historical geography of the "empire of slavery." Moving
backward in time and eastward in space—and thus against the conventional
spatiotemporal direction of history—Brown's lecture counters narratives of
historical progress with a palimpsestic history of oppression and resistance.
For Brown, the whole "gloomy history of human servitude," traceable in the
New World to the arrival of Columbus on Hispaniola—the island that would
become the site of the Haitian Revolution—and rooted in the slave societies
of the deeper past, is manifest in the present oppression and the prospective
revolutionary violence of enslaved people in the United States.

As it had appeared to Garnet and David Walker before him, *this* was the
legacy of Western history: a tradition of exploitative violence only thinly
veiled by the rhetoric of liberty such violence afforded the "privileged citizen" of these regimes; and the best these societies had to offer, at least for
the historian writing from the perspective of the oppressed and the enslaved,
was the spectacle of their own ruination. To this end, Brown excerpts from
Bulwer-Lytton an elaborate description of the destruction of Sparta. "That
city in ruins," as Brown recounted in his lecture, presented "one of the sub-
limest and most awful spectacles in history." With "the earth still trembling,"
and "the grim and dauntless soldiery collected amid piles of death and ruin,"
the "earthquake became" for the helots "the watchword of revolt," rendering "the multitude, sensible, not of danger, but of wrong, and rising, not to
succor, but to revenge." The passage here combines a spectacle of ruin with
a story of resistance, the righteousness of which is established through the

linkage of the earthquake with the slave revolt. Slavery, the passage suggests, is not only immoral but unnatural—so much so that it was "as if the great mother herself had summoned her children to vindicate the long-abused, the all inalienable heritage derived from her; and the stir of the angry elements was but the announcement of an armed and solemn union between nature and the oppressed."[101]

Brown's appropriation of Bulwer-Lytton's passage not only counters the theory of exceptionalism by positioning the US slave economy squarely within "the long and gloomy history of human servitude," but also situates enslaved African Americans within a revolutionary countercurrent to that history, aligned with both natural law and the laws of nature. According to this logic, the only "natural" state for a slave society is ruination. Brown takes this logic from the descriptive register of Bulwer-Lytton's account of the helot revolt and renders it prophetic in its application to the United States. The helots had been roused to revolution by "the all-inalienable heritage" of freedom, but while Americans claimed a similar grounding in natural law and unalienable rights, their postrevolutionary government "incorporated slavery and the slave-trade," and thus "aided in giving strength and vitality to an institution that" would ultimately "rend asunder" the free republic the Revolutionary War was fought to establish.[102] Unlike Toussaint's revolutionary government, which "made liberty its watchword" and "Freedom universal amongst the people," the American founders wrote slavery into the Constitution and thus made it constitutive of the nation they founded. The scene Brown conjures up, then, of a city utterly in ruins, points not merely to the destruction of the institution of slavery, as if it were some aberration to be excised from an otherwise healthy republic, but to the razing of the nation itself.

The Sepulchers of the Fathers

Brown's prediction of a catastrophic rending of the national fabric immediately follows the sublime spectacle of Sparta's destruction, a sequence that invited readers—as the *Colored American* had done in both word and image throughout its pages—to envision the abstract political disintegration of the "Union" through the material reality of a city in ruins. As the rest of the chapter will show, this prophetic evocation of ruins is characteristic more generally of Brown's writing about cities and their architecture, both of which he understands as sites of contestation with respect to historical narratives. Just as the *Weekly Advocate* had presented a straightforward "Description of the United States," anchored by the image of the Capitol as a symbol of unity and

the progress of American civilization, which at the same time revealed the
fractures and fault lines invisibly threatening the structural integrity of "the
people's house," Brown's writing about cities and monuments likewise illuminates the destabilizing contradictions embedded within them.

As we have seen, Brown participated in the tradition of juxtaposing the
Capitol with the Washington slave pen in order to highlight American hypocrisy, and in his *Narrative* the Bunker Hill Monument functioned similarly.
Like the Capitol, the Bunker Hill Monument, insofar as it was a monument
to the triumph of revolutionary forces over British imperial domination, was
a sign of the progress of the American nation and its founding principle of
freedom.[103] But the experience of the enslaved author, with respect to both
the ideology and the geography of the United States, led to a different conclusion about historical progress. Though he knew it would "sound strangely,"
Brown explained to his readers that it was "nonetheless true that an enslaved
American was forced to flee "from a democratic, republican, Christian government, to receive protection," whether in Canada or eventually the British
Isles themselves, "under the monarchy of Great Britain."[104] To flee in the
name of freedom, from a supposedly free republic to the protection of the
empire that republic had supposedly overthrown, was to journey symbolically
backward in time. The fact that fugitives like Brown and Frederick Douglass
would eventually be forced to travel eastward to England and the European
continent, moving against the direction of history according to the theory of
translatio imperii, in order to evade the Fugitive Slave Law, only reinforces the
point: that from the perspective of black people in America, whether enslaved
or nominally free, historical progress amounted primarily to the replication
of the slavery and empire the nation would claim to have escaped and moved
beyond. While the Bunker Hill Monument fit squarely within an American
historical discourse consisting of "boasting declarations in favour of freedom,"
which "extol the genius of Washington" and "the patriotism of Henry," for
Brown both the monument and the larger discourse were at best nationalistic
bluster and markers of hypocrisy, and at worst a standing threat to a tenuous
state of freedom.[105] As he observed in his *Narrative*, "While the people of
the United States boast of their freedom, they at the same time keep three
millions of their own citizens in chains; and while I am seated here in sight of
Bunker Hill Monument, writing this narrative, I am a slave, and no law, not
even in Massachusetts, can protect me from the hands of the slave-holder!"[106]

If we recall Brown's earlier evocation of the "American slave-trader, with
the constitution in his hat and his license in his pocket," marching "his gang
of chained men and women under the very eaves of the nation's capitol," we

can see how he acknowledges the Bunker Hill Monument and the Capitol as anchoring architectural features of the linear narrative of American progress, but at the same time refigures the monuments as coordinates within a competing historical narrative. This counternarrative looks to the monuments not for the ways they bespeak American "greatness" or the progress of civilization, but for the way they signify—through the imposing terms of their architecture and the Egyptian and Roman allusions embedded within them—their essential continuity with the spatiotemporal landscape of Garnet's "empire of ruin."[107]

While Garnet's spatialized vision of history is abstract and generalized, Brown's is grounded quite specifically in the solid reality of the monuments he encounters, and a clearer sense of what we might call Brown's historical geography emerges if we attend to the way Brown links American monuments not only to one another, but to their models and precedents in Europe. In *Three Years in Europe*, his travel narrative published in 1852, Brown draws the connection explicitly when he refers to the "Column Vendome" as "the Bunker Hill Monument of Paris." The Vendôme Column was built to celebrate the military conquests of Napoleon, and "the bas-relief of the shaft," as Brown describes it, "displays, in a chronological order, the principal actions of the French army, from the departure of the troops from Boulogne to the battle of Austerlitz." As if to add insult to the injuries of the defeated, the "metallic composition" for these outer decorations consisted of "cannons, guns, spikes, and other warlike implements taken from the Russians and Austrians by Napoleon," and the column's overall design follows the model of Trajan's Column in Rome. It is perhaps this combination of hubristic metallurgy and deliberate imitation of the Roman Empire, along with the later facts of Napoleon's history—the retreat from Russia, the defeat at Waterloo, his final exile on St. Helena—that led Brown ultimately to deem the column a "monument to folly."[108]

While Brown draws much of his description of the Vendôme Column, more or less verbatim, from a contemporary travel guide to Paris, both this last conclusion and the comparison to the Bunker Hill Monument are entirely his own. The original text of the guidebook presents the Vendôme Column to the English-speaking traveler with no historical commentary, describing it merely as "one of the most remarkable monuments in Paris," affording from its upper platform "an excellent view of the French capital and its many monuments."[109] While the average tourist is invited to appreciate the full sweep of French monumental grandeur from the pinnacle of one of its "most remarkable" examples, the column allows Brown to construct a rather different historical constellation, linking the American "empire for liberty" to imperial Rome and Napoleonic France through the concept of folly. Just as the Vendôme Column was a hubristic monument to a conquering hero who would end his career in ignominious defeat, the Bunker Hill Monument celebrated the triumph of a principle of freedom that had been betrayed and subjugated. By triangulating contemporary Boston, Paris of the recent past, and Rome in the time of Trajan, Brown invited his audience, as Garnet had done with his 1848 address, to view these historical coordinates all at once, as part of the "vast unfinished plot" of empire and slavery in which all Americans were implicated.

Brown deals similarly with the "celebrated obelisk of Luxor" at the Place de la Concorde, though he is more direct in expressing his suspicion that the latter monument was erected less to celebrate national achievement than deliberately to cover up the national crimes committed in that place. Referring to the Place's history as the site of the guillotine during the Reign of Terror, Brown recounts feeling a "shudder" as he "passed over its grounds," and speculates that the French erected the obelisk in order "to take from one's mind the old associations of this place."[110] But as Brown notes, the obelisk merely covers over the violence of domestic terror with the violence of empire. This monument was not *modeled on* but *was in fact* a relic of the ancient world. While the obelisk was not colonial plunder per se—it was given to France as part of a complex exchange of antiquities tied to contemporary geopolitics— Brown depicts the monument as emblematic of the persistence of empire and slavery across a very *longue durée*, from the ancient Egyptian slave society to the imperial pressures of the West upon North Africa and the Levant.[111] Much as David Walker had done in presenting his own condensation of white history, Brown employs apophasis to draw attention to what he purports to pass over in silence:

> It would be tedious to follow the history of this old and venerated stone, which was taken from the quarry 1550 years before the birth of Christ; placed in Thebes; its removal; the journey to the Nile, and down the Nile; thence to Cherbourg, and lastly its arrival in Paris on the 23d of December, 1833—just one year before I escaped from slavery. The obelisk was raised on the spot where it now stands, on the 25th of October, 1836, in the presence of Louis Philippe and amid the greetings of 160,000 persons.[112]

For Brown, the path of the obelisk mirrors the course of empire across space and time, as the "old and venerated stone" is first put in the service of the pharaohs, before being transferred to the modern West in order to fulfill the neoclassical desire for monuments from the ancient world. Brown is deliberate in noting not only that the obelisk was ultimately situated in the Place de la Concorde to cover over the memory of the Revolution and its aftermath, but also that its dedication took the form of a nationalistic ritual involving a sitting monarch and a cheering crowd. Brown's account of this counterrevolutionary spectacle, through which an imposing imperial monument obscures with nationalist grandeur the failure or abandonment of the principles for which a revolution was carried out, resonates with his earlier linkage of the Bunker Hill Monument to the Vendôme Column and Trajan's Column in Rome. It apprehends the ideological function of classical monumentalism as a means of justifying and celebrating authoritarianism and empire, and by observing the coincidence of his escape from slavery and the obelisk's arrival in Paris, Brown merges the history of the obelisk with his own, situating the enslaved American—and by extension the nation at large—within the long global history of empire and slavery that exceptionalist narratives aimed to disavow.

In moving from the *Narrative* to *Three Years in Europe*, Brown passes geographically from his primary scene of writing in the shadow of Bunker Hill to historic sites in Paris that allow him to deepen the critique the American monument had originally inspired. Brown's observation concerning the hypocrisy of slavery in the United States, as exemplified by the ironic juxtaposition of the monument to freedom with the fugitive narrator writing "in sight of" it, aligns precisely with the more common practice of contrasting the US Capitol with the Washington slave pen. The critical force of these juxtapositions relies upon the affirmation of the normative messages encoded within the monuments; for the hypocrisy to be clear, we must accept the Capitol and the Bunker Hill Monument on the terms on which they were constructed—as symbols of freedom and American progress. But just as the *Colored American* allowed its readers to map the idea of Nineveh in ruins back onto the "beautiful engraving" of the "View of the Capitol at Washington," so too would Brown's meditations on the Parisian monuments to "folly" allow a reinterpretation of the meaning of the monument at Bunker Hill. By linking the Bunker Hill Monument to monuments from the ancient world and the imperial West, Brown retroactively imbues the obelisk at Bunker Hill with a second significance. Beyond its role as a symbol of freedom that generates, by contrast with the slave narrator in its shadow, an ironic rebuke to American hypocrisy, the Bunker Hill Monument also signals the nation's affinity with the follies of empires past, and thus projects a spectral image of its own future existence as a ruin.

Brown brings this historical sensibility to bear in *Clotel* through the use of Washington, DC, as a powerfully symbolic landscape. Though the novel is episodic and assembled, as Ivy Wilson has argued, as something of a "bricolage," the various episodes function as a prelude to a definitively climactic scene in the nation's capital—the destination toward which the eponymous character has been inexorably moving.[113] Like Brown's physical relocation to England and Europe and his imaginative historical journeying in the travel writing and the lecture on Haiti, Clotel's journey is backward in time and against the westward course of imperial history. As the novel's subtitle suggests, Clotel is the daughter of Thomas Jefferson. Having been sold at auction after Jefferson's death, Clotel lives first in Virginia as mistress to the apparently benevolent white planter Horatio Green, with whom she has a daughter. Though faithful for a time, Green develops social and political ambitions, and ultimately betrays Clotel, marrying a white woman of means and influence who insists he sell Clotel down the river. Clotel ultimately finds herself separated from her daughter and sold into slavery in the deepest South.

The course of her life thus far has moved her farther and farther from the figure of Jefferson, the city of Washington, and the supposedly unalienable rights for which both man and city stood as powerful symbols. The concluding chapters of the novel reverse this course, with Clotel's fatal journey bringing her back to Virginia and finally to Washington. This northeastward movement is at the same time a symbolic movement toward the central characters and landscapes of the nation's founding mythology—a journey to both the seat of American power and the origins of the American idea. As the daughter of the "Founding Father" Thomas Jefferson, Clotel is a symbol for the nation itself. In returning to Virginia, where the state capitol and the house at Monticello—both designed by Jefferson—stand as neoclassical national monuments, her physical trajectory aligns with the critical orientation of the novel, which has been pointing toward Jefferson all along.

Beyond evoking the specter of Jefferson throughout the novel as the father of "the President's Daughter," Brown—like David Walker before him—directly addresses Jefferson's most prominent writings within his own text. Brown chose Jefferson's most famous words for the novel's epigraph—the lines from the Declaration of Independence in which he asserted as "self-evident" the "truths" that "all men are created equal; that they are endowed by their Creator with certain inalienable rights"—and in a later chapter he included the passage from Query XVIII of *Notes on the State of Virginia* in which Jefferson laments slavery's effects on the "Manners" of both enslavers and the enslaved. This is the passage Jefferson concludes with his dark premonition of the fate of the enslaving nation itself. Brown emphasized this premonition by printing it twice in the same chapter, the second time standing alone: "I trem- ble for my country, when I recollect that God is just, and that His justice can- not sleep for ever" (155).[114] By reiterating these well-known remarks, Brown at once highlights the problem of slavery in the "empire for liberty" and signals a turn in the late chapters of the novel toward the trope of the ruins of empires, which had already informed his meditations on European monuments, as it would his lecture on the Haitian Revolution.

This turn becomes explicit shortly thereafter, in a chapter entitled "A True Democrat." The "Democrat" is Henry Morton, a white doctor from Vermont who purchases Thomas Jefferson's other daughter, Althesa, in order to marry her and remove her from slavery. The two live happily in New Orleans, where Morton's democratic nature, expressed through his opposition to slavery, makes him from time to time "obnoxious to private circles, owing to the denunciatory manner in which he condemned the 'peculiar institution'" (178). At a party one evening, finding himself subjected to the discourse of a slave owner on the "glory and freedom of American institutions," Morton denounces slavery by way of analogy to ancient Rome. His tirade, through which he argues that "unless slavery was speedily abolished, it would be the ruin of the Union," is itself a bricolage of sources ranging from Walker's *Appeal* to any number of essays and articles from the abolitionist press (178). "Behold," Morton intones:

> the once proud fabric of a Roman empire—an empire carrying its arts and arms into every part of the Eastern continent; the monarchs of mighty kingdoms dragged at the wheels of her triumphal chariots; her eagle waving over the ruins of desolated countries;—where is her splendour, her wealth, her power, her glory? Extinguished forever. Her mouldering temples, the mournful vestiges of her former grandeur, afford a shelter to her muttering monks. Where are her statesmen, her sages, her philosophers, her orators, generals? Go to their solitary tombs and inquire? She lost her national character, and her destruc- tion followed. The ramparts of her national pride were broken down, and Vandalism desolated her classic fields. Then let the people of our country take warning ere it is too late. (181)

In its use of rhetorical questions, Morton's peroration echoes quite faithfully the essay in the *Colored American* "On the Mutability of Human Things," but it is emblematic of the discourse of imperial ruin more broadly. Over the course of the novel it functions both generally, as the kind of ominous warning this rhetoric always presented, and specifically as a means of framing the story's conclusion within the city of Washington, in which the forms and methods of black classicism I have traced thus far merge in the set piece of Clotel's dramatic suicide, "a tragedy" that Brown pointedly describes as "enacted . . . within plain sight of the President's house and the capital of the Union" (217).

Here Brown reiterates the common juxtaposition of the Capitol building with the business of slavery conducted in its shadow. But read in relation to Morton's tirade, Brown's juxtaposition of the Capitol with slavery does more than merely highlight the hypocrisy of slavery in the United States; it also renders the building an ominous foreshadowing of imperial decline and ruination. This prophecy of ruin is reaffirmed in more explicit terms through the voice of George, another enslaved child of another "American statesman," who had also been owned by Horatio Green, the ambitious politician who betrayed Clotel and the daughter they had together. George had been involved in Nat Turner's rebellion, and in his defense before the court he appeals to the principles of the Declaration of Independence. "I have heard my master," he tells the court, "read in the Declaration of Independence 'that all men are created free and equal,' and this caused me to inquire of myself why I was a slave. I also heard him talking . . . about the war with England, and he said, all wars and fightings for freedom were just and right. If so, in what am I wrong?" (224). While the entire novel is concerned with the betrayal of these revolutionary principles, here George becomes, as Wilson has observed, "the only character who explicitly adopts and deploys the iconographic language of the American Revolution to frame his polemic for black emancipation."[115] But in his defense he also echoes Brown's previous writings on monumental culture, extending the critique beyond the fact of hypocrisy with respect to revolutionary rhetoric to the ideological underpinnings of American exceptionalism and its attendant imperial project.

Using language appropriated from the Massachusetts minister Charles Shackford's condemnation of the Mexican War—in a lecture that Douglass would publish across three issues of the *North Star* in February and March of 1848—George warns the tribunal that neither nationalistic celebrations nor monumental architecture "will save you," nor will it "do to praise your fathers and build their sepulchres" (225).[116] The word "sepulchre" here—in both Shackford's original and Brown's appropriation—conjures up the scene of Daniel Webster at the dedication to the Bunker Hill Monument, where he suggested that he and the citizens in attendance were "among the sepulchres of our fathers"; and in recalling the Bunker Hill Monument, George's speech comes into alignment with Brown's wide-ranging skepticism regarding monuments in general.[117] The speech definitively extends Brown critical view of Bunker Hill to the landscape of Washington, and brings them both under the larger discourse of empire and ruin rooted in the example of Rome.

Given that Brown situates this speech in the chapter just after Clotel's suicide in the shadow of the White House and the Capitol—which in turn had followed closely on Morton's discourse on the "mouldering temples" and "solitary tombs" of the Romans—George's reference to the sepulchers of the fathers incorporates the buildings and monuments of Washington under the umbrella concept of the tomb. George would seem to affirm this conceptual association in his own peroration, which is inflected, like Morton's, with the rhetoric of ruin. Similar to the rebel Gabriel before him, George figures his uprising as an act of patriotism, the failure of which portends the failure of the nation he had hoped to save from itself. Taking an elevated historical perspective, much like Garnet's view of the empire of ruin, George laments the future of America "from the mount of vision," where "the genius of a true humanity, beholding you with tearful eyes . . . shall fold his wings in sorrowing pity, and repeat the strain, 'O land of Washington, how often would I have gathered thy children together, as a hen doth gather her brood under her wings, and ye would not; behold your house is left unto you desolate'" (225).

Here Brown again plagiarizes Shackford for George's alteration of a passage from the Gospel according to Matthew, which contains Christ's warning to his disciples not to be taken in by the Pharisees, who "say, and do not."[118] In Matthew's account, Christ goes on to develop a monumental image for the hypocrisy of the Pharisees that resonates powerfully with George's defense, likening them "unto whited sepulchres, which indeed appear beautiful outward, but are within full of dead men's bones, and of all uncleanness."[119] In a previous chapter of *Clotel*, which recounts the cycle of violence set in motion by Turner's rebellion, Brown again suggestively plagiarizes—this time from John Relly Beard's *Life of Toussaint L'Ouverture*—similar terms to describe the only monument to the freedom struggle of the enslaved: "No graves were dug for the negroes; their dead bodies became food for dogs and vultures, and their bones, partly calcined by the sun, remained scattered about, as if to mark the mournful fury of servitude and lust for power" (214).[120] These latter two are precisely what the American Pharisees entomb in the "whited sepulchres" of the national monuments that mark the landscape of the "land of Washington." With Morton's discourse on the fall of Rome in the background, along with Christ's warning to "Jerusalem, Jerusalem . . . that killest

the prophets, and stonest them which are sent unto thee," we can see how
the rebel George—whose name inevitably recalls the rebellious "Father of his
Country"—undoes in a single trenchant passage both the biblical and the
classical typological underpinnings of the American mission, while at the
same time imaginatively rendering the monumental landscape of Washington
little more than a graveyard in which the nation's ideals are buried along with
its crimes.[121]

Within Plain Sight

It is against this landscape of Washington that Clotel meets her tragic fate.
Having been captured in Richmond, Clotel is transferred to Washington to
be sold, and not surprisingly, given the contexts we have been developing, the
slave pen in which she finds herself "stands midway between the capitol at
Washington and the president's house" (215). Rather than submit to a return
to southern slavery, Clotel decides to make a break for freedom. Literally fleeing the city that had been consecrated to freedom, but finding herself trapped
between slave catchers pursuing from both north and south, Clotel leaps to
her death from the Long Bridge, which linked Washington to Virginia across
the Potomac River.[122]

By choosing death over slavery, Clotel claims the mantle of Patrick Henry,
the American Revolution, and the legacy of Cato that had so powerfully
informed them both, but she also enacts what Brown suggests is the darker
truth for the American slave that the climactic chapter's title—"Death Is
Freedom"—would seem to suggest. Within the entrenched regime of chattel
slavery and white supremacy, liberty or death is not a living option for enslaved
people. The "appalling tragedy" of Clotel's death reveals that death *is* freedom
in two distinct yet related senses: in the more conventional sense that death is
a release from the bondage—whether literal or figurative—that is mortal life;
but also in the historical materialist sense, embraced by the likes of Calhoun
if denied by the likes of Jefferson, that black death—again either literal or
figurative, bodily death or the social death that chattel slavery produces—
underpins white freedom. As David Walker observed, whites had determined
that "the sons of Africa" are "and *ought to be* SLAVES to the American people and their children forever!! To dig their mines and work their farms; and
thus go on enriching them, from one generation to another with our *blood*
and our *tears*!!!!"[123] Walker suggests that black labor amounts to the transformation of black bodies into white riches, the material human resource into
the abstraction of wealth.[124] Clotel leaps to her death in the shadow of white

monumental buildings consecrated to freedom and constructed in large part by the labor of enslaved people. The "blood" and "tears" that constitute that labor are incorporated into those buildings, which George will figure in the following chapter as the "whited sepulchres" of the nation's "fathers." Just as enslaved labor everywhere was invisibly incorporated into both white monuments and the "enrichment" of whites themselves, and enslaved bodies were incorporated into the body politic through the logic of the three-fifths compromise, Clotel's dead body is unceremoniously "deposited" in "a hole dug in the sand" by the bank of the river, entombed—though with a grave unmarked—within the very land of Washington (218).

Clotel's suicide and burial occur "within plain sight" of the most prominent monumental features of the Washington landscape—buildings her own father had helped to design, and in which he had lived and worked, presiding over the economic and geopolitical affairs of the "empire for liberty" he had imagined. But just as Brown had drawn the story of imperial "folly" from the triumphal monuments he visited in Paris, so too does the choreography of Clotel's fatal flight, with the convergence of northern and southern slave catchers on the enslaved woman trapped at the center point of the supposedly divided nation, all in the shadow of the White House and the Capitol, allow him to project a story of American slavery and empire onto these neoclassical monuments that had been putatively consecrated to freedom and democracy. The juxtaposition of Capitol and fugitive is reiterated in the Grace Greenwood poem Brown appends to the end of the chapter, in which "Columbia's daughter flees" from "Columbia's glorious capitol," seeking "sanctuary God has given" in the "sheltering forest trees," and it is visually reaffirmed in the famous image of "The Death of Clotel," which appeared as the frontispiece to the novel (fig. 2.4). In this engraving, we see Clotel, caught between slave catchers moving in from the north and the south, in the act of leaping upward and *eastward*—moving like Brown and other fugitives against the spatiotemporal grain of history—and against the backdrop of the city.

Through Clotel's suicidal leap in plain sight of the Capitol, Brown simultaneously refigures that building as a monument to slavery rather than freedom and aligns his heroine with Nat Turner and Gabriel as the proper inheritors of the Catonic image. In both her self-sacrificing act of resistance and the unsung nature of the act, however, Clotel may also recall us to the earlier story, which Douglass had printed in the *North Star*, of the enslaved man in Alabama who similarly had died in a river while trying to escape. Just as Clotel had claimed her liberty through the act of dying, the Alabama fugitive was "a poor despised, sorrow-stricken man, who acts out the sentiment"

THE DEATH OF CLOTEL. *Page* 218.

FIGURE 2.4 "The Death of Clotel." Frontispiece image for William Wells Brown's *Clotel; or, The President's Daughter* (London: Partridge & Oakey, 1853).

of Patrick Henry.[125] The *North Star* went on to suggest that fates such as those befalling Clotel and the enslaved man in Alabama, in spite of their dramatic aspects, were not even considered tragic within the predominant narrative of national progress. They were business as usual, collateral losses quite common to the economy of slavery—matters for accounts and ledgers rather than monuments and historiography.

While Brown superficially follows the *North Star* in lamenting the absence of "proper" monuments to the dead, Clotel's burial beneath the riverbank— like the bones of Nat Turner's compatriots and the martyrs of the Haitian Revolution, all "scattered about" and "calcined by the sun"—constitutes a new kind of natural monument, marking "the mournful fury of servitude and lust of power" (214). Considering the situation of the novel within the context of the prevalent discourse of imperial ruin, Clotel's interment, literally beneath the foundations of the seat of American empire, both unsettles and reveals the nature of those foundations.[126] And given George's warning that no amount of what Henry David Thoreau called the "hammered stone" of nationalist construction could "save" the nation from itself, we can understand Clotel's incorporation into the earth as the germ of something like the earthquake that provided the ancient helots with a "watchword of revolt" and a sign of

Sparta's impending ruin.[127] Her riverbank grave thus threatens the stability of the monumental landscape above, but it also stands as an alternative monument, marking the transnational and transhistorical union of "nature and the oppressed"—a union that contrasts starkly with the economic alliance of North and South, situated within and celebrated by the imperious Roman forms of its monumental buildings, and bound together by the commodified body of the slave.

Ancient History, American Time

CHARLES CHESNUTT AND THE SITES OF MEMORY

AS ITS VARIOUS appearances in abolitionist discourse and antebellum African American literature make clear, the US Capitol was a site of contestation from the time of its construction through the coming of the Civil War. In this regard both the Capitol and the larger monumental landscape of Washington, DC, are what the French historian Pierre Nora has called *lieux de mémoire* (typically translated as "sites of memory"). For Nora, the site of memory is a capacious category, encompassing not only monumental structures like the Pantheon and the Arc de Triomphe, but also "commemorations" and "celebrations" of historical figures and events. Sites of memory might also include those figures themselves—like Napoleon Bonaparte or the "Founding Fathers"—and the sites at which historic events transpired, such as the battlefield at Gettysburg or "the Wall of the Fédérés, where the last defenders of the Paris Commune were massacred in 1870."[1] Ferzina Banaji has usefully defined the *lieu de mémoire* as "a metonymic site in which traces of the past are commemorated or celebrated and the collective memories of a particular group located, their meaning crystallised into a single authoritative interpretation of history."[2] The single authoritative interpretation of US history has been prominently on display in both the Capitol and the city of Washington since their conception, but as Nora notes, while there are "dominant . . . *lieux de mémoire*" that contribute to this kind of authoritative narrative, there are also those that offer resistance to domination. The former, like the Capitol, are "spectacular and triumphant, imposing and, generally, imposed—either by a national authority or by an established interest, but always from above," while the latter "are places of refuge, sanctuaries of spontaneous devotion and silent pilgrimage, where one finds the living heart of memory."[3] In this second category we might include both the unmarked site of Clotel's burial as well as the novel called *Clotel*.[4] But these alternative sites of memory do something more than provide refuge, a space outside the culture of domination. Since these alternative sites—Clotel's unmarked grave beneath the city of Washington, and *Clotel*'s irruption within the canon of national literature—emerge from and are part of the same literal and figurative geography of the larger "American" narrative, they fundamentally reconfigure that geography. Clotel's burial alters the composition of the *lieu de mémoire* that is the city of Washington, even as the grave itself becomes a site of memory in its own right.

This chapter will consider the ways this contest over sites of memory extended to the project of postbellum national reconciliation, which involved the proliferation of monuments and celebrations commemorating not only the Civil War, but the entire course of the nation's history. This nationalist project entailed major renovations and commissioned artworks at the Capitol, as well as the construction of other prominent buildings and monuments in Washington, DC, and around the country. This wave of construction and renovation effectively perpetuated an imperial mode of American classicism that had developed across the earlier part of nineteenth century, one that drew on ancient history and employed a classical aesthetic to both justify and celebrate the expansion of an American empire. And just as William Wells Brown and others had done before the war, many black writers after Reconstruction recognized that this representational strategy aligned with a political one—that continental and global empire, grounded in entrenched ideologies of national exceptionalism and white supremacy, were the means through which reconciliation were to be achieved.

Geopolitically, the era Charles Chesnutt would name "Post-bellum, Pre-Harlem" encompassed not only the closing of the frontier but also the formal and informal projection of American power into the Caribbean and across the Pacific, a concerted imperial project that Pauline Hopkins identified as part of a global "battle . . . between the Anglo-Saxon and the dark-skinned races of the earth."[5] And writers like Chesnutt and Hopkins attended not only to these geopolitical developments, but also to the monumental structures and historical celebrations that served to enable and justify that imperial agenda. Beyond their authorizing function with respect to the project of empire, these forms of commemoration—for occasions such as the centennial of George Washington's inauguration, or the four hundredth anniversary of the arrival of Columbus in the "New World"—also served as sites of memory through which blacks and their enslavement could be elided from the historical record, and around which whites could rally to re-establish a racialized progress narrative for the nation.[6]

As the nation recommitted to the projects of continental and global empire, monumental culture and nationalist commemorations—from the renovation and decoration of the US capitol in the 1860s and 1870s to the construction of the "White City" for the Columbian Exposition in 1893—aimed to re-establish the exceptionalist narrative of progress that had been temporarily interrupted by the Civil War. What follows in this chapter will consider Charles Chesnutt's early work in relation to this resurgent imperial culture of the postbellum United States. While monumental constructions and public rituals commemorating national history aimed to reassert the Jeffersonian notion of the "empire for liberty," Chesnutt's early fiction—in alignment with the writings of contemporaries like T. Thomas Fortune and Pauline Hopkins—reads these cultural rituals and artifacts as evidence of the persistence of the "empire of slavery" by another name.

Chesnutt in the Temple of Liberty

At twenty-one years of age, Charles Chesnutt was ambitious and determined, as he wrote in his journal, to "go to the Metropolis, or some other large city, and like Franklin, Greely [sic] and many others," he would make his mark there. As a first step in this direction, Chesnutt travelled to Washington, DC, in 1879, and as he set out for the capital he was "buoyed up with high hopes of success and bright visions of the privileges and rights enjoyed by colored men in the blessed land to which my steps were turned."[7] As this passage from his journal suggests, Chesnutt undertook this first foray into the metropolis as both a pragmatist in search of opportunity and a pilgrim to the "blessed" shrine of American freedom. In both regards his trip was quintessentially "American," informed by an optimism typically associated with figures like Benjamin Franklin and Horace Greeley and embodied by the monumental landscape of Washington, DC. Just prior to his trip, Chesnutt had expressed this optimism in a letter to the Congregationalist *Christian Union*. In the letter, never published but recorded in his own journal, Chesnutt had enthusiastically envisioned a future in which "the Colored Man in America" would "be considered . . . a friend and brother," and in which he might "become a strong pillar in the Temple of American Liberty."[8] In this optimistic vision, no longer would African Americans be included in the nation—as Clotel had been—through their anonymous burial within it; instead black citizens would be legitimately incorporated into the architecture of democracy.

Chesnutt's optimism with respect to the figurative "Temple of American Liberty" remains apparent in his reflections on its material embodiment in the US Capitol. The building was, in Chesnutt's estimation, "worthy to be Capitol of a great nation," with its "tall dome pierc[ing] the sky," and the "Goddess of Liberty" looking "down upon the broad land which acknowledges her sway." He was impressed with the classical architecture and the "truly imposing" nature of "the vast marble pile." Beyond its monumental structure, Chesnutt was struck by its many adornments, including the "historical paintings . . . on the stairways, and around the rotunda." Among these paintings was Emanuel Leutze's *Westward the Course of Empire Takes Its Way*, a mural in the stairwell in the House wing of the Capitol (fig. 3.1). Commissioned in 1861 and completed the following year, the mural quite literally redirects the nation's gaze from its fraught North-South axis to the expansive territory of a newly acquired West. The scene is of a wagon train crossing the western mountains at the point at which the Pacific Ocean first becomes visible. A forward scout stands off in the middle distance, elevated on an outcropping of rock and waving one arm in triumph, while another man reaches upward with an American flag they intend to plant at the site. Closer in, a man in a coonskin cap gently encourages the women and children nearby, who seem

FIGURE 3.1 Emanuel Leutze, *Westward the Course of Empire Takes Its Way*, stereochrome mural, 1862. House Wing, west stairway, US Capitol. Image courtesy of the Architect of the Capitol.

wearied by the journey, to continue along the path. Another man on a horse, his gun resting across the back of his saddle, indicates to the rest of the party that the ocean—their destination and their destiny—lies just ahead.

Leutze's mural is perhaps the quintessential image of Manifest Destiny, combining the iconography of both the biblical and classical strains of American typology. Surrounding the romantic imagery of the central composition is a frame that includes a variety of historical and allegorical figures, along with textual inscriptions, that announce these typological relations. The figure of Moses, included in the left-hand frame, reinforces the visual allusion to the journey of the Israelites to the Promised Land, which finally could be viewed from the pinnacle of Pisgah.[9] If the biblical elements of the image refer to the supposedly sacred nature of the American mission, the classical references develop the secular foundations of American empire. This is most obvious in the title itself, which Leutze drew from George Berkeley's 1752 poem "On the Prospect of Planting Arts and Learning in America." As I have shown in chapter 1, Berkeley's poem encapsulated for eighteenth- and nineteenth-century readers the classical historical concept of *translatio imperii*, according to which the seat of empire moved inexorably westward—from Rome, in the predominant American conception, to London and then to the New World. While Berkeley's famous phrase is prominently inscribed across the top panel, Leutze reaffirmed its imperial message through the less conspicuous inclusion of an equally famous passage from Jonathan Sewall's epilogue to Joseph Addison's *Cato*. As we have seen in the previous two chapters, these lines—"No pent up Utica contracts our powers, but the whole boundless continent is ours"—provided a rallying cry for patriots during the Revolutionary War and for national expansionists across the following decades. Situated at the bottom-left corner of the surrounding frame, Sewall's declaration invited statesmen and citizens to envision the consummation of US empire as both the legacy of the American Revolution and the ameliorative future that only awaited the resolution of the Civil War.[10]

If Leutze's mural speaks to a presently fractured nation through a reparative vision of the future, Constantino Brumidi's *Frieze of American History*—which circles the interior of the Capitol Rotunda—works to effect that reparation through a depiction of a collective narrative of the past. And like Leutze's mural, the *Frieze* was commissioned by the federal government specifically for this reconciliatory purpose. While Brumidi had been initially commissioned in 1865 for the fresco adorning the interior of the building's dome—itself a richly classical composition entitled *The Apotheosis of George Washington*, in which the first president is elevated to the status of a god—it is perhaps not surprising that he was reinstated as a full-time artist at the Capitol in the immediate aftermath of the Compromise of 1877, which resulted in the election of Rutherford B. Hayes to the presidency and the de facto abandonment of Reconstruction. At that time Brumidi was tasked with executing the *Frieze*, which he had sketched out twenty years earlier—just prior to the election of Lincoln and the outbreak of the war—as a sequence of twenty scenes that would visually narrate the history of "America" from the arrival of Columbus to the California Gold Rush.[11] If this commission seemed to reiterate the narratives already expressed in Leutze's mural and other decorative elements of the Capitol—for example, Thomas Crawford's *Progress of Civilization*, the sculptural frieze above the entrance to the Senate chamber (fig. 3.2)—this reiteration corresponded to what was emerging as the effectual re-entrenchment of sectional conflict over slavery and its aftermath. For African Americans and their allies, the Compromise of 1877 echoed in unsettling ways the insidious compromises of the antebellum period, revealing a persistent willingness, if not an outright determination, to sacrifice the interests of African Americans to the project of "American" unification. Just as Leutze's mural had encouraged viewers to orient themselves to the West, looking beyond the inconvenient fissure of civil war to the national narrative such a westward orientation implied, Brumidi's *Frieze* obscures the unfinished business of history in order to advance a linear and progressive historical view.

The frieze is an elaborate trompe l'oeil, painted in fresco to appear as sculpture, which links it to Crawford's actual sculpture above the entrance to the Senate. Crawford's sculpture essentially encapsulates the history of settler colonialism through a series of figures depicting the displacement of Native Americans in favor of Anglo-European forms of agriculture, science, and military power. Taken together, the two "friezes" marry the ideas of "America" and "Civilization" through the forms of classicism and the idea of race. While Crawford's sculpture had represented white conquest through emblematic figures, each frame of Brumidi's *Frieze* depicts a recognizable event from the history of Anglo-European colonization of the New World. But in spite of

FIGURE 3.2 Thomas Crawford, *The Progress of Civilization*. Marble. 1863. Senate pediment, east front, US Capitol. Image courtesy of the Architect of the Capitol.

its historical specificity, Brumidi's *Frieze* functions similarly to Crawford's *Progress*, in that it assimilates all specifics to its larger aim, which is to render "American History" and "The Progress of Civilization" essentially synonymous and coextensive. Beginning with the "Landing of Columbus," proceeding through the exploits of the Spaniards Cortés, Pizarro, and de Soto, the arrival of the English Pilgrims, and the famous battles of the Revolutionary War, and culminating in the triumph of the United States over Mexico and the discovery of gold in California, the *Frieze* narrates the inexorable rise of an "American" empire (figs. 3.3 and 3.4).

In his account of his trip to Washington, Chesnutt does express a genuine admiration for these interior artworks and the general grandeur of the Capitol and the capital city, yet there are already hints of a more critical mode that would eventually emerge in his stories and novels. While he was impressed with the "historical" images that he saw, he also took note of what he didn't

FIGURE 3.3 Constantino Brumidi, "Landing of Columbus." *Frieze of American History.* 1877–1880. Rotunda, US Capitol. Image courtesy of the Architect of the Capitol.

FIGURE 3.4 Constantino Brumidi, "American Army Entering the City of Mexico." *Frieze of American History.* 1877–1880. Rotunda, US Capitol. Image courtesy of the Architect of the Capitol.

see, namely representations of slavery and the Civil War, none of which, as he remarked in his journal, "can be admitted to the Capitol."[12] The American landscape as depicted in the Capitol at the time that Chesnutt arrived was dominated not by the recent rupture of the war, but by the ideas of civilization's progress and the achievement of an American continental empire, all presided over by the apotheosized specter of George Washington. And this nationalist aesthetic entirely obscured the 250-year history of slavery upon which the country had been built. This conspicuous absence would seem to have confirmed for Chesnutt a sentiment he had copied out, not long before his trip to Washington, from his reading in Voltaire: "We love the truth, but the ancient proverb says 'Not all truths are good to say.'"[13] This Voltairean idea certainly informed Chesnutt's view that "the reason" for the absence was perfectly "obvious."[14] Slavery and Civil War may have been historical truths, but they remained unspeakable within "Temple of American Liberty." Chesnutt's "obvious" point is that public history demands distortion—a point he elaborates through the example of Brumidi's *Apotheosis*, which he attends to in greater detail than any of the other artworks in the Capitol (fig. 3.5).

The project of expanding and renovating the Capitol had begun in the 1850s, but with the onset of the war its completion took on a sense of existential urgency, as the building stood increasingly as a figure for the nation.

FIGURE 3.5 Constantino Brumidi, *The Apotheosis of Washington*. Fresco. 1865. Rotunda, US Capitol. Image courtesy of the Architect of the Capitol.

Completed at the end of 1865, Brumidi's *Apotheosis* would provide the finishing touch to both the Capitol and the war. The fresco aimed at national reconciliation through its celebration of Washington and its classical aesthetic, both of which recalled the nation's founding: the former evoking the common struggle of the Revolution and the latter recalling the typological association with the precedent of republican Rome that had animated the revolutionary generation. The focal point of the composition is Washington himself, who sits on a cloud flanked by the goddesses of Victory and Liberty. On a white banner above the general's head is emblazoned the nation's Latin motto—*E pluribus unum*. Radiating outward from Washington is a series of allegorical scenes, drawing on figures from classical mythology to depict, in a manner similar to Crawford's design for the pediment frieze, the arts and sciences, commerce, and military power as the emblems of American progress. Each of these emblems is visually linked to its attendant god from the Roman pantheon, with Washington, now apotheosized as a god in his own right, presiding over them all.

In his own remarks on the fresco, Chesnutt forgoes appreciation in favor of noting a potent irony about Brumidi's "allegorical painting": perhaps like the history depicted in the other paintings around the Capitol, the *Apotheosis* gets less appealing the closer you look at it. "From below," as Chesnutt observed, "the figures appear of life-size, and the coloring is very chaste, but on ascending the dome to within a few feet of the picture, the figures are large and ugly, and the coloring coarse. But in this the art consists, as they were painted to be viewed from below, [at] a distance."[15] The art consists in controlling the way we see it, keeping us at a distance and covering the coarseness of reality with the illusion of virtue. While the critique here is focused narrowly on Brumidi's aesthetic effects, in the context of his observations about the politics of representation in the Capitol these remarks indicate Chesnutt's more general apprehension that the apotheosis of Washington and the invisibility of slavery were part and parcel of the same representational agenda, evidence less of the truth of history than of the predominance of a certain historical method.

Brumidi was still at work on the *Frieze of American History* when Chesnutt visited the Capitol in 1879, and the young writer in fact noted the presence of the "gray haired artist," precariously "perched upon a slender scaffold half way up the dome," still applying "his brush industriously" to the task at hand.[16] If African American literary-historical engagements with hegemonic forms of classicism and monumental culture—from Phillis Wheatley's ironic revision of classical typologies to William Wells Brown's reframing of the American architecture of freedom and democracy as an architecture of slavery and empire—indicate a long-standing pattern of contestation at the sites of memory through which the "authoritative interpretation" of American history has been produced, the simultaneous presence of the aging Brumidi working away on the *Frieze of American History* and the young Chesnutt observing and remarking on the distortions inherent in this kind of work presents a compelling image for this historiographical contest.

Chesnutt's apprehension of the aesthetic sleight of hand at work in the *Apotheosis of George Washington* would carry over specifically to a critique, which he would sketch out in a pair of short pieces published in the humor magazine *Puck* in 1889, of the tradition of venerating the Founding Fathers in general and General Washington in particular. Much as Walker's *Appeal* and Brown's *Clotel* had intervened in the official "play of memory and history" that constituted the public life of Thomas Jefferson as a site of memory, Chesnutt's stories tapped into the collective memory of enslaved people in America to destabilize the most stable figure—the *lieu de mémoire* par excellence—within the pantheon of American public history. In doing so he presented a challenge to the nation's increasing determination to dispense with the history of slavery and obscure its ongoing legacy.

This determination was on full display early in 1889. April of that year marked the centennial of George Washington's first inauguration, and Americans spared no expense—material or sentimental—to celebrate the occasion. New York City hosted a three-day extravaganza that "reverently acknowledged" not only Washington, but an entire "century of prosperous progress."[17] The festivities included a five-hour military procession, an "industrial parade," and what one observer would later describe as "the greatest banquet known to modern times."[18] As a preemptive counterpoint to this patriotic festival, the humor magazine *Puck* dedicated its April issue to satirizing both Washington and the centennial celebration. This issue included Chesnutt's "The Origin of the Hatchet Story," a short fiction that compared the "father" of America to the sociopathic child of an Egyptian pharaoh—a child who amuses himself by murdering and mutilating the palace slaves as if they were so many cherry trees. By figuring Washington as an Egyptian despot, Chesnutt's satire inverted the widely held view of Washington as an American Moses, divinely appointed to deliver his people from their captivity to the English Crown.[19] Later the same year, in a story entitled "A Roman Antique," Chesnutt reversed the other conventional allegory of the nation's founding—the struggle of Roman republicans against the tyranny of Caesar—which provided the foundations for the concept of American freedom from the Revolution onward. While Washington had been commonly compared to Cato—Caesar's fiercest rival— Chesnutt's story likens Washington to Julius Caesar himself.[20] Chesnutt draws the connection to Caesar through a supposedly nineteen-hundred-year-old black narrator, once the "fav'rite body-sarven'" of "Mars Julius Caesar," who tells the story of his extremely gradual emancipation; and both stories from 1889 link Washington to ancient imperial rulers through the institution of slavery.

This appeal to the distant past aims to illuminate the unfinished business of more recent American times: the Civil War and the slavery it had been fought to abolish. Chesnutt anticipated in the "Hatchet Story" and confirmed in "A Roman Antique" that the celebration of the Union would elide the inconvenient fact of the four-year hiatus in that Union's existence. Under the guise of remembrance, it was a ritual of forgetting not only the war but also the legacy of slavery and the failures of Reconstruction. As he had been for Brumidi's fresco during the war, Washington remained in its aftermath the perfect figure around which to rally for a ritualistic affirmation of national continuity. As tensions between North and South failed to dissipate during Reconstruction, the need for Washington as a symbol of union likewise re-emerged. In 1876, the year that would culminate in the disputed election of Hayes, the memory of Washington was central to celebrations of the centennial of American independence. At that time, a full eleven years since the end of the war, deep divisions had remained within the supposedly reunified nation, and "national consensus was limited to Washington."[21]

By 1889, the national outlook was somewhat different. In his own inaugural address, President Benjamin Harrison clearly articulated a shift in focus from the old conflict between North and South to the westward trajectory of national expansion. Noting the rising population in the West and the development and diversification of an industrial economy nationwide, Harrison relegated the "prejudices and paralysis of slavery" to the past, urging the nation to heal its residual wounds through the "peaceful agencies of commerce." Harrison concluded his address in the optative mood, conjuring a vision for America's future that would redeem the sacrifices of the past. With a difficult history behind them, the American people could look forward with "unalloyed pleasure" to "swift development" and national "increase."[22]

This increase, as Harrison noted, would also apply to the size and strength of the US Navy, the principal instrument in the extension of American power beyond its continental bounds. Ellen Goldner has argued that Chesnutt's stories from 1889 to 1899 develop a critique of emergent American imperialism, and this is surely true of the Washington satires; but the immediate target of

Chesnutt's critique in the stories of 1889 is the already imperial display of the centennial celebration, not the least part of which was the parade of ships from Harrison's navy.[23] In addition to these military-industrial parades and processions, the commemoration included the construction of the Roman triumphal arch that stands at the northern entrance to Washington Square Park in New York City; and this arch provides the unmentioned backdrop for "A Roman Antique," which is set in Washington Square (fig. 3.6).[24] This Roman monument was consistent with a long tradition of Washington veneration, which applied to him an intensely classical iconography. This tradition included Horatio Greenough's 1840 sculpture of Washington—which

FIGURE 3.6 Triumphal arch at Washington Square, *Magazine of American History* 22.1 (July 1889): 3. Image courtesy of the American Antiquarian Society.

was modeled on Phidias's *Zeus*, one of the "wonders" of the ancient world—as well as Brumidi's *Apotheosis*, which, in the sleight of hand Chesnutt had identified as essential to its "art," mirrored aesthetically the political function of the centennial celebration itself. Much as Brumidi had covered a "coarse" reality with virtuous illusion, the centennial aimed to obscure the unresolved conflicts of the first American century with visions of the unbounded promise of the second.

With its deliberate and elaborate staging of celebratory remembrance and its construction of a classical monument in Washington Square, the centennial celebration can be understood as a site of memory in Nora's sense as well as an example of monumental culture broadly conceived. Monumentalism might be expressed in actual structures or in other representational forms, but such cultural artifacts are generally meant to evoke "awe and reverence," as the viewer is called to affirm the authority of the grand narratives encoded in the objects.[25] And the grand narratives encoded in Washington's centennial and his triumphal arch were national unity and progress, abstractions made manifest in the geographic expansion and economic "increase" that Harrison had celebrated in his inaugural address. The centennial displays of classical iconography and imperial power adopted the imagery of the past to project an American future that would surpass its ancient models. Chesnutt, by contrast, draws ancient history into American time in order to highlight the consistent narrative of enslavement and oppression that these ceremonies and monuments to progress tend to obscure, and by extension to assert a skeptical view of the idea of historical progress itself.

The reversal of the meaning of classical history and iconography for the contemporary American context recalls one of the critical methods of black classicism that prevailed—as we have seen in the previous chapter—throughout the antebellum period, from the pages of the *Colored American* to the various writings and performances of William Wells Brown. This critical orientation toward American cultural forms and practices, which persisted beyond the war and would inform Chesnutt's writing throughout his career, directly challenged the mainstream function of classicism in this period. As Caroline Winterer has shown, postbellum Americans understood Greece and especially Rome as antecedents in a narrative of progress, in which the United States was emerging into Western civilization's highest stage of development.[26] In his stories satirizing the centennial Chesnutt rejects this historical view, suggesting instead that imperial celebrations and Roman arches did not signify "the passing away of the old and the incoming of the new," but rather revealed both ancient and American history as very present concerns.[27]

Hardly passed away, slavery was a persistent reality for African Americans after 1876. Structural racism formed, as Chesnutt wrote in his journal, a barrier to the nation's "moral progress," and the South, expending all its energies "to prevent the rise of the Negro," remained "in a semi-barbarous condition."[28] Taking this into account, the allegorical connections to Caesar's Rome and Ramses's Egypt affirm Chesnutt's view of the United States as adhering to archaic strategies of oppression and of the progress of "civilization" as a dubious proposition.

Race and the Ideology of the Classical

Situating Chesnutt's early stories within the context of monumental culture and national celebration shows how his engagement with classical models works to critique not only the history of slavery and its aftermath, but also the way this history was obscured by or assimilated to the outward forms of public memory. In this regard, Chesnutt's work with classical materials is neither separate from nor even corollary to his more obviously political engagement with the white supremacist social and economic order of the postbellum United States—it is integral to it; and fully elaborating the relation between engagement with classical tradition and engagement with other structures of oppression is a central concern of what follows on Chesnutt and of this study as a whole. Chesnutt provides something of a fulcrum for the literary history this book develops, in that from his work we can discern not only the continuities in the political and social conditions between the antebellum period and the postwar rise of Jim Crow, but also how various forms of African American literary classicism after the war are linked or indebted to the critical practices of the antebellum writers we have considered in the previous chapters. In drawing these connections—between classical culture and racial politics, between antebellum and postwar practices—I hope to deepen and complicate our understanding of Chesnutt's relation to Western history and literature, while emphasizing his own apprehension of the ways classical tradition operated as a language of power within the imperial culture of the United States.[29]

Toward the latter goal, my readings of Chesnutt in this chapter and the next one frame his use of classical tradition—much as I have framed the classicism of William Wells Brown and the writers in the antebellum black press—as a critique not only of the institution of slavery and the project of empire, but also of the ways they had been at once obscured and justified by a dominant narrative of American history. This dominant narrative, at least since the Revolution, had deified its "great men" and relied upon a typological understanding of national destiny, in which the United States was both a New Jerusalem and a New Rome, related to historical precedents but destined to surpass them through the redeeming force of American exceptionalism. Chesnutt's classicism, by contrast, links the nation's history and its Founding Fathers to what Stephanie Smallwood has called a "deep chronology" of slavery and empire.[30] This sense of a deep chronology both recalls the temporal understanding we have already noted in the nineteenth-century works of David Walker, William Wells Brown, and Henry Highland Garnet, among others, and relates to central concerns in American studies today. Garnet powerfully expressed this sense of historical time by linking the United States to the Atlantic world since Columbus through the idea of the "empire of slavery," a spatiotemporal figuration tightly correlated to his conception of history more broadly as an "empire of ruin"; and Matthew Frye Jacobson adapted this view to our present moment in the equally trenchant claim, with which he began his presidential address to the American Studies Association in 2012, that "empire *is* US history."[31] Attending to the ways classical tradition informs the dark comedy of Chesnutt's political satires—and to the historical consciousness these satires reveal and develop—contributes to our understanding of how the histories of slavery, empire, and resistance have appeared from the contrasting perspectives of the white center and the black margin of American thought after the Civil War.

As I have outlined in the foregoing chapters, from the Revolution to the Civil War, "the classics" were central to the perspective of the center. The historian Carl Richard has called this the golden age of American classicism, during which classical styles and allusions abounded in American nationalist poetry, art, and architecture, and there was a widespread identification—in terms of both republican government and civilizational progress—with ancient Rome. By contrast, for African Americans in the age of New World slavery, dominant claims to a Roman lineage had little to do with either republicanism or civilization, but rather with the continuation of the systemic oppression on which such ideas and institutions relied.

This view of Rome as a precedent for social stratification and oppression rather than general progress was reinforced through the segregation—by race *and* class—of classical education. Even among whites, real classical training—which included instruction in the Greek and Latin languages and the history and literature of the ancient world—was essentially reserved for a small elite with access to higher education. Even after the Civil War, when college attendance increased significantly among white Americans, enrollment figures were still only 2 and 3 percent of the male and female populations respectively.[32] These postwar decades were also marked by the rising utilitarian ethos of the Gilded Age, which led colleges and universities to de-emphasize the relevance of classical training to the demands of the new industrial world, relegating the classics to the category of "high culture." Where it had once been seen by poets and statesmen as essential for civic participation, in the postwar years classical education became for white elites what it largely remains today, a form of intellectual privilege and a marker of social class.[33]

Even with the rise of black colleges during and after Reconstruction, classical training was not widely accessible for African Americans. In the debates over how best to improve the conditions of formerly enslaved people and their descendants, powerful whites—even philanthropic northerners like John Fox Slater and the former president Rutherford B. Hayes—along with black leaders like Booker T. Washington, advocated strongly for industrial, agricultural, and other kinds of manual training, as opposed to "classical studies, the higher mathematics, and other college studies."[34] The message was that a classical education held little value for black students, but this message might have seemed curious, given the high regard in which white social and political authorities continued to hold the classics for themselves—as a sign of elite status for individuals, and of a grand historical lineage for both the nation and the race.

This cultural and historical authorization is the kind of ideological work the idea of the classical has always performed. As Seth Schein has argued, the classics have served "to legitimate . . . values that are commonly associated with western civilization and 'our' western cultural heritage."[35] The meaning of "our" here is crucial. For white politicians and scholars, especially those in the South, whiteness and civilization were linked through appropriation of the classical tradition to the American context. Like John C. Calhoun and George Fitzhugh, both of whom appealed to classical models explicitly to legitimate slavery as a "positive good" before the Civil War, southerners after the war similarly claimed a connection between whiteness, classics, and civilization itself.[36] And the new postwar status of the classics as high culture for the educated classes only reinforced the connection, further stratifying the field of social relations and separating economically valuable types of education from those that represented the higher values associated with the upper echelons of society.

Given this background it is not surprising that Chesnutt had trouble finding an instructor to teach him Latin in North Carolina in the 1870s. As he wrote in his journal, though he yearned for the "advantages of a good school," that schooling would have to "wait for a future opportunity," since the "first class teachers" in his town "would not teach a 'nigger' and I would have no other sort." With "no learned professor or obliging classmate," Chesnutt nonetheless pursued classical study on his own.[37] Just as Frederick Douglass had famously discovered the threat that black literacy posed to the social order that withheld it, Chesnutt understood that the cultural literacy an education in the arts and humanities provided was likewise a source of social and political power. With this in mind, he set out to acquire this education on his own, developing in the process an ironic view of both the classics and the larger culture that claimed them as its special inheritance.

Chesnutt's autodidacticism afforded him an unconventional relation to the classics, one he would express most often in his work through surprising revisions, merged with African American forms, and often operating on what Ralph Ellison would call "the lower frequencies."[38] This relation set him somewhat apart from African American contemporaries like William Sanders Scarborough and Anna Julia Cooper, who gained access to the academy. Scarborough was a scholar of the classics who advanced the cause of equality through orthodox channels. He studied at Oberlin College, mastered Latin and Greek, published widely in philology, and then spread his knowledge to a broad range of African American students as a means of advancing and uplifting the race. In the process, as Michele Valerie Ronnick has argued, he discredited racist theories about black capacity to excel in the humanities.[39] Cooper also attended Oberlin and studied the classics, which, as Eric Ashley Hairston has argued, not only prepared her for an extended tenure as a Latin teacher in Washington, DC, but also contributed "a classical component" to her "uplift message."[40]

Though Chesnutt was entirely convinced of the power of higher education to elevate a people, he was equally convinced that it was not *his* race that needed uplift, and the task he set for himself as a writer was in fact "the elevation of the whites," whose racism and "spirit of caste" he took as evidence of their arrested moral development.[41] Among the weapons in his arsenal of "elevation" were the languages he had learned for himself: the contemporary vernacular of the black folktale and the supposedly dead language of the classics. If Scarborough had become, through formal education, a master of the archive of Western culture, Chesnutt set about remastering that archive from the perspective of the oppressed and the enslaved, rendering it less a validation of Western cultural and political authority than a demonstration of the arbitrariness of claims to such authority.

As one aspect of this project of "elevation," Chesnutt aimed to cut the prerogative of whiteness down to size with a new black language, which both refigures and supersedes the white one. In "A Deep Sleeper" (1893), for example, Chesnutt deploys an unexpected "Roman" vocabulary, modified through the vernacular of the black storyteller who narrates a story within the story. This layering of narration—whereby the black storyteller (Uncle Julius) tells stories to the white "author" (John), who transcribes them for his own presumably white audience—is the standard form for Chesnutt's "conjure tales." The tale here concerns a family of slaves named Skundus, Tushus, Cottus, and Squinchus, which Julius claims are " 'Hebrew names en' wuz tuk out'n de Bible.' " These names, derived from Latin numerical adjectives, are examples of a common naming convention and of the perverse sense of humor peculiar to American slave-owners.[42] John and his white family mock Julius's claim that the names come from the Bible; but this is only because these names are unfamiliar, unrecognizable to white listeners as names in any language at all. Despite the mockery, Julius's story implicitly directs us to the "chapter and verse" in which these names appear, answering in earnest the disingenuous bibliographical demand of Julius's condescending white listeners. There are, it turns out, many characters named Secundus in the Bible—including one who figures in the story of Eutychus, the "deep sleeper" to whom Chesnutt's story obviously alludes—and men named Tertius and Quartus appear in two consecutive verses of Paul's Epistle to the Romans. In this epistle, Paul preaches inclusiveness to a multiethnic audience of every social class, including Romans and Greeks, Gentiles and Jews, women and slaves. Tertius, a figure biblical exegetes describe as Paul's amanuensis, even announces his presence and his role as the *author* of the text: "I, Tertius, who wrote this epistle, salute you in the Lord."[43]

His explicit self-identification notwithstanding, Tertius and the others surrounding Paul are neither seen nor heard by Julius's white listeners. The biblical characters named for numbers are like the slaves on the plantation: invisible to the "master" class, even when their names are written in the classical language these "masters" claim as their own. But Julius, as John Edgar Wideman has suggested, marks the language in a way that renders it no longer recognizable to the powerful and therefore no longer available as a mechanism of power.[44] From this point of view, "Skundus" is not a mispronunciation but a neologism, and Julius's language is neither Latin nor English but a language all his own that contains the histories of both.

This is the language in which Julius, himself the bearer of a classically imperial name, casts his new epistle to the "New Rome" of the United States, a letter delivering a satirical critique of slavery and empire that echoes the earlier satire in "A Roman Antique." As Julius tells us in "A Deep Sleeper," Skundus's mother would rather have chosen a different name for her child, "sump'n plain en' simple, like 'Rastus' er 'Caesar' er 'George Wash'n'ton.' " Like the other "mispronunciations," this series of names is meant to be funny, but beneath the comedic veneer, which already serves to critique the sense of humor to which these linguistic "jokes" appeal, there is the serious business of history. Julius reveals the workings of a culture that both glorified itself and denigrated its slaves through appeals to classical tradition so common-place as to render the name "Caesar" (or, for that matter, "Julius") something "plain en' simple." Moreover, following Chesnutt's unflattering comparison of Julius Caesar and George Washington in "A Roman Antique," the easy rela-tion Julius draws in "A Deep Sleeper" between the two historical generals is neither incidental nor purely a matter of slave-naming convention; instead, it elaborates a vision of the American nation not as something exceptional but rather as another iteration of the familiar structures and practices that have marked the long history of empire and slavery in the West.

Glory and Magnificence and Power

Chesnutt's path to this vision of history began with self-education. He devised his own rigorous course of study, learning French, German, and Latin, and immersing himself in classical literature. He counted learning Latin the most difficult and important accomplishment of his life, and his journals contain extended passages of transcription and commentary on Latin texts. On the subject of Rome, he tackled Virgil in the original and read widely in eighteenth- and nineteenth-century histories, including Charles Merivale's *General History of Rome*.[45] With this self-education, he was taking deliberate steps not only to improve his prospects as a writer but also "to know and to test," as W. E. B. Du Bois would put it, "the power of the cabalistic letters of the white man."[46] To know this power was not to accept the master nar-rative of Western cultural history but rather to see how this narrative had been, as Nora has noted with respect to "dominant" sites of memory, con-structed and "imposed . . . from above."[47] Understanding that construction freed Chesnutt to construct a new literature from the full range of materials at his disposal, to dialectically oppose black folklore and the lived experience of African Americans to the hegemonic narratives of Western culture and American progress. As Chesnutt noted in his journal in 1880, his "intimate friendship with literature," along with "a fair knowledge of the classics, a speaking acquaintance with the modern languages," and personal experience "in one of the most eventful eras of [the nation's] history," had all uniquely positioned him as a writer for his time. From Chesnutt's point of view, both white and black traditions were "material," means to the end of his literary "crusade" against the "insidious" and "unjust spirit of caste" in America.[48]

This political approach to literary and historical materials is character-istic of Chesnutt's classicism. "A Roman Antique" is a classical tale, but its Roman elements serve to critique both racial politics and the politics of pub-lic memory in the United States. "The Origin of the Hatchet Story" draws on scriptural and classical sources, but Chesnutt's interest in scripture is less theological than historical; and his historical concern is less with excavating the buried truth of the past than with exposing the ideological function of the past in the present. Chesnutt's stories highlight the ways both biblical and classical history served the dominant culture as authorization for white supremacist policies at home and abroad, simultaneously eliding and justify-ing the violence of slavery and empire in the name of preconceived typologi-cal and teleological narratives linking the United States to the ancient world.

The centennial celebration of George Washington's inauguration, with its nationalist speeches, imperial processions, and triumphal arches (a total of four spanned Fifth Avenue for the parade) did precisely this, eliding the history of slavery and the experience of African Americans and affirming a single progressive narrative. Hamilton Fish, a former Secretary of State and the president of the Centennial Committee, offered a near-perfect con-densation of this story, describing the nation's first century as the seamless "operation" of "the machinery of the glorious Constitution under which the government has prospered and enlarged across the continent, insuring peace, security, and happiness to more than sixty millions of people, and not a single slave."[49] Having reduced the fraught history of American slavery to the fact of its legal abolition, Fish allowed the pageantry to do its work, celebrating in Roman fashion both the institutions of a free republic and the progress of imperial power.

To Chesnutt the centennial suggested a different relation between America's present, its recent past, and the deeper history of the ancient world. Throughout his fiction, antebellum American slavery seems to have resur-faced in the wake of Reconstruction, just as ancient slavery had been reborn in the New World. By connecting America and Washington to classical slav-ery, Chesnutt's stories powerfully articulate two common postbellum under-standings among African Americans: first, that the "old snake" of slavery, as Frederick Douglass feared it might, had indeed "come forth" again; and, second, that American slavery should be contextualized within a broader and longer history of empire, traceable through New World colonialism back to ancient Rome.[50] By bringing slavery to the foreground of both ancient and modern history, Chesnutt's writing illuminates the darker side of America's claims to classical heritage. As opposed to mythic or millennial narratives of racial or national exceptionalism, Chesnutt's focus on slavery reveals a story of economics and power; moreover, it shows how claims to a classical cultural inheritance serve specifically to occlude these underlying material facts.

"A Roman Antique" highlights the material history that the Washington centennial obscured with nationalistic spectacle. The story follows the typical structure of Chesnutt's conjure tales, in which an older black narrator—a former slave—tells a story of the days of slavery to a white man from the North. These tales typically end with a twofold revelation: that the story within a story has resulted in some material payoff for the teller *and* that it has incisively critiqued the history and culture the white listener both represents and reproduces. The stories the ex-slave tells are generally confined to the setting of the antebellum American plantation, but in "A Roman Antique" Chesnutt extends the historical range of the black storyteller to situate the American experience within a deeper chronology. Set in Washington Square Park in 1889, the centennial year, the story opens with a scene in which an old black man sits wearily down on a bench and strikes up a conversation with a white man he finds there. As they talk, both men reveal that they are from "Rome," though they mean different things by this. The white man is from Rome, New York, and on discovering this the black man spins out a Roman history of his own. He says he is nineteen hundred years old, that he was "Mars Julius Caesar's fav'rite body-sarven," and that he faithfully served the great general in the wars, even saving his life in the heat of battle. In return Caesar gave him a quarter and "lef' directions in his will fer me ter be gradu'lly 'mancipated, so I 'ud be free w'en I wuz a hund'ed years ole. Ah, but dem wuz good ole times!' he added, with a sigh of regret."[51]

The reference to a hundred-year plan of emancipation satirizes the centennial, but the style and content of the story, in which a former slave demonstrates loyalty to his master and nostalgia for the "good ole times" of slavery, suggest that another object of its critique is the plantation genre of fiction. This genre was, like the centennial celebration itself, in the business of historical revision. Though it did not obscure the centrality of slavery to antebellum American life, the plantation tradition, which rose in popularity alongside the increase in legal discrimination and extralegal violence that characterized the post-Reconstruction South, tended to depict the institution as a benign and practical—if not desirable—form of social organization. Chesnutt's ironic treatment of this genre has been widely discussed by scholars, but these readings have taken little note of the extension of the critique in "A Roman Antique" to a longer history of classical appropriation by mainstream American culture, and thus its extension to the larger problem of nationalist historiography.[52]

The specific target of Chesnutt's satire in "A Roman Antique" is Thomas Nelson Page's story "Marse Chan," which appeared in 1884 in *Century Magazine*—a prominent journal of literature, history, and culture—and later in Page's popular collection *In Ole Virginia* (1887).[53] In this story a faithful slave follows his master into battle against the Union Army, a situation Chesnutt adapts to the classical context of "A Roman Antique." Chesnutt's story thus links the histories of American and classical slavery to the revisionist historical impulse that characterizes the plantation tradition exemplified by Page. And the thread that ties these elements together is the unique voice of the slave narrator himself. This narrator recognizes not only the parallels between ancient Rome and modern America but also the white listener's investment in claiming a Roman heritage as evidence and validation of his social, economic, and political privileges. By employing the kind of subversive irony that characterizes all of Chesnutt's tales, this Roman narrator appeals to his listener's claim to historical authority in order to undermine that claim.

The title of the story itself may reinforce this apparent critique of the function of the classical through another example of the kind of multilingual signification we have seen in "A Deep Sleeper." Taking "Roman antique" in its English sense, we understand the old narrator himself to be the antique. But in French *roman antique* refers to a subgenre of medieval romance (also known as *roman d'antiquité*), which consists of anachronistic renderings of Greek and Roman myths and histories, versions that reconfigure the heroes for the chivalric settings familiar to medieval audiences. The *roman antique* performed the same function for aristocratic audiences of the Middle Ages that the old man's story performs for the white listener in Washington Square Park, providing a classical antecedent for contemporary culture. Since the plantation tradition, as exemplified by "Marse Chan," also made use of medieval ideas and conventions, especially those of chivalric romance, Chesnutt's title seems to refer all at once to the plantation genre, the Roman Empire, and the *roman antique*, layering the antebellum, the classical, and the medieval to reveal a continuity of slavery and the cultural elitism that justifies and depends on it.[54]

While Chesnutt invokes ancient history to satirize the plantation genre and, by extension, American pretensions to a classical heritage, "A Roman Antique" also signifies on another well-known and peculiarly American genre: the story recounted by George Washington's slaves or their descendants, a genre with many sources in many forms. Perhaps the most famous was P. T. Barnum's notorious display of an elderly black woman named Joice Heth, who claimed to be the 160-year-old former nursemaid to Washington.[55] Part of Heth's performance was the recollection of old stories, including the famous incident of the cherry tree. Similar performers telling similar tales abounded in the nineteenth century.[56] Richard Stanup, for example, a free blackman living in Urbana, Ohio, told a story nearly identical to the one in "A Roman Antique," in which he claimed to have been wounded in Washington's service during the French and Indian War and the American Revolution. Stanup was a local hero in Ohio (where Chesnutt lived) and he was considered reputable and authentic. The Urbana chapter of the Daughters of the American Revolution erected a Stanup memorial, and in the bicentennial year of 1976 a Pennsylvania congressman inquired into establishing a monument to Stanup at Valley Forge.[57] Less sensationally, many black caretakers at Mount Vernon cultivated the impression—by telling stories to visitors for money—that they had been in Washington's personal service.[58]

Mark Twain picked up on this popular tradition in "General Washington's Negro Body-Servant" (1868), his mock biography of the general's "favorite body-servant." In Twain's story, this body servant (also named "George") has died, according to newspaper reports, at least six times since Washington's passing. With each successive death the old man seems to age in both directions, living a few years longer but recollecting events from the more distant past. Originally recalling only the second inaugural and Washington's death, at his latest passing (in 1864) the old man "distinctly" remembers everything from "the surrender of Cornwallis" to "the landing of the Pilgrims." The "biographer" thus concludes that the body servant was "two hundred and sixty or seventy years old when he departed this life finally." In short, by 1889 Washington's body servant was a familiar character, a fact to which the editors of the centennial edition of *Puck* attested when they asked, "Where is that immortal colored body-servant? A hundred barouches should be reserved for him in the parade."[59]

Chesnutt's revision of the plantation story aligns ancient Rome with New York City in the Gilded Age, conjuring a classical model that affirms the white listener's view of his own cultural world. But the simultaneous revision of the body-servant story links Washington to Rome through the status he shares with Caesar as imperial tyrant and owner of slaves. Chesnutt's invocation of Roman history thus emphasizes not the high culture expressed in classical monuments but rather the culture of slavery such monuments repress. The white "Roman" misses the references to American slavery and the plantation genre in the old man's story, to say nothing of the larger critique of American classicism that applies to the listener himself. But this is the storyteller's objective: his story, like those told at Mount Vernon, is a pitch for money, and the way to make money is to give listeners what they want—in this case confirmation of a grand historical lineage. "A vision of imperial Rome rose up before me," the white listener recounts, "with all its glory and magnificence and power." Noting the white man's "fit of abstraction," the storyteller asks him for a quarter. Henry Wonham calls this a "thinly veiled plea for reparations," the legitimacy of which the white man "inadvertently acknowledges" when instead of a quarter he hands over twenty dollars.[60] Before the white man can recover his senses, the old storyteller has taken the money and "disappeared behind a clump of shrubbery in the direction of Sixth Avenue."

This "fit of abstraction" results from the black narrator's understanding not only of historical events but also of the forms and functions of history in the imagination of the ruling class. The storyteller plays to predominant tastes for revisionist tales of slavery in the Old South and grand monumental visions of Rome in America. He generates a useful state of awe and reverence in the spectator by tapping into the white man's imperial inclinations, while dramatizing the de facto gradualism of the emancipation. Washington's body servant dies many times in Twain's story, while in Chesnutt's he seems to live forever, but both cases suggest the presence of slavery's past, in spite of monumental celebrations of its passing. And Washington, as the story makes clear, bears a large measure of responsibility for slavery's survival. Though he did support gradual emancipation and made provisions for the manumission of his slaves, like the other founders Washington left emancipation as an inchoate idea for an uncertain future.[61] A century later full freedom still seemed a gradualist proposition, but the white listener does not dwell on the grim failures that mark the history of the American republic. Instead, he takes refuge in a glorious vision of empire, epitomized by the monumental architecture of Rome and replicated in the arch at the entrance to Washington Square Park—an arch built to commemorate a hundred years of "prosperous progress" and "not a single slave."

Myths and Origins

While "A Roman Antique" thus casts a skeptical eye on classical monumentalism as a form of public memory, "The Origin of the Hatchet Story" takes aim at the kind of mythic narratives that monuments tend to reinforce. The story is a coming-of-age tale, in which we follow the development of a young man's moral consciousness in relation to the origin myths of the nation—specifically the account, popularized by Mason Locke Weems, of the young George Washington, the cherry tree, and the little hatchet with which he hacks it down. Like most nineteenth-century American children, the narrator of "The Origin of the Hatchet Story" has been raised on Weems's account, but the model of young Washington has hardly served him as a felicitous example. Rather, over the course of his early years, some unspecified authority has "dinned" the story "into [his] ears . . . very frequently in a close and painful personal connection." Through this incessant dinning, a story meant to inspire love and admiration for the nation's "father" leads the narrator "to hate the very name of Washington."[62]

The nature and power of the critique here rest on a question: what is this "close and painful" connection? Given that Chesnutt was working at the time to place his story "Rena Walden"—which would later become his tragic novel of passing and racial genealogy *The House behind the Cedars*—and that he published his quasi-satirical essay "What Is a White Man?" almost simultaneously with "The Origin of the Hatchet Story," it is clear that the ambiguities and secrecy attending the fraught question of racial identity were present concerns. If the moral of Washington's story is the imperative to be honest and Chesnutt's focus is the problem of the color line, it is fair to assume that the narrator's pain derives from the web of dishonesty and illegitimacy in which the unspoken history of race in America ensnares men and women of ambiguous racial identity. And if we consider the link between his ambiguous race and the story of Washington, a more radical hypothesis emerges: that the narrator may trace his mixed racial ancestry to Washington himself.

This genealogical reading is strengthened if we consider the other prominent source for the cherry tree story, which Chesnutt's tale also follows very closely. Published in 1863, *The Farmer Boy, and How He Became Commander-in-Chief* is another hagiographic "biography" of Washington, written by Morrison Heady, under the name Uncle Juvinell, for the moral instruction of children growing up in the shadow of the Civil War.[63] Heady's version of the cherry tree story raises the ethical stakes by drawing Washington into the orbit of slavery. As in Weems's story, little George hacks down his father's tree, but in Heady's tale the enraged father heads straight for the slave quarters, brandishing his whip as he searches for someone to blame. George intervenes at the last moment, owning up to his deed and saving the young slave Jerry, who had been singled out for a whipping. Witnessing the boy's virtuous confession, the father exonerates the son, but while Weems's version offers the cherry tree story as a lesson learned by father, son, and his young white readers, Heady's proud father turns the lesson on the slaves, dinning it into their ears: "Look on him, my black children, look on him and be as near like him as you can, if you would have the love of your master and the good-will of all around you."[64] Heady most likely intended "my black children" to carry the metaphoric sense implied by the patriarchal institution of slavery, but it is impossible for us, as it would have been for Chesnutt, to avoid considering the literal meaning as well.

In 1889 the open suggestion of a slave's family connection to Washington would have been radical indeed, and such an allegation would have no public hearing until 1999, when the descendants of a Mount Vernon slave named West Ford claimed Washington as an ancestor. Even then the claim only drew the attention it did because it came in the wake of DNA evidence confirming the biological relation between Thomas Jefferson and the descendants of Sally Hemings—a relation that had been routinely dismissed by professional historians. Only DNA, that irrefutable stuff of modern forensics, could convince white skeptics determined not to believe it. Jefferson's relationship with Sally Hemings, though, had been known widely enough in the nineteenth century that it had provided the central, taken-for-granted historical context for Brown's *Clotel*, which in turn further disseminated the story among its readers. Washington, by contrast, had enjoyed an unsullied reputation in this regard until the Ford claim was made public.[65]

The Ford family, however, had its own version of the Washington story all along, a version passed down through the generations, unknown to mainstream scholars until it was revealed two hundred years after Washington's death.[66] That Chesnutt entertained the notion of such an entanglement is clear from a lecture he delivered on Abraham Lincoln, who, unlike Washington and Jefferson, "had no Negro women to play with." With respect to Lincoln, unlike the others, the nation could rest assured that "no bastard daughter of his ever defamed her sire," and "The Origin of the Hatchet Story" intimates the possibility of precisely this sort of defamatory tie.[67] Whether the narrator, like Heady's "black children," is a figurative descendant of the father of his country or a literal descendant of the Washington line, the sense of a brutally painful connection is nonetheless clear. The narrator's repressed pain, rooted in such a source, is both personal and national, held as a family secret that is also Washington's lie.

The boy in the story grows up into a man very much like Chesnutt, who takes an interest in the ancient world. Later in his life, during an archaeological expedition in Egypt, the narrator gains a measure of liberation by discovering the surprising "origin" of Washington's myth. Going downriver, the "Nile steamer" runs out of fuel, and to feed the furnace the captain buys "a job-lot of mummies from a speculator near Bab-el-Mezook." The humor here does little to conceal the grim logic of slavery that predominates. Bought from a speculator, these nonwhite human bodies will provide the fuel for white progress; but just before they are cast into the furnace, a scroll drops from a mummy's wrapping: an ancient Egyptian text that holds—like the hidden histories of the Hemingses and Fords—an American secret. The text, which the narrator translates from hieroglyphics, provides a new source for the Washington myth—a source that asserts a black version of the story rooted in the experience of bondage. In this original, the son of pharaoh Ramses appears as the model for the young Washington. Given a scimitar by his father, "Little Rammy" proceeds to wreak havoc around the royal court, attacking and mutilating his father's slaves until he takes his "experiment" a step too far, decapitating "his father's favorite Hebrew slave, Abednego." The enraged pharaoh demands to know the culprit, and as in Heady's version he interrogates and threatens the other slaves until Little Rammy confesses: " 'Sire,' he said, 'I cannot tell a lie. I did it with my little scimitar.' " And as in Heady and Weems, the boy's honesty elicits the father's absolution: "I would rather you had killed a thousand Hebrew slaves than to have told a lie." Here Chesnutt lifts the narrative framework from Weems and Heady, but the violation and destruction of enslaved human bodies instead of trees makes apparent the real historical violence that is hidden in such hagiographic and nationalistic accounts of the country's founding.

As "A Roman Antique" does by connecting Washington to Caesar, "The Origin of the Hatchet Story" counters the celebration of an American century with a message from across deeper time. This message replaces the exceptionalist myth of Washington's honesty with the historical reality that all such national mythologies are constructed to suit the needs of the day. The "Hatchet Story," the narrator concludes, "was merely one of those myths which, floating down the stream of tradition, become attached in successive generations to popular heroes," just another of the "lies," as Ralph Ellison would later put it in *Invisible Man*, that power "keep[s] [its] power by."[68] Given that the myth attached to Washington is a parable about the fundamental honesty of the founder, and therefore about the good faith of the nation he founded, Chesnutt's revision comments ironically on the facts of American history and on the fiction that inheres in any nationalist historiography.

If Weems and Heady contribute to the construction of the "Hatchet Story" as a dominant *lieu de mémoire*, the stories of the Fords and Hemingses, like the interment of Clotel and the revealing scroll of the disinterred mummy, contribute to a collective narrative of resistance animated by "the living heart of memory." And if we return to Chesnutt's early journals, where he both noted Brumidi's sleight of hand in his depiction of Washington's *Apotheosis* and recorded Voltaire's pithy remarks on the politics of speaking the truth, we will clearly apprehend the roots of his critique of the construction of both Washington and the centennial as sites of national memory. In response to such nationalist modes of historical commemoration, Chesnutt proposed the opposite. As he noted in his journal, slightly altering a passage from Voltaire, "Quand on écrit l'histoire, il faut n'être d'aucun pays": "When writing history, one must be of no nation at all."[69]

Ancient History, American Time

By linking Washington to ancient Egypt, Chesnutt reiterates a common identification of enslaved African Americans with the Israelites in bondage, but at the same time he suggests a more unique identification of American slaves with Egyptian mummies. These two perspectives—of the Hebrew slave and the Egyptian mummy—emerge from the mummy's scroll to provide two complementary revisions of the dominant American story. From the first point of view Washington appears as an Egyptian tyrant, which by extension renders America a despotic Egypt, the violent oppressor of captive slaves. From the second the mummy is analogous to the unfortunate Abednego and Washington's tree, and Egypt is both the origin of an alternative history and a site of transnational identification for the subjects of contemporary imperialism.[70]

Neither of these perspectives ignores the fact that ancient Egypt was itself a slave society, the monuments of which were constructed by the coerced labor of the oppressed; but for Chesnutt, as it did for Du Bois and other black writers and intellectuals, Egypt also served as a counterpoint to white American classicism and the historical narratives such classicism enables. The normative discourse of *Classica Americana* held that Greco-Roman civilization was the root of all later civilization worthy of the name and that the white American "empire for liberty" was its ultimate expression. According to this view, Greece and Rome did not derive from Egypt but simply displaced it in an inevitable step toward white ascendancy, a process that culminates in the global hegemony of Western culture in its American form. By tracing American origins to the mummy's scroll, Chesnutt criticizes the despotic "Egyptian" elements of white American culture, challenges that culture's claims to biblical and classical heritage, and advances a black historical narrative linked to Egypt.

This link to Egypt both stakes a claim to a black classical history prior to slavery and establishes a contemporary connection between the internal colonization experienced by African Americans and the colonization of modern Egypt by Western forces. These forces included the classical archaeologists who had, two years before the publication of Chesnutt's Egyptian allegory, established a regime of incarceration and torture in order to discover the location of Ramses's tomb. As the American writer and photographer Edward Wilson approvingly described this approach in *The Century* magazine, "Arrest after arrest was made, and the bastinado was applied to many a callous sole which had never felt even shoe or sandal," and eventually a combination of bribery and threats of summary execution produced the desired intelligence.[71] These "scientists" thus perpetrated unspeakable violence on the living and the dead in order to add, quite literally, the bodies of the colonized to the empire's body of knowledge. This was "history" in the making, the assimilation of ancient Egyptian material—whether the obelisk transferred to the Place de la Concorde, about which William Wells Brown had written in 1852, or the corpses of kings in the museum collection at the end of the century— to a narrative that renders the imperial West both the rightful inheritor of a living tradition of Roman power and the proper curator of the material relics of a dead African civilization.

Chesnutt's mummy interrupts this narrative by reanimating Egypt as a multivalent symbolic landscape, at once an analog for American slavery and empire and a site of black civilizational origins that undermines exclusive white supremacist claims to the foundations and the future of civilization. In this regard, Chesnutt's satire anticipates in miniature what Pauline Hopkins would more fully elaborate in her 1903 novel *Of One Blood*, a novel in which, as Scott Trafton has argued, Egypt "is represented as a figure of the double": "both itself and America . . . both a site of literal excavation and a metaphor for the problematic of African American racial identity."[72] Like Chesnutt's story, Hopkins's novel features a "passing" protagonist who joins an expedition set on archaeological discovery and material gain. Similar to the transatlantic journeys of Frederick Douglass and William Wells Brown, whose eastward trajectories constituted a form of symbolic travel back in time, moving against the geographic and temporal "course of empire," Hopkins's exploring party travels upriver toward the source of the Nile and the origin of civilization. Under the direction of the white Professor Stone, the group thus backtracks literally and figuratively from Egypt toward "the mother country" of Ethiopia, hoping to uncover not only "the ancient records of Ethiopia's greatness," but also "the riches of her marvelous mines."[73] And though the party's objective is the collection of artifacts of value within both the fiscal and epistemological economies of the imperial West, what emerges—as with the mummy's scroll in Chesnutt's story—is a twofold revelation: first, of an African origin of civilization that upends white supremacist historiographies of antiquity; and, second, of the fraught familial dynamics the regime of racial slavery everywhere produced.

These revelations culminate the novel's transhistorical oedipal drama, in which the hero, Reuel Briggs, is revealed as both the hereditary monarch of an ancient Ethiopian empire and an American slave-owner's son who has unwittingly married his own sister. The monarchical line passes through the "New World" via the figure of the conjure woman Aunt Hannah and her daughter Mira, where it is corrupted but not effaced by its contamination—through the routine sexual violence of plantation slavery—with whiteness, and Reuel attributes his tragic situation to "the bond that bound him to the white race of his native land."[74] The sister, Dianthe, dies the conventional death of the tragic mulatta, but order is ultimately restored through Reuel's marriage to an Ethiopian queen and his re-establishment as ruler of the kingdom of Telassar. While the expedition had set out to claim the relics of a dead empire for the museums and coffers of a living one—and Reuel himself had set out to secure the wealth that would ironically provide a veneer of bourgeois respectability to his incestuous marriage—the novel concludes with two vital civilizations in opposition. Though Reuel eyes, "with serious apprehension, the advance of mighty nations penetrating the dark, mysterious forests" of what he has adopted as "his native land," this imperial encroachment remains in tension with an earlier prophetic warning.[75] Confronting the white trespassers at Telassar, the high priest of the city rhetorically asks: "Fair-haired worshippers of Mammon, do you not know that you have been weighed in the balance and found wanting? that your course is done?"[76]

This type of warning recalls the rhetoric of imperial ruin that pervaded the antebellum writings we encountered in the previous chapter, and reveals its ongoing salience within a discourse of resistance to entrenched structures of white supremacy in the post-Reconstruction United States. Both before and after the Civil War, black writers routinely prophesied the end of American civilization by conjuring images of ancient empires in ruins. While the dominant mode of classical monumentalism had been aggressively employed—from the decorations of the Capitol to the construction of triumphal arches in New York—as a means of directing the nation's gaze away from the intransigent problems of its North-South axis and onto the glorious imperial prospects made manifest by the seemingly limitless landscape of the American West, the critical mode of black classicism persistently redirected that gaze. While the former insisted, as did Harrison in his inaugural address, that the nation's history was synonymous with the progress of both freedom and civilization, the latter advanced a contrary view of that history as a recurrent pattern of oppressive bondage and imperial overstretch inexorably unfolding into ruination. From this point of view, monuments such as the Washington Square arch did not signal the triumph of American democratic freedom, but rather projected an image of a future America in ruins.

Frederick Douglass essentially took up this perspective in his critical remarks on the occasion of the Columbian Exposition in 1893. Though nominally commemorating the four hundredth anniversary of the arrival of Columbus in the "New World," the exposition was more than anything another showcase for American progress, designed to demonstrate "just how wonderful," as Alan Trachtenberg has put it, "America had become." The physical manifestation of the wonderful progress of America was a planned "city" of predominantly neoclassical architecture and a near "uniform whiteness."[77] The completed city looked not unlike the one Thomas Cole had depicted in the "Consummation" painting of his "Course of Empire" series, and while a "general classicism" predominated throughout the city's design, there was, as Stanley Applebaum has observed, "a particularly strong tinge of Roman Empire styling in its triumphal arches, arcades, domes, applications of architectural sculpture and painted panels, among many other features" (fig. 3.7).[78] Given this prevailing "Romanism," it is perhaps unsurprising that a visitor like the white American writer Owen Wister would react much as the white listener had to the vision of "glory and magnificence and power" the old man had conjured in "A Roman Antique." As Wister recorded in his diary, in the "White City" he was "seized" by "a bewilderment at the gloriousness of everything," and "dazzled" by "the total consummate beauty and grandeur of the thing."[79] But as with President Harrison's speech and the decorations at the Capitol, what was studiously elided in the design and the events of the Columbian Exposition was any trace of African American life.

FIGURE 3.7 "Columbian Exposition, Grand Basin." Photo by C. D. Arnold. Image courtesy Ryerson & Burnham Archives. Art Institute of Chicago.

Douglass attested to this exclusion in his introduction to Ida B. Wells's critical counterpoint to the fair, aptly entitled *The Reason Why the Colored American Is Not in the World's Columbian Exposition*. For Douglass, the exclusion of blacks from the Columbian Exposition in 1893 only reaffirmed the critique he had advanced in 1852, revealing once again the "flagrant contradiction" between the "boasted" ideals of "American Republican liberty and civilization," and the racist reality of the nation's political and social organization. In stark contrast to Wister's bedazzlement, for Douglass the White City, "with its splendid display of wealth and power, its triumphs of art and its multitudinous architectural and other attractions" was nothing but "a whited sepulcher."[80] While this phrase refers first to its biblical source—through which it identifies the White City primarily as a site of hypocrisy—it also echoes William Wells Brown's evocation of the "sepulchers of the fathers" in *Clotel*.[81] In both cases, nationally significant buildings and monuments are refigured as tombs, not only signaling the figurative burial of the nation's supposed ideals, but also providing a memento mori for the nation itself. Douglass reinforces the latter function of the White City by recalling—as Brown had also done in *Clotel*—Thomas Jefferson's well-known prophecy: "Jefferson, himself a slaveholder, said he 'trembled for his country' when he reflected 'that God is just and that His justice cannot sleep forever.' "

Douglass's rhetoric transforms the triumphal "Romanism" of the White City into a site of national entombment and ruination. This view of the Roman styling of American monumental culture as evidence of an underlying commitment to empire and slavery had emerged in the black press and across a wide array of antebellum writings, and the view remained persuasive to African American readers and writers after the war. T. Thomas Fortune, the editor of the *New York Globe*, made this view explicit in his 1884 polemic *Black and White: Land, Labor, and Politics in the South*. In that book, Fortune lays out an essentially Marxist critique of land monopolies and the exploitation of agricultural labor in the South after the war, with the express aim of drawing American racial inequity into the discourse of the global struggle between labor and capital. Establishing a continuity with the antebellum rhetoric of imperial decline, Fortune links the oppressive forces of the postbellum South with a long history of empire. To understand "the terror which walked abroad in the South" from the end of the war up to the time of his writing, Fortune argued that we should turn to "other lands than our own, where the iron hand of the tyrant, seated upon a throne, cemented with a thousand years of usurpation and the blood of millions of innocent victims, presses hard upon the necks of the high and the backs of the low." He draws comparisons to more recent "dynastic villanies [*sic*] of the house of Orleans or Stuart, or that prototype of all that is tyrannical, sordid and inhuman, the Czar of all the Russias," but always in the background is the example of ancient Rome.[82]

As Fortune argues, the white perpetrators of racial terrorism in the American South, who had by the time of his writing effected the practical annulment of the black freedom and citizenship rights so recently established by the Reconstruction amendments to the Constitution, had risen to "power by the most approved practices of the most odious of tyrants," in the process shedding "as much innocent blood as the bloody triumvirate of Rome."[83] Though Fortune adds an important new element to the rhetoric of imperial decline that had predominated prior to the war, focusing not only on the institution of slavery but also on the expansion of land monopolies that necessitated the expansion of slavery in Rome, he draws the historical analogy in order to present the same prophetic warning about the American future. The politically and economically powerful classes in America, like "the nobility of Great Britain," who "dance and make merry while the people starve," were no better than "Nero," fiddling "while Rome was one vast blaze of conflagration and horror."[84] In Fortune's view, which echoed his antebellum predecessors, the slavery and exploitation underpinning Roman ascendancy were in reality the pillars of an unsustainable economy that led inevitably to ruin. The United States, then, "having adopted at the beginning the system which hastened the downfall of Rome after she had spread her authority over the known world," was in for a similarly catastrophic collapse. Illustrating his own materialist vision with a natural analogy that echoes Brown's account of the volcanic rebellion of the helots, Fortune goes on to warn his American readers that a people's revolution would soon enough "burst upon us as Mount Vesuvius burst forth upon Herculaneum and Pompeii"; and reiterating Garnet's sense that American slavery had "crossed its Rubicon," he concludes, "It is too late for America to be wise in time. 'The die is cast.'"[85]

The contrast could hardly be any starker, between the "gloriousness of everything" as it appeared to Wister at the Columbian Exposition and the dark visions of decline and ruin that appear in the works of Douglass, Fortune, Hopkins, and Chesnutt. What President Harrison and the white elite of an imperial "Gilded Age" America could describe as a hundred years of "prosperous progress," aptly represented in the unalloyed neoclassical whiteness of the White City, for post-Reconstruction African American writers indicated only the extension of the "empire of ruin" across the continental geography of the United States. If the White City constituted the apogee of white classicism and monumental culture, the black classical tradition in the wake of Reconstruction continued to recast such dominant cultural productions as evidence of an unexceptional imperial agenda in the present, ominously foreshadowing a future American empire in ruins.

Just as the ruins of antiquity had famously "spoken" to C. F. Volney in his *Meditations on the Revolution of Empires*—a text that had in turn spoken powerfully to the antebellum discourse of resistance—Hopkins's lost civilization and Chesnutt's ancient narrators render the past both present and articulate.[86] The mummy bearing a message across time and space is a near-perfect figure for this articulate and present past, but the "antique" storyteller in Washington Square plays an analogous role. As artifacts and artificers, these figures bear witness to the violence endemic to history as events—the course of "New World" empire and slavery since the arrival of Columbus—and their representation, as in the imperial Roman architecture of the White City celebrating that arrival. The first involves the dark legacy of slavery, the "unspeakable things," in Toni Morrison's phrase, that to a large extent remain "unspoken." The second takes up what Morrison calls the "history of history" itself, the ways in which the past is continually reconstructed—in paint and stone, patriotic pageants and monuments worthy of Rome—to serve and justify the needs and desires of the present.[87]

4

Crumbling into Dust

CONJURE AND THE RUINS OF EMPIRE

AS THE PREVIOUS chapter has shown, in his early sketches and stories Charles Chesnutt frequently employed ancient artifacts—a nineteen-
hundred-year-old narrator, the exhumed body of an Egyptian mummy, and
the text his burial wrappings conceal—to upend both the theory of American
exceptionalism and the historiography of progress. This historical method,
through which Chesnutt conjures images or figures from the past—whether
the recent past of legal slavery or the deeper history of classical antiquity—
to comment critically on the present would be central to Chesnutt's fiction
throughout his career. This method is most consistently applied in the "conjure tales," in which the former slave Uncle Julius tells stories that attest to the
living presence of slavery even after the Civil War and Reconstruction, but
perhaps the most striking example of Chesnutt's engagement with antiquity
occurs in *The Marrow of Tradition*, the fiction in which he most explicitly
attends to the political crisis of the present.

Like the narrator of the "Hatchet Story," the protagonist of *The Marrow of
Tradition* travels toward his own point of origin, a literal movement through
space that is also a figurative journey into the past. Dr. Miller, an African
American surgeon trained in the medical schools at Paris and Vienna, is
returning from New York to his hometown of Wellington, North Carolina,
to open a new hospital for the black population. After crossing into Virginia,
Miller's relegation to the Jim Crow car affords him the opportunity to
reflect upon the racial dynamics of American life as well as their geopolitical and world-historical implications. While reading an item in the newspaper about American imperial expansion resulting from the recent war with
Spain, he is interrupted by the arrival of an imperious white antagonist from

Wellington—Captain George McBane—who breaks the racial barrier with impunity in order to smoke his cigar and spit on the floor of the Jim Crow car, before returning to the elegant refinement of the car reserved for whites.

Later in the journey, Miller is joined in the "colored" car by a group of black laborers heading home from a job. The group is "a jolly, good-natured crowd" who "enjoy themselves after their own fashion." They play music and dance in the aisle, and though Miller, who has internalized the social and cultural elitism of his white counterparts in the bourgeoisie, finds the crowd "noisy . . . dirty, and malodorous," he nonetheless can also appreciate that they are, in spite of the oppression and poverty that characterizes their material lives, to some extent "happy," exhibiting "a cheerfulness of spirit which enabled them to catch pleasure on the wing," and thereby to "endure with equanimity the ills that seemed inevitable." As a man of science, Miller seems to recognize this "ability to live and thrive under adverse circumstances"—circumstances imposed and maintained by the likes of the white supremacist McBane—as an evolutionary advantage, and perhaps "the surest guaranty of the future."[1]

This evolutionary thinking comes together with the figure of McBane and the newspaper report from the frontiers of American empire to precipitate for Miller an imaginative journey to antiquity. Spurred by his experience on the train, Miller's reflections range from the deep past to the present and into the future, leading him to conclude that the "race which shall at the last inherit the earth—the residuary legatee of civilization—will be the race which remains longest upon it," and therefore to take comfort in the historical endurance of "the negro," who "was here before the Anglo-Saxon was evolved." From the dawn of history, Miller suggests, "the negro" has "looked out from the inscrutable face of the Sphinx across the sands of Egypt while yet the ancestors of those who now oppress him were living in caves . . . and painting themselves with woad."[2] Although Miller is responding to the events around him on the train, and by extension to the racial violence and inequity that characterized the emergent era of Jim Crow, the spatiotemporal grammar of his thinking suggests something more than a lesson drawn from the past to apply to the present. Instead, the grammar renders distant historical times and places coincident, bringing them together in a transoceanic and transhistorical palimpsest that counters any linear or stadial view of social or civilizational progress. Here and throughout *The Marrow of Tradition*, Chesnutt challenges what white Americans had taken for granted: the ideological triad of whiteness, progress, and civilization. The passage specifically opposes the teleological view of America's "Manifest Destiny" through an ancient icon that conjures no glorious vision of future imperial grandeur, but rather the spectral presence of the ruins of empires past. And for Miller, the past, where "the negro was" in the days of the Sphinx, is not "there" but "here"—and "the negro is here yet." Miller thus effectively inhabits the perspective of the Sphinx to step outside the controlling temporality of the historiography of progress and reconfigure the linear narrative of the course of empire as a spatial landscape, much like Henry Highland Garnet's antebellum figuration of history as a "vast empire of ruin."[3]

This extension of a commentary on contemporary racial politics back to the ancient world is typical of Chesnutt's career-long engagement with classical material. While the last chapter focused on the ways Chesnutt's early reading and educational experiences—along with his encounters with neoclassical national monuments and nationalist commemorations of an imperial cast— all contributed to his critical view of the American empire and the various ways it was justified and celebrated, this chapter situates Chesnutt's writing within a continuous tradition of black classicism as political engagement and historical critique extending from the antebellum period to the twentieth century and beyond. By reading Chesnutt as a figure at the crossroads of multiple historical times and cultural forms, this chapter examines his manipulation of multiple mythic traditions into a cohesive and unsettling vision of history as unfinished business, a past that is far from past. Chesnutt's triangulation of contemporary racial antagonism, the ruined civilization of ancient Egypt, and the precivilized past of the Anglo-American "race" demonstrates precisely this vision of the present past—a vision that brings together these seemingly incongruous historical situations as integral parts of a collective story. Assembling this story from the transhistorical perspective of "the negro" within "the Sphinx," Chesnutt echoes a nineteenth-century tradition that included Garnet, David Walker, William Wells Brown, and various writers and editors for antebellum black newspapers, while at the same time anticipating a later anti-imperial discourse generated by writers such as Richard Wright and Toni Morrison. Situated in this way, Chesnutt provides a fulcrum for a collective African American literary history that has emerged as a prophetic counterpoint to the prevailing historical consciousness in America.

As I noted in chapter 2, though this countertradition emerged before the idiom of Marxism, it nonetheless situates the struggle of American slaves and postslavery African Americans within the collective story Marx and Engels would delineate, of "freeman and slave, patrician and plebeian, lord and serf . . . in a word, oppressor and oppressed," a conflict destined to culminate either in "a revolutionary reconstitution of society . . . or in the common ruin of the contending classes."[4] In black abolitionist writing the idea of ruination routinely accompanied the critique of slavery, and these writers drew on classical models to suggest a direct causal relationship between the economics of slavery and the ruin of empires, and to highlight the historical continuities between ancient and American slavery. On this latter point, black writers were in ironic alignment with southerners like John C. Calhoun, George Fitzhugh, and T. R. R. Cobb, who argued that both freedom and civilization depended upon the existence of slavery, "that there never has yet existed," as Calhoun proclaimed, "a wealthy and civilized society in which one portion of the community did not, in point of fact, live on the labor of the other."[5] But where Calhoun and others made this point to argue in favor of this notion of civilization and the slavery that made it possible, black writers and orators pointed to slavery as evidence of a fundamental problem within this idea of civilization itself. The civilization Calhoun described was marked by greed and therefore by moral and political corruption—the fatal flaws to which C. F. Volney, in his influential book *The Ruins*, had attributed the fall of every empire.[6] For antebellum black writers, slavery was hardly the foundation for the "empire for liberty" Thomas Jefferson had imagined, stretching to the "thousandth generation" of the future; it was instead the flawed foundation of an unsustainable economy that historically had led to the ruin of empires.[7]

In Chesnutt's early sketches, prophetic narrators seem to irrupt out of the ruins of Roman and Egyptian antiquity, demonstrating the continuing relevance of the antebellum theory after the Civil War and Reconstruction, when Frederick Douglass's grim premonition seemed to have been realized: African Americans had escaped "slavery to individuals, only to become the slaves of the community at large."[8] The view that slavery had been reestablished under different terms was widely shared; and as a result there was also widespread acknowledgment of the need, as Douglass perceived it, for continuing "antislavery work."[9] W. E. B. Du Bois affirmed this view, advocating higher education and full enfranchisement as the only effective means of resisting a "second slavery."[10] Chesnutt himself, surveying in 1903 the ever-expanding "catalogue of lynchings and anti-Negro riots," which "day after day" grew "more appalling," concluded that the country stood "face to face with the revival of slavery."[11] Given this apparent revival of the conditions of the antebellum past, many black writers returned to the imagery of fallen empires of ancient history to offer a dark vision for the American future.

Chesnutt's delineation of this layered history—of antebellum and postbellum, ancient world and modern America—in *The Marrow of Tradition* speaks powerfully to the continuing presence of slavery in the lived experience of African Americans at the turn of the century. Perhaps because of its power it was an unwelcome notion in the predominantly white literary marketplace. In the ten or twelve years prior to the novel's publication, Chesnutt had become one of the most prominent black literary figures in American history to date, publishing individual stories with the *Atlantic* and two collections and a novel with the prestigious publishing house of Houghton Mifflin in Boston. But as he would discover through the critical response to *The Marrow of Tradition*, this success was largely predicated on his work being agreeable to the political and racial sensibilities of the northern literary establishment these publishers represented; and the measure of his agreeability tended to track with the degree to which white readers could assimilate his work to their established views. While scholars and general readers today almost universally understand Chesnutt's conjure tales as subverting the conventions of the plantation genre—wherein genial old slaves reminisce fondly about the days of slavery—his contemporary white readers were more likely to construe the stories as realism.

This misreading of Chesnutt's critique of both antebellum and post-Reconstruction America as a humorous affirmation of the historical vision of the plantation genre constitutes the phenomenon Gene Andrew Jarrett has called "minstrel realism."[12] Chesnutt's rise to literary fame was in large part due to the support of William Dean Howells—the so-called dean of American letters at the time—who was himself in large part responsible for establishing and disseminating minstrel realism as an interpretive model. Following Howells, who had written an influential review of Chesnutt's stories in the *Atlantic* and another essay on Chesnutt and some of his contemporaries in the *North American Review*, white readers could delight in Chesnutt's ability "to enjoy the negro's ludicrous side as the white observer enjoys it," without seriously entertaining the possibility that "their amiability" might "veil" any kind of critical opposition to political or cultural white supremacy.[13] Indeed, Howells's confidence to the contrary is strong enough that he does go on to entertain this possibility quite explicitly, only to quickly dismiss it as a ludicrous idea. "What if," Howells asks, "upon some large scale they should be subtler than we have supposed? What if their amiability should veil a sense of *our* absurdities, and there should be in our polite inferiors the potentiality of something like contempt for us?" Having introduced this "notion," which he admits is too "awful" to contemplate, Howells happily concludes that in any case "we may be sure that they will be too kind, too wise, ever to do more than let us guess at the truth, if it is the truth."[14]

Howells's assessment of Chesnutt as "too kind" to deal openly with the ugly truths of American racism appeared in the August 1901 issue of the *North American Review*. By the December issue, which included his review of *The Marrow of Tradition*, Howells had completely changed his tune. In that review Howells essentially accused Chesnutt of breaching the racial contract of minstrel realism. In place of a pleasurable and unthreatening tour of the "ludicrous side" of black American life, Chesnutt had produced an incendiary critique of racism in America, closer in its aesthetic and political affiliations to literary naturalism than anything resembling the minstrel realism Howells knew and loved. In the dean's estimation, *The Marrow of Tradition* was "bitter," and the literary marketplace at large was inclined to agree. Sales of the novel were meager, and there is more or less a scholarly consensus that the radical nature of *The Marrow of Tradition* ended Chesnutt's career as a writer who might appeal to both sides of the color line.

Chesnutt would publish only one more novel—*The Colonel's Dream*, released by Doubleday, Page in 1905—and a handful of stories between 1901 and 1915. Perhaps because they had served almost precisely the opposite of their intended purpose, appealing to a taste among white readers for minstrel realism rather than successfully challenging the racial ideology underpinning this aesthetic, none of the stories published over this period were conjure tales. But Chesnutt would return to the form for a final story published not for the predominantly white audiences that had fueled the success of his early career, but for the predominantly black audience of the *Crisis*, the journal of the NAACP. Du Bois, head of the NAACP and editor of the *Crisis*, had admired Chesnutt for decades, and in the early twenties he sent multiple letters to Chesnutt soliciting a story from him for the journal.[15] In 1924, Chesnutt sent in the manuscript for "The Marked Tree," along with a note informing Du Bois that the story "is in my earlier manner, but I think it has a thread of interest which might be interesting to your readers."[16] By his "earlier manner" Chesnutt means the story is a conjure tale, and it is significant here that he explicitly suggests the "thread of interest" this kind of story might hold for readers in the mid-1920s.

Like the earlier conjure tales, "The Marked Tree" is a critique of both slavery and its representation in the plantation genre, which recalled the institution as a benign and familial social arrangement, consisting of benevolent patriarchs and contented slaves. Sharply breaking with the conventions of the genre, "The Marked Tree" tells the story of an enslaved woman who takes revenge on the plantation owner for the sale and subsequent murder of her son. Through the use of conjure, a variation of African magic practiced by enslaved and free blacks in the New World, the enslaved woman destroys the slave owner, his family, and the entire plantation, leaving this once illustrious house of slavery in ruins. Narrating an actual attack by an enslaved person against a slave plantation, the story presents Chesnutt's most explicit literary attack on the institution of slavery, its intransigent legacy, and the manner in which the plantation genre had framed it within the national imagination.

In the 1880s and 1890s the plantation genre was both popular and influential in shaping American impressions of slavery, the Civil War, and Reconstruction, and Chesnutt's critical revision of the genre in his early stories capitalized on its reach and power. Although by 1924 the genre had receded somewhat in its popularity, the ideology of the plantation remained in force through the regime of Jim Crow, and Chesnutt's note to Du Bois seems to assert his story's relevancy within this sociopolitical context. In recalling a form appropriate to the conditions of the turn of the century, Chesnutt implies the persistence of those conditions, just as the earlier conjure tales had aimed to demonstrate the living presence of slavery even after emancipation. Chesnutt's return to the conjure tale in 1924 thus evokes two different eras of recent history: the nadir of the turn of the century, when a "second slavery" was normalized through legislation, judicial sanction, and extralegal violence; and the era of chattel slavery itself. For Du Bois's black readers in Jim Crow America, this past was both present and alive, and it was to this sense of a living residual history that Chesnutt's historical fiction could appeal. But as previous works such as *The Marrow of Tradition* and his early satires suggest, this residual history ran deeper. Like those earlier works, "The Marked Tree" connects the 1920s to the world of classical antiquity, recalling ancient empires of slavery through the rhetoric of antebellum antislavery resistance, which emphasized the ruin to which such empires were always reduced.

For Whom?

The George Washington centennial celebration in 1889 had provided the occasion for the early development of Chesnutt's critique of both the imperial character of US expansion and the historical narrative asserted by the centennial celebration itself. That celebration, marked by a conspicuous display of American military power and the appearance of Roman triumphal arches in New York City, performed the typical function of nationalist commemorations, generating the impression of national unity and presenting the nation's history as a narrative of progress. Such commemorations produce "consensus," as the art historian Christopher Thomas has put it, even among the most severely "divergent" and "conflicting groups."[17] After the Civil War these divergent groups included waves of recent immigrants, but the most pressing and fractious conflict was still to be found in the unresolved history of the war itself. As Chesnutt's early satires suggest, the Washington centennial—and the Harrison administration for which it provided something of a stage— aimed to achieve reconciliation by drawing national attention away from the war and its unresolved conflicts and onto the bright prospects of western set- tlement and economic growth. In this regard the centennial was of a piece with the redecoration of the US Capitol and the construction of the extrav- agant White City for the Columbian Exposition in Chicago, all of which aimed to advance a narrative of national reconciliation and progress through a classical monumentalist aesthetic. And if the triumphal arches in New York and the neoclassical buildings of the White City made clear the continuing importance of classical forms to American nationalism in the years following Reconstruction, nothing could make clearer their ongoing relevance in the early twentieth century than the design and construction of the most explic- itly classical monument in Washington, DC, the Lincoln Memorial.

Given that he presided over national dissolution and civil war, it is per- haps not surprising that it took some time for Lincoln to emerge as an accept- able figure for a national monument. Unlike Washington, whom both sides in the Civil War could claim as a "father," Lincoln was only a hero to some Americans. But as the tragedy of the Civil War was slowly replaced in the public consciousness by the triumph of industrialization, the closing of the continental frontier, and the increasingly global projection of American power, the controversial historical Lincoln gradually dissolved into some- thing more like the "mythical persona" of Washington, an "ideal President" and an appropriate symbol for a nation attaining its ascendancy as "a world power and force for good."[18]

Economic and geopolitical successes provided American elites with not only much to celebrate but also powerful incentives to do so in such a way as to put the nation's troubled past behind them. As W. E. B. Du Bois dryly observed in *The Souls of Black Folk*, following Reconstruction the nation "was a little ashamed of having bestowed so much sentiment on Negroes, and was concentrating its energies on Dollars."[19] Du Bois's parallelism here emphasizes the reinscription of slavery's commodification of African Americans within the postwar economy, making clear by implication that reconciliation would consist in what Susan Mizruchi has described as the sacrificial rendering of "Black Americans as the casualty of national advance."[20] In light of this sacrifi- cial logic, for African Americans neither economic nor imperial growth were anything to celebrate. To the contrary, as Chesnutt's allusion to the extension of American empire—through the newspaper item Dr. Miller reads on the train—within the context of a narrative of domestic racial terror would seem to imply, imperialism abroad and white supremacist violence at home were closely correlated phenomena.

Contrasting starkly with the outlook of *The Marrow of Tradition*, the Lincoln Memorial was conceived as the monumental symbol of both the nation's progress as an economic and geopolitical power and the reunion and reconciliation that seemed to have facilitated that progress. As Thomas has observed, the positioning of the memorial at the end of the mall—aligned with the Washington Monument and the Capitol and connected to the Arlington Cemetery by a bridge across the Potomac—made it "a point of symbolic reunion for the nation," while the classical architecture and the overall scale of the new designs for both the monument and the mall as a whole were indeed "imperial . . . befitting the great power America was fast becoming."[21] If the Capitol building—in both its neoclassical architecture and the classicism of its interior adornments—was the original temple of the Jeffersonian empire for liberty, then the new memorial would be consecrated to what Lincoln prophetically described as "a new birth of freedom."[22]

Though architect Henry Bacon modeled the memorial on the type of Greek temple exemplified by the Parthenon in Athens, he made various alterations to align the monument with the Roman architecture and iconography that predominated in the capital. As Thomas observes, Bacon was keeping with a "Roman theme" that was "strong and old in American public architecture," which contributed both "civic" and "imperial" dimensions to the form.[23] The specific model for the memorial was likely the Temple of Concord, which Augustus had rebuilt in order "to celebrate the unity and prosperity he had bestowed on Rome and its empire."[24] Through these allusions—to Roman sacred architecture in general, and more specifically to the Pax Romana rising from the ashes of civil war—the Lincoln Memorial invited its visitors to celebrate a "new birth of freedom" and of American empire.

Bacon emphasized the ideas of rebirth and reunion through the thirty-six columns that surround the building, which correspond to the number of states in the Union at the end of the Civil War, as well as the various inscriptions throughout the interior. Unlike the Capitol, the Lincoln Memorial could obviously not evade the subjects of slavery and civil war. Most prominently, the Second Inaugural Address, in which Lincoln gravely reflected that perhaps "every drop of blood drawn with the lash" might eventually be "paid

by another drawn with the sword," is printed in its entirety on the northern interior wall. But accompanying the address is a mural depicting "unity"
and reconciliation rather than emancipation and blood sacrifice, and strikingly inscribed just above the head of the seated Lincoln is the Memorial's
dedication:

IN THIS TEMPLE

AS IN THE HEARTS OF THE PEOPLE

FOR WHOM HE SAVED THE UNION

THE MEMORY OF ABRAHAM LINCOLN

IS ENSHRINED FOREVER

In both word and image, the focus on "union"—as opposed to emancipation—
served the purpose of foregrounding white reconciliation at the expense of the
historical and ongoing experience of African Americans.[25] The mural above
the Gettysburg Address, which is inscribed on the southern wall, is entitled
"Freedom," but the ambiguity of the text of the address—a new birth of freedom for whom?—raises a salient question about the inscription above the
statue's enormous marble head: "for whom," exactly, had Abraham Lincoln
"saved the union"?

This question was relevant as ever when the memorial was dedicated in a
public ceremony in 1922, as the coverage of the event in the *Crisis* powerfully
demonstrates. The magazine's account of the dedication appeared among
other news items on a single page of the July 1922 edition. The first article
on the page reported the lynching of three black men in Kirwin, Texas, while
another consisted of a series of letters by various mayors, governors, university presidents, and other public figures urging the Senate to enact the Dyer
Anti-Lynching Legislation. This latter piece was entitled "Memorial to the
Senate," and though in this context it means a "reminder" or "admonition," it
also suggests a monument to a thing of the past, as if the institution itself were
already dead and gone. This sense of memorial as monument is reinforced by
the item's proximity to the notice of the dedication of the Lincoln Memorial,
which described the ceremony as yet another outrage against the dignity and
citizenship status of African Americans. If the massive Greco-Roman temple itself was evidence of the continuing importance of a classical aesthetic
to constructions of national identity and projections of national power, few
things could more clearly illustrate the abiding historical contradiction at the
heart of that identity than the fact that the dedication celebration was segregated along the lines of race.[26]

Although intensely ironic for a commemoration of the "Great Emancipator," the segregation of the spectators mirrored the implicit historiographical imperative of both the monument's design and the ceremony itself. Eliding the issue of slavery, the program adhered to a narrative of union and reconciliation. This was perhaps made clearest in the censorship of Robert Moton's speech for the occasion. Moton, the successor to Booker T. Washington as the principal of the Tuskegee Institute and one of the most prominent African American figures in the country, initially submitted a speech to the event committee that addressed directly the unfinished business of the Civil War and Reconstruction. This original speech began by evoking a contrast, which had been commonly deployed in antislavery writing of the antebellum period, between the nearly simultaneous arrivals of the *Mayflower* in Massachusetts and the first slave ship in Virginia in the early seventeenth century. Moton's contention was that although Americans could be "proud of our achievements at home," and there was "abundant cause for rejoicing that sectional rancours and racial antagonisms are softening more and more into mutual understanding," the nation nonetheless remained "half privileged and half repressed . . . half free and half yet in bondage."[27]

As with the memorial itself, the theme of Moton's speech—even in its original draft—had been the idea of union, but extended to all American citizens regardless of race. Considering the relative conservatism of that position, however, the original draft of the speech concluded on a surprisingly radical note. Similar to his evocation of the contrasting ships arriving in the New World, Moton drew on the rhetoric of antebellum resistance to energize his conclusion. Echoing Frederick Douglass's fiery 1852 oration "What to the Slave Is the Fourth of July?," Moton went as far as to suggest that "unless we can make real in our national life, in every state and in every section, the things for which" Lincoln had died, then "this memorial which we erect in token of our veneration is but a hollow mockery" and "a symbol of hypocrisy."[28] But in the speech he actually delivered at the event, this scathing admonition was excised, and Moton's remarks were easily assimilated to the ceremony's insistent and familiar theme: that reconciliation had already been achieved and that the past was definitively past.

The entire spectacle—a white marble monument to American freedom and unity, modeled on classical buildings in which religion and empire converged, and dedicated before a segregated audience and celebrated in speeches excising slavery from the national narrative—was perhaps all too familiar in its ironies. It recalled the symbolic dissonance of the US Capitol and the Washington slave pen—a contrast routinely identified in antebellum abolitionist writing—as well as the more recent exclusion of African Americans from the neoclassical White City of the Columbian Exposition of 1893. In response to the exclusion from the Exposition—and thus from the historical narrative of progress it was designed to advance— Ida B. Wells edited a volume elaborating *The Reason Why the Colored American Is Not in the World's Columbian Exposition*. It was in this volume that Douglass had argued that "to the colored people of America" the White City, "with its splendid display of wealth and power, its triumphs of art and its multitudinous architectural and other attractions," was really "a whited sepulcher." As antebellum abolitionists had done with the monumental landscape of Washington, DC, Douglass's rhetoric transformed the White City—intended as it was to signify the idea of the progress of civilization— into a symbol of its own future existence as ruins.[29]

The *Crisis* effects a similar transformation of the Lincoln Memorial in a striking photograph in the same issue in which the indignities of the dedication ceremony had been recounted. While the Lincoln Memorial had been inserted geographically into a preexisting monumental axis, linked through the Washington Monument to the Capitol, and though by the time of the dedication it was fully integrated into the landscaped grounds at the western end of the National Mall, the photo in the *Crisis* situates the monument in a desolate setting (figs. 4.1 and 4.2). The building stands all but alone on an empty plain, joined by a single tree that is entirely black in contrast to the white monument and the bleached gray sky. Decontextualized from the modern city, it appears an intact relic of the ancient world. Framing it this way, the *Crisis* transforms the neoclassical monument to a reconciled and ascendant America into a ghostly specter of ruin. If the monument and ceremony suggested to a reunified white America the imperial grandeur of the nation Lincoln had supposedly died to save, they suggested to readers of the *Crisis* that Lincoln's prophecy of a new birth of freedom might only materialize when the American empire was dead.[30]

The monument and its dedication exemplify the ways classical tradition had been used to cultivate a national image; and the revision the *Crisis* makes to the monument's symbolism provides a visual analogue to Chesnutt's revisionary practice in "The Marked Tree." The photo of the monument in the *Crisis* is taken from the perspective of the margins, a perspective that reflects the physical displacement of the black guests to the outskirts of the dedication ceremony, as they were "placed nearly a block away from the memorial in the grass and weeds."[31] The marginalization of African American spectators, like the censoring of Moton's speech, was part and parcel of the ceremony's

FIGURE 4.1 "Lincoln Memorial Dedication Taken from the Washington Monument." 1922. Harris & Ewing. Photo courtesy of the Library of Congress.

underlying if unspoken purpose: to celebrate national reconciliation by rendering slavery invisible and silent. Chesnutt's twentieth-century resurrection of two critical narrative strategies—the magic of conjure along with the rhetoric of the ruin of empires—that had been originally tailored to nineteenth-century conditions constitutes a direct challenge to this nationalist occlusion of inconvenient and intransigent historical realities. Future-oriented nationalism would quite literally entomb the nation's past in the classical architecture of its monuments, creating a clear separation between the past and the present. By contrast, Chesnutt's story articulates a multilayered view of

THE LINCOLN MEMORIAL

FIGURE 4.2 "The Lincoln Memorial," *Crisis*, July 1922, 128.

historical stagnation on the issue of racial justice in America, linking the 1920s to the post-Reconstruction and pre–Civil War eras, and back to the ancient slave societies that the United States had taken as models for its own.

This layered historical consciousness expresses itself in "The Marked Tree" through an allegory of imperial decline of the kind that appeared frequently in antebellum black writing, as well as in post-Reconstruction works such as T. Thomas Fortune's *Black and White*, Pauline Hopkins's *Of One Blood*, and Chesnutt's early stories.[32] Following this long-established tradition, Chesnutt's late story and Du Bois's journal share an apprehension of Western history as the accumulation of ruin, and of the modern West not as the proper inheritor of the democratic ideals and high culture associated with classical antiquity, but rather as a reiteration of the imperial civilizations created by the same logic that would later destroy them. In its depiction of a representative house of slavery fallen into a state of ruination, Chesnutt's story is itself representative of the type of revision antebellum African American writers made to the typological underpinnings of the American historical narrative. Where the dominant narrative depicted ancient Rome and modern America as type and antitype in a narrative of liberal progress, black writers and orators refigured them as sedimentary layers in a single transhistorical empire of slavery that was always unfolding into an empire of ruin.

The Mark and the Blow

In "The Marked Tree," Chesnutt reiterates the skepticism of *The Marrow of Tradition* regarding the notion of progress after the war and Reconstruction; and he articulates this view by appealing to a rhetoric of imperial decline that—as we have seen in chapter two—was widely employed in the antebellum era. The rhetoric of decline drew heavily on C. F. Volney's *The Ruins; or, Meditation on the Revolutions of Empires*, which had presented a straightforward and essentially materialist theory of the rise and fall of empires. "Men," Volney argued, "always greedy and improvident," developed imperial societies based on conquest and enslavement, which led to a general state of tyranny followed by degeneration and collapse.[33] Antebellum abolitionist writers shared and frequently reiterated this straightforward theory: that greed led to slavery, upheaval, and decline.

In the American context, as works such as Walker's *Appeal*, Brown's lecture on the Haitian Revolution, and Garnet's "Address to the Slaves" make clear, the rhetoric of decline pointed toward slave revolt or some other cataclysmic event.[34] Such prophecies were to some extent realized in the Civil War, but just as the American Revolution had failed to liberate slaves, the Civil War and Reconstruction would prove less than revolutionary with respect to positive liberty for African Americans. Du Bois explicitly identified, in the opening chapter of *The Souls of Black Folk*, the looming threat of a second slavery in the twentieth century, thereby establishing a continuity between the antislavery struggle and his own; and he reaffirmed this sense of continuity through an epigraph to a subsequent chapter, in which he argued against the accommodationist politics of Booker T. Washington. For this epigraph, Du Bois drew on a passage from Lord Byron's *Childe Harold's Pilgrimage* (1818) that would have had a powerful resonance for his African American readers. The lines—"Hereditary bondsmen! Know ye not / Who would be free themselves must strike the blow?" (IV.73–76)—were for Byron an exhortation to contemporary Greeks, at the time "enslaved" by the Ottoman Empire, to claim their inheritance as the descendants of the ancient founders of the very idea of Western freedom; but in the antebellum period they had been adopted repeatedly by African American writers as a battle cry against American slavery.[35] *Childe Harold's Pilgrimage* was also the most extended poetic treatment of the central themes of Volney's *Ruins*, and Canto IV, from which these famous lines are drawn, devotes considerable space to the contemplation of ruins and the historical lessons they impart. In both regards— its commitment to revolutionary politics and its alignment with Volney's theory of history—Byron's poem held a powerful appeal for black writers both before and after the Civil War.

These pairs—ruins and resistance, Volney and Byron—provide an allusive counterpart to the conjure-tale framework of "The Marked Tree." Following Chesnutt's "earlier manner," the story is narrated by John, the white northerner who has migrated to North Carolina after the Civil War. Although he takes pride in his northern industriousness and entrepreneurial spirit, John also admits to being enchanted by the South. He is taken with the native indolence of its people, the "laissez-faire customs of [his] adopted state," and the picturesque qualities of the landscape.[36] So while he approaches the old Spencer slave plantation with an eye to buying and improving it, he is drawn not only by its potential as an investment, but by its aesthetic value as a ruin. John takes evident pleasure in describing the "exhausted" fields, "neglected grapevines ... and gnarled and knotted fruit-trees, smothered by ruder growths about them" (I:59). And his pleasure only increases in describing the house, which is now little more than an absence: "Destroyed by fire many years before," the only remaining traces were "a crumbling brick pillar here and there ... the dilapidated, ivy-draped lower half of a chimney, of which the yawning, blackened fireplace bore mute witness of the vanished generations which had lived and loved—and perchance suffered and died, within the radius of the genial glow" (I:59).

This is the wreckage of American slavery: the soil exhausted by unsustainable agriculture, the human society extinguished by its adherence to an inhuman and unnatural system. But while the context is decidedly American, the landscape evokes a deeper history of decline, and John's account of his entrance into the ruin echoes Volney's description of Palmyra. John even sits on a stump that recalls the "shaft of a column" on which Volney's narrator seats himself to begin his "profound reverie" on the revolutions of empires.[37] Developing the parallel, Uncle Julius—the formerly enslaved black narrator who will relate the history of the plantation as a story within the story— becomes the equivalent of Volney's "apparition," a ghostly figure who appears and recounts the history of the ruins, accompanied by "refreshing night breezes ... the howlings only of the jackal, and the solemn notes of the bird of night."[38] Similarly, as the night comes on, Julius tells John the story of the old plantation to the "accompaniment of night-time sounds—the deep diapason from a distant frog-pond, the shrill chirp of the cicada, the occasional bark of a dog or cry of an owl" (I:61). And like Volney's apparition, Julius imparts the lessons of these American ruins, explaining the living history of slavery to whites like John who insist on believing it is dead.

The ruin of the plantation is bound up with the ruin of the tree, and it is the stump that prompts Julius to tell their connected stories. The stump, as John notes, is "in a good state of preservation, except for a hole in the center, due, doubtless, to a rotten heart, in what had been in other respects a sound and perfect tree" (I:59–60). It will become apparent that the stump represents an otherwise "perfect Union" blighted by the "rotten" institution of slavery; but we only gather this symbolism through Julius's version of the tree's history. As Julius tells it, years ago two children were born on the plantation on the same day, one to the white mistress of the house and one to an enslaved black woman named Phillis, and the implication is that Aleck Spencer—master of the plantation and patriarch of the Spencer clan—is the father of both. The mixed-race child is living testimony to the domestic transgressions and sexual violence that were common in plantation life, and following the common pattern, punishment for the crime is meted out to the black mother and her son Isham. Although Phillis had been a house servant, sometime before Isham is born Mrs. Spencer—the outraged wife—remands her to the cotton fields. Then, years later, Spencer sells Isham—again, on the advice of his wife—in order to finance the extravagant wedding of the "legitimate" son. In short, the black son is sold to pay for the white one, and the black child ultimately pays the price with his life.

The wedding celebration for young Johnny Spencer and his bride recalls the earlier celebration of his christening. Both events take place under the family tree, an impressive oak beside the big house that had been the site of Spencer weddings and christenings for generations. Like the "colored citizens" at the dedication ceremony for the Lincoln Memorial, the plantation slaves were invited to witness the christening from the margins. Phillis, the new mother to Johnny's black brother Isham, stood along with the other field hands "out on de edge . . . fuh dey wuz all 'vited up ter take part," though their celebratory feast was "out in de yahd" while "de white folks wuz eatin' in de house" (I:61). When the time comes to celebrate Johnny's wedding, this scene is essentially repeated, with the slaves invited to witness from the outskirts and enjoy the remnants of the feast after the whites had finished. As the celebration is in progress, Isham is mortally wounded while trying to escape the brutal new master to whom Aleck Spencer had sold him. In spite of his injuries, Isham manages to make it back home, where he dies in his mother's quarters, within earshot of the festivities at the big house. In response, Phillis bears witness to the murder through an act of inscription that attacks the system that demands and sanctions it. Through an act of conjure, Phillis "marks" the Spencer family tree, transforming it from a symbol of the family's power into the agent of its destruction. Through various mechanisms, the conjured tree kills off the entire Spencer family and finally burns the plantation to the ground.

Phillis's mark is an act of conjure, but the marking is also figured in the story as an act of writing. This writing is in a language of her own that remains illegible to the white narrator as anything but a mark, but is legible to readers through its very notable effects, as it both marks and constitutes the transformation of the Spencer tree from a sign of ascendancy to vehicle of ruination. Throughout the conjure stories, Chesnutt implies an analogy between magic and storytelling, between conjure and conjure tale. Julius's stories work like magic, usually achieving some material gain or strategic advantage in relation to his employers. But "The Marked Tree" figures the act of conjure more explicitly as a performative act of writing as resistance. This is emphasized, quite literally, through the use—uncharacteristic for Chesnutt—of italic text. Phillis "*marked de Spencer tree*," and the italicization of this act of retribution draws our attention to a prior act of resistance, when Isham "achully *hit his marster!*"[39] These separate acts—striking the blow and marking the tree—merge through the visual emphasis on the written marks on the page, becoming both causally and thematically related. The blow causes the mark, and the mark in turn strikes a blow.

As a "family tree," the oak is a genealogical figure for both the Spencer family and the American nation. Before Phillis marks the tree, it serves to commemorate a glorious past and celebrate a promising future; and in typical American fashion, the monumental tree, like the buildings and monuments in the city of Washington, derives important aspects of its symbolism from classical models. The oak is associated with Jove, most powerful of the Roman gods, a fit symbol for a representative family of the master class. Its ancient roots and upward growth represent a deep history and the manifest destiny of this exceptional family. More pointedly, with respect to the imperial strain of American classicism, the oak is also the tree to which Virgil likens Aeneas in his steadfast resistance to the claims of Dido—the lover he betrays in the name of his own manifest destiny. By "marking" this tree, Phillis alters its symbolic function, much as a simple change in perspective had rendered the Lincoln Memorial a scene of ruin rather than reconciliation. No longer an image of ascendancy, exceptionalism, and power, the marked tree becomes a symbol of catastrophe and decline.[40]

When she changes the tree's symbolism, Phillis also changes its name. Although it had been the "Spencer Oak," Julius now calls it the "U-pass" tree—a name he learned years earlier from Aleck Spencer himself, who dubbed it a

"Upas" after it had killed off most of his family. Sensing the trace of the literary in Julius's oral recollection, John tells us the Upas is "the fabled tree of death," referring to a poisonous tree that appears in at least four eighteenth- and nineteenth-century texts (1:60). Most notable among these is Canto IV of Byron's *Childe Harold's Pilgrimage*, which I have already mentioned as perhaps the most prominent literary meditation on the revolutions of empires and a major text in African American intellectual history.[41] While the whole of Canto IV of *Childe Harold* shows the influence of Volney, the stanza on the Upas emphasizes his specific claim that "human nature," if Western history is any indication, has become both unnatural and unsustainable. In Byron's poem this nature is a "false one," out of sync with the "harmony of things." This disconnection from a natural state—which *The Ruins* reminds us is a state of "equality"—constitutes our "uneradicable taint of sin, / This boundless upas, this all-blasting tree, / Whose . . . leaves and branches be / the skies which rain their plagues on men like dew"—plagues that include not only "disease" and "death," but "bondage" (IV.1126–32).[42]

While it seems that Phillis has marked the tree with a layered literary allusion, we must remember that this allusion is only produced in the mind—and the second-order narration—of the white narrator of the story. In this sense the allusion is in fact a kind of useful illusion, generated through the subversive application of conjure (to the tree) and conjure tale (to the narrator and the dominant symbolic system that informs his narration). The word "U-pass/Upas" signifies differently to different people, since Phillis's mark is written in a language that remains illegible to John but is legible to us, as it would have been to black readers of the *Crisis*, through its material effects—effects that go far beyond the destruction of the master's house to rupture the symbolic order upon which white claims to mastery are founded. If the tree and the house are symbols of ascendancy, monumental anchors to a narrative of American power and progress, Phillis and Julius alter quite radically, through a kind of collective authorial intervention, the supposedly providential course of this familiar and national story.

Just before Phillis marks the tree, Spencer offers a toast—to both the family and the tree—that affirms the dominant American narrative: "May it last anudder hunded yeahs, an' den anudder, an' may it fetch good luck to my son an' his wife, an tuh deir child'en an' deir child'en's child'en" (II:110). The toast echoes the words of Jefferson's first inaugural address, in which he envisioned an empire of liberty "for our descendants to the thousandth and thousandth generation." But Phillis disrupts the Spencer family ritual of power by marking it with a powerful ritual of her own, which signifies in multiple registers and has multiple effects. First, in its evocation of the "Upas" tradition it appeals to John's sense of himself as a man of letters, his taste for romantic meditations on ruins, and his own penchant for offhanded literary allusion. John is a bourgeois literary snob, and he takes pleasure in drawing obscure connections between Julius's tales and canonical texts of the Western tradition. Second, the allusion to Byron in particular links Julius's story of the Spencer plantation to the related rhetorics of resistance and ruination that black writers had developed in opposition to slavery, and which Du Bois and Chesnutt had elsewhere invoked in response to worsening conditions in the wake of Reconstruction.

The allusion to *Childe Harold* thus not only recalls Byron's place in African American intellectual history, but it also reveals the elitist and racially exclusive literary conditioning of the white narrator. John is not aware, we can assume, of David Walker, William Wells Brown, and the African American historiography of decline, nor is he aware that *Childe Harold's Pilgrimage* was an important text for black writers of the antebellum period. His response to Volney and Byron is informed by what he considers his disinterested aesthetics, rather than any political history, and there is certainly no pressing sense for him of the living presence of American slavery or the slave economy of ancient empires in the wreckage of the Spencer family home. John's inability or reluctance to read Julius's stories politically—and his more general tendency to separate the political from the aesthetic and the present from the past—demonstrates a view of history deeply conditioned by his privileged position within the hierarchy of power.[43]

From this dominant point of view, John understands Phillis's mark only in terms of its apparent allusions to his own tradition. Like Julius's oral storytelling tradition, her mark is to John nothing but an anachronism. But as Julius is trying to explain to him, Phillis is not from another time but from *their* time. Likewise, Julius's story of the ruined tree is not a nostalgic reflection on the lost glories of the antebellum world or the lost power of an irretrievable African heritage, but rather a critical intervention that asserts the living presence of both antebellum oppression and African American forms of resistance. And the vehicle for this assertion is the "language" of conjure—as acts of magic and writing as symbolic action—a language to which Chesnutt deliberately returned in 1924 and which, he suspected, retained a critical interest for readers of the *Crisis*.

Chesnutt's return to conjure therefore asserts not only the primacy of a black literary voice but also an alternative sense of historical time. In both of its functions here—as open rebellion (for Phillis) and as subversive literary language (for Chesnutt)—the art of conjure may be linked to the complex struggle Walter Johnson has discerned between the various temporalities that have framed the experiences of the African diaspora and the prevailing temporal framework of the imperial West. This struggle is not a negotiation for space for the black voice within white canons, or for equal access to the dominant political economy and its progressive narrative of history, but rather, as Johnson suggests, part of a larger war "for control of the New World," and a concerted effort "to force Euro-Americans into another place in time."[44]

The Mansions of the Dead

Julius's story constitutes at least a minor victory in this kind of war, as it forces John to rethink his—and his race's—supposed mastery of historical time. As John narrates the story, which takes place in three distinct time frames of its own—the entrance into the ruin, followed by Julius's story, then later by John's narration—he betrays a dawning awareness of a complex and multilayered history of which he is only a part and over which he holds no dominion. For the first time, he recognizes in Julius's tale not merely a simple, if tragic, recollection of the era of slavery. As the word "U-pass" conjures the poetry of Byron, which draws us back through Volney to the ancient world, Julius's moral fable draws John's meditations through the recent past of slavery to the long history of the fable itself. "He took," John observes, "the crude legends and vague superstitions of the neighborhood and embodied them in stories as complete, in their way, as the Sagas of Iceland or the primitive tales of ancient Greece. . . . Had Julius lived in a happier age for men of his complexion," he concludes, "the world might have had a black Aesop" (I:60–61). John's sudden apprehension of Julius as Aesop, a foundational figure in the Western tradition, simultaneously leads him to question the relative state of his own civilization. Perhaps Julius *would* prove the new Aesop for a higher culture than John can presently imagine: "Who knows," he wonders, "whether our civilization has yet more than cut its milk teeth, or humanity has even really begun to walk erect?" (I:61).

Among the ironies here is the fact that Chesnutt had figured Julius as a black Aesop from the earliest story in which he appeared—"The Goophered Grapevine" in 1887. Julius, like Aesop, emerges from enslavement to become a moral adviser to powerful people. Aesop has also been traditionally viewed as an ethnic or racial outsider.[45] In the "Life of Aesop" that prefaces the 1865 Hurd & Houghton edition of the *Fables*, Aesop self-identifies as "Negro," and is described in the language of stereotype: "His head was long, nose flat, lips

thick and pendent, a hump back, and complexion dark, from which he con-
tracted his name (Æsopus being the same with Æthiops)."[46] These characteristics are part of the Aesop tradition, but in the American contexts of slavery
and Jim Crow they signify in a particularly loaded way. For Chesnutt, who
developed a new kind of American fable by signifying on precisely such stereotypes, this ancient African figure, whose narrative powers were celebrated
in his day and throughout history, resonated profoundly with the figure of
the African American storyteller of his own time and place.[47]

While there are many similarities between Aesop and Julius, most relevant to the matter of the politics of African American literature is that
both undergo the transition, through a supposed emancipation, from field
labor to the labor of narrative. Both earn their livings through telling stories and providing counsel to powerful men; and in each case the storytelling
"career" begins with a fable of a plantation economy that withholds, in a literal sense, the fruits of slave labor from enslaved laborers themselves. In "The
Goophered Grapevine," the grapes are conjured with a spell to prevent the
slaves who grow them from eating them, while Aesop is wrongfully accused of
stealing his master's figs. Although Julius and Aesop's stories serve to establish
a measure of authority—and therefore a measure of freedom—in relation to
the plantation owners, both authority and freedom remain under constant
threat. Indeed, in spite of his initial story's "truth," Aesop is sold (as if "down
the river") specifically because his master fears retaining a truthful slave; and
for Julius, the occasion of "The Goophered Grapevine" is his de facto re-
enslavement to white economic interests. Yet Julius, like Aesop before him,
resists this second slavery by telling stories—stories intended, as Chesnutt
said of his own project as a writer, to effect "the elevation of the whites,"
whom he perceives to be in a state of arrested moral development.[48]

For Julius, then, storytelling is *work*: it is both the source and the practice
of his freedom, and for all its humor it is a serious business indeed. By contrast, for John the production and consumption of art and culture are contingent upon his possession of leisure, and therefore on the power relations that
supply and ensure it. At the beginning of "The Marked Tree," John attributes
this view—which "celebrate[s]" the "dignity of ease"—to Horace, whom he
describes as "a gentleman and a philosopher, with some reputation as a poet"
(I:59). For John this is like a literary joke, an ironic expression of his aesthetic
cultivation, but the real irony lies in what it says in the context of the place in
which he stands. On the plantation this is the view of the slaveholder. Beneath
it lies the oppressive logic that constructs freedom on the basis of slavery, and
by extension justifies the sale of the black child to secure the privileges of the

white. It is a logic that can describe a tree with a "rotten heart" as otherwise "perfect." This view of culture as contingent on freedom, as freedom is contingent on slavery, is rooted in a classical tradition that Americans strongly claimed as their own; and John's appeal to Horace attests to the persistence of this claim.

While proslavery southerners openly embraced the idea that liberty depended on slavery, northerners like John tended to obscure this dependency as part of a broader cognitive dissonance on the meaning of freedom in America. John is of the class that lamented slavery even as it relentlessly compromised with it in the name of national unity and economic growth. John loves Horace and the leisure he espouses, but he ignores the slavery upon which Roman freedom was built. John's race and class allow him to consider the problems of history as separate from himself, and artifacts from the past as matters of pleasurable and apolitical contemplation. He is a tourist in the ruins, one who returns to the comforts of his piazza when he grows weary of their melancholy lessons. Chesnutt, on the other hand, renders the historical ties between the ancient world and modern America from the perspective of the oppressed and the enslaved, countering John's Horace with Julius's Aesop.[49] To Julius, a free black man in the wake of the Civil War, re-enslaved by the alignment of social, economic, and political forces to which his access is denied, history is indeed a nightmare from which it is impossible to awake. American slavery has survived the war just as ancient slavery survived in antebellum America. Julius is not a tourist in a historical landscape but what Volney would call the resident "Genius" in the "mansions of the dead."[50] Although disempowered within the structures of American society, Julius nonetheless bears powerful witness to what John's historical vision elides. Julius does not share with John the privileges of full citizenship in the exceptional nation, which include the luxury of disavowing the centuries of oppression and exclusion upon which those privileges rest. This disavowal is at the heart of exceptionalist thinking, which says, along with Herman Melville's quintessentially American Captain Delano—who is himself the protagonist of a story that draws the United States into a deep and haunting history of slavery and empire—"the past is passed; why moralize upon it?"[51] Julius, on the other hand, is what Saidiya Hartman and Tina Campt would call a "child of empire," suffering acutely "the knowledge that the past is not yet past."[52]

This sense of history's presence and relevance underlies both Chesnutt's redeployment of conjure and his engagement with classicism. This historical consciousness also informs the earlier writings of Walker, Brown, and Garnet, younger contemporaries such as Langston Hughes and Claude McKay, and literary descendants like Ralph Ellison and Toni Morrison. We see it in the temporal sensibility of Hughes's "The Negro Speaks of Rivers," published in the *Crisis* in 1921, as well as in McKay's "America," which echoes Chesnutt's earlier vision of the Sphinx. McKay's poem imagines an ascendant America transformed into a state of ruin, as the speaker gazes "darkly . . . into the days ahead," where "beneath the touch of Time's unerring hand," America's monuments, its "granite wonders," appear as "priceless treasures sinking in the sand."[53] Both Hughes and McKay might be said to "conjure" images from the past, which they then rework into a new literary historiography that rejects the teleology of exceptionalism. As Chesnutt had done with the Sphinx, this next generation of poets applied the "dark gaze" of an African American perspective to the history of empire.

Some fifty years later, just following the nation's bicentennial celebration, Morrison would demonstrate the continuing power and relevance of this critical perspective. Applying another dark gaze to the aftermath of another incomplete revolution in civil rights, Morrison constructs a scene in *Song of Solomon* that echoes "The Marked Tree" in many respects. As in Chesnutt's story, the critical event is the murder of a black man—Macon Dead, a former slave who presents a challenge to the economy of white supremacy by moving north after the war and becoming a successful farmer—who refuses what legal scholar Anthony Farley calls "the commodity form" enslaved people "had been assigned."[54] The novel as a whole advances a completely different symbolic system that refuses to name and value the human as commodity, and as in Chesnutt's story the new system is advanced by a woman who illuminates both the material and the cultural dimensions of American slavery.

Morrison's character is named Circe, a name that exemplifies the typical usage of classical material within the slavery regime. As Morrison has said in an interview, she generally alludes to Western tradition only "to show that something has gone wrong" or "to signal something being askew," and Circe's name fits within a pattern of classical allusion in the novel that demonstrates less the cultural heights to which a civilized people might ascend than it does the deep pathologies of whiteness.[55] As another character suggests, white people "know they are unnatural. Their writers and artists have been saying it for years. Telling them they are unnatural, telling them they are depraved. They call it tragedy" (157). The manifestation of this depravity in the historical world of the novel is the economy of slavery and white supremacy. Though set in the 1960s, Morrison's present story still inhabits the same "slave world," as Houston Baker has called it, that provides the setting for Chesnutt's conjure tales; and Circe, a character some have related to the genre of magical realism, would be equally at home in the context of conjure.[56] Like Chesnutt's Phillis, who takes on—through her associations with Phillis Wheatley, classical precedent, and African culture prior to enslavement—a transhistorical aspect, Morrison's Circe is of indeterminate age, and bears witness to the continuity of slavery across deep stretches of time and space. Also like Phillis, she seems to have "marked" a white "house" for destruction.

Circe lives within the ruins of a house that stands for American history. If the founding moment of this history, as Farley has argued, is neither the "Discovery of America" nor the landing on "Plymouth Rock," but the arrival of slave ships in Virginia and the marking of black bodies as commodities within an economy of slavery, in Morrison's historical allegory it is the murder of the liberated slave Macon Dead that marks the ritual reestablishment after the Civil War of the same economic and legal regime.[57] Macon Dead carves a self-sufficient agrarian life out of the landscape, embodying the Jeffersonian ideal of the yeoman farmer. But in the slave economy, which persists beyond the legal abolition of slavery, the black yeoman is out of line, and it is the very success of his Jeffersonian endeavor that makes him an affront to the dominant culture to which that model was meant to apply. Dead is murdered by his white neighbors, the Butlers, who "owned half the county." As a witness recounts, "Macon's land was in their way," so they kill him and take it, all in the course of expanding their family empire by conquest. If Macon's murder echoes the murder of Phillis's son, Circe's revenge echoes Phillis's revenge upon the Spencer family and its tree. After the murder, Circe, who is a servant in the Butler house, undertakes a long-term project of what the locals call "evening up" (233). As Phillis does with the Spencers, Circe renders the white imperial family a barren line. The money disappears, the mansion decays, and the Butler estate falls into ruin.[58]

This ruin serves as home for the last two inhabitants, the mistress and the servant. As time passes, the two women become more and more equal, not by the black woman's acquisition or accumulation of property or rights, but by the progressive deterioration of these ideological pillars of white power. Mrs. Butler ultimately commits suicide rather than descend any further. "She couldn't stand," as Circe tells it, "to see the place go to ruin," and she "killed herself rather than do the work I'd been doing all my life!" (247). That this telling occurs amid the very ruins Mrs. Butler would never tolerate situates the scene within the long African American literary tradition I have tried to delineate, which includes Fortune, Hopkins, Chesnutt, Hughes, and McKay after the war, and Brown, Garnet, Walker, and the black newspapers before it. For all of these writers the ruins of empire, from Egypt to Rome to the

United States, are the inevitable results of a commitment to what the historian William Appleman Williams identified as "empire as a way of life."[59] This way of life is characterized by greed—the popular terms in the earlier part of the tradition are "avarice" and "cupidity"—the familiar fetishizing of the commodity and the commodification of the human. The Butlers lived and died in order to acquire property and other people to care for it. "They loved it," Circe says: "Stole for it, lied for it, killed for it." And in the years since the murder of Macon Dead, Circe's gradual retribution ultimately culminates in the ruin of the Butler family and their monumental house. Even after the Butlers are dead and gone she insists on remaining in the house to ensure that "everything in this world they lived for will crumble and rot" (247).

By the end of "The Marked Tree," John comes to understand an analogous point: that no real progress is possible while any vestige of the deadly Upas tree remains. Completing the process Phillis began, John orders "the stump of the Spencer Oak extracted," which proves "a difficult task even with the aid of explosives" (II:113).[60] Just as this literal destruction transforms the physical landscape, the literary work of conjure reworks the symbolic one. In both of its manifestations—Phillis's mark and Julius's story—we can see how the language of conjure revises past and present into a new reality with which whites must come to terms, and in light of which they must reconsider what Alain Locke called the "root-idea" of their philosophy and culture—an idea "which never was soundly in accordance with the facts."[61] This root idea is "supremacy," the desire for and the assertion of which have driven the history of American slavery and empire.

Chesnutt and Morrison counter this root idea with what Baker calls the "root-work" of conjure. This work has as its ultimate aim not only "to *re-form*" the "slave world" created by the imperial West, but also the "progress and survival of a genuinely Afro-American *sound*."[62] This sound is the voice of conjure, which rejects the authority of the root idea of Western history because it emerges from outside that history, and thus can view it in all its contingency. And as the project of conjure reveals this contingent status, it simultaneously elaborates an alternative conception of history—traceable to a time prior to enslavement, prior to classicism or contact with the West—as a field of contestation between competing narratives and temporalities. Both conjure and black classicism can thus be seen as examples of what Walter Johnson calls "historical counter-practices," which serve as "irruptive reminders of the possibilities suppressed by the forcible superimposition of European history that began with the slave trade."[63]

In "The Marked Tree," we witness just such an irruptive reminder, which effectively forces the white narrator into a place in time that necessitates a different view of what he calls history and tradition; and this new perspective requires of him a different kind of action. John's new commitment to using any means necessary to obliterate the fabled tree of death exceeds the demands of his economic self-interest, and suggests a burgeoning realization that it was not the rotten heart of a perfect tree, but the tree itself that was rotten; that any empire—for liberty or otherwise—built on slavery would eventually join the historical landscape of the "empire of ruin."

Crumbling into Dust

By appealing to the nineteenth-century trope of the revolutions of empires, Chesnutt and Morrison allegorize, through the depiction of literal ruination, the sort of "mental revolution" Locke believed was necessary to usher in a "new world."[64] This transformative vision echoes Garnet's 1848 address "The Past and the Present Condition, and the Destiny, of the Colored Race," in which he invited his listeners and readers not only to contemplate the "empire of ruin" that is history, but also to imagine an alternative future where "truth, love, and liberty are descending the heavens, bearing the charter of man's destiny to a waiting world."[65] Some ninety years later, though in a language less Romantic, Richard Wright would articulate a similar assessment of the possibilities for revolutionary black writing: the writer "may, with disgust and revulsion, say *no* and depict the horrors of capitalism encroaching upon the human being. Or he may, with hope and passion, say *yes* and depict the faint stirrings of a new and emerging life."[66] Whether the "social voice" of the writer emphasizes the negative or the positive, the ruins of the past or the vision of the future, what is "overheard" for Wright is the author's "faith."[67] This faith develops through a restored sense of "heritage," which appears when the black writer can "ascend," in Garnet's phrase, the "eminence" of the present and survey history from this perspective. For Wright, "perspective" is "that fixed point in intellectual space where a writer stands to view the struggles, hopes, and sufferings of his people."[68] With these things in sight, black writers will begin "to feel the meaning of the history of their race as though they in one life time had lived it themselves throughout all the long centuries."[69]

This is the apprehension of history we find in Hughes's "soul," "ancient as the world and older than the flow of human blood in human veins," as well as in Chesnutt's vision of the Sphinx and his elegiac rendering of Uncle Julius as a black American Aesop.[70] And like McKay's "America," both *The Marrow of Tradition* and "The Marked Tree" present apocalyptic visions rooted in the historical theory of imperial decline. Yet Chesnutt's writings also offer "faint stirrings" of a hope that can at least be "over-heard." This hope is embodied in the figure Julius-Aesop, the black storyteller who works the roots of multiple traditions, tilling the ground from which a new collective tradition could be born. Wright argues that the key to black literary power lies in harnessing black "folklore" to the project, and Chesnutt was the first writer really to do this—asserting a black mythology in a black voice, even as he put this mythology in what Ralph Ellison would call "antagonistic cooperation" with the white Western tradition.[71]

The figure of black Aesop embodies and reiterates the two central lessons of Chesnutt's Sphinx: faith and resilience. By modeling Julius partially on Aesop, Chesnutt expresses his faith in a future culture guided by the ethos of such a founder; but since Aesop and Julius both lived in "unhappy" times for men of their literal or figurative "complexion," resilience and resistance would continue to be the primary modes of their lives and struggles. The works of writers such as Ellison and Morrison attest to the continuing relevance of these lessons for later articulations of black classicism within African American cultural production. If white American authorities—whether political or cultural—would continue to construct hierarchies of race and nation through an imagined relation to a classical past, drawing on the classical arts as the basis of a racialized cultural elitism, and classical histories as enabling precedents for the project of American empire, black classicism would respond with a vision of that empire's inexorable fall into ruin.

During his time at the American Academy in Rome, Ellison noted that classicism revealed the "myth and ritual business" lying "beneath the foundations of the West"; and Morrison and Chesnutt both share with Ellison this understanding of the deep connection between a nation's cultural and political histories.[72] "Canon building is Empire building," as Morrison has put it, and Chesnutt earlier argued that to "know a nation" we must "read its books."[73] But by extension, the works of these writers suggest a corollary: to *change* a nation, *change* its books. The kind of critical engagement with classical tradition and monumental culture we have seen in the fiction of Chesnutt and Morrison, the poetry of Hughes and McKay, and the theoretical work of Locke, Wright, and Ellison contributes to a changing of the books. This critical engagement resonates not only with the antebellum rhetoric of imperial ruination, but also with the simultaneous "deconstruction" and "reconstruction" Hartman and Campt locate at the heart of more recent anticolonial writing, twin processes that reveal "literary production as a site of struggle in an age dominated by the color line, capitalism, and empire."[74] This struggle ideally results in a creative destruction through which the blighted wood of cultural white supremacy is cut away and left, like the history-laden timbers in another Chesnutt story, haunted by the ghost of yet another murdered slave, to "crumble' inter dus'."[75]

5

National Monuments and the Residue of History

IN THE DECADES following the segregated dedication of the Lincoln Memorial, the site of that monument would continue to be what Christopher Thomas has aptly described as "racially contested ground."[1] Like the US Capitol, the Bunker Hill Monument, and the Washington Square arch, the Lincoln Memorial is in this regard an exemplary *lieu de mémoire*, a site, as the historian Scott Sandage has defined it, "where we struggle over tensions between our experience of the past (memory) and our organization of it (history)."[2] Given the entrenched racism and racial segregation of US history in both of its senses (i.e., as historical events and their representation) the Lincoln Memorial is more specifically a site of struggle between the "official" or hegemonic white culture implicitly addressed by the monument's inscription—the people "for whom" Lincoln had supposedly "saved the union"—and the challenge presented by African American artists and activists to this dominant culture's conception of the nation's history.[3]

From one perspective, the contest that unfolded across the twentieth century at the site of the memorial could be shaped into a narrative of the inexorable progress of liberalism. In such a progressive narrative, the monument serves as a stage upon which major events in the movement for civil rights play themselves out. The first major episode in this story took place on Easter Sunday in 1939, when the internationally acclaimed singer Marian Anderson—in an act of protest against her exclusion from other racially segregated venues in Washington—performed from the steps of the monument (fig. 5.1). By opening her set with the patriotic song "America," and performing with Lincoln in his temple prominently visible behind her, Anderson effectively revived the antebellum strategy of juxtaposing images of slavery and

FIGURE 5.1 Marian Anderson Performing at the Lincoln Memorial, 9 April 1939. Photo courtesy of the Library of Congress.

the US Capitol in order to illustrate the significant gap between the nation's stated principles and its practices.[4]

The linkage to the antebellum period is intensified if we recall that the African American poet James Whitfield had ironically revised the lyrics of "America" in his own poem of the same title in 1853. For Whitfield, the "boasted land of liberty" was anything but "sweet"; it was instead a "land of blood, and crime, and wrong," where "the black man," torn "from his soil," was "Chained on . . . blood-bemoistened sod, / Cringing beneath a tyrant's rod."[5] Whitfield went on to evoke—in the tradition of David Walker, Henry Highland Garnet, William Wells Brown, and others in the antebellum period—the fates of ancient empires to develop a grim prophecy for an unregenerate America. Likening American slavery to its Egyptian and Babylonian precedents, Whitfield suggested that a "darker doom than Egypt felt, / May yet repay this nation's guilt."[6] But as Garnet had done in "The Past and the Present Condition, and the Destiny, of the Colored People," Whitfield tempered his dark prophecy with a vision of an alternative future.[7] The poem ends with an appeal to God in a collective voice; and this collective comes not "in the panoply of war," hoping "in blood to wash out blood, / Through wrong to seek redress for wrong," but rather "in the sacred name of peace, / Of justice, virtue, love and truth."[8] Though Whitfield's conclusion is rooted in a commitment to nonviolence that would resonate with Martin Luther King Jr.'s strategy a century later, it also shares with King a commitment to not only emancipation but *reparation*. In Whitfield's "America," the struggle will continue until "the bonds of every slave" have been broken *and* "the wrongs we bear shall be redressed."[9]

Anderson's rendition of "America" on the steps of the memorial demonstrated that Whitfield's conditions were far from being met, and the performance itself marked the beginning of a new stage in this ongoing struggle that would play itself out through a series of protests and performances at the Lincoln Memorial that "constituted," as Sandage has argued, "a formidable politics of memory," which transformed the monument from a marker of white reunification after the Civil War to a powerful symbol of the unfinished business of emancipation.[10]

This tradition of performative protest reached its apogee with the 1963 March on Washington, which culminated in what has become one of the most indelibly inscribed images in US history: Martin Luther King Jr. delivering the "I Have a Dream" speech from the steps of the memorial. In his speech that day, King followed Anderson in capitalizing on a long tradition of juxtaposing the black liberation struggle with a white monument to the freedom that was putatively the nation's hallmark. In his speech King cited the founding documents and nodded toward both the Founding Fathers and Abraham Lincoln, the "great American in whose symbolic shadow" he was standing as he addressed the crowd. And in his conclusion, King evoked both Anderson's earlier performance and the presence of the antebellum past through his own recitation of the lyrics to "America," which Whitfield had so powerfully reconfigured in his abolitionist revision of the song. King imagined a "day when all of God's children will be able to sing with new meaning, 'My country, 'tis of thee, sweet land of liberty,'" before drawing on an element of the song's refrain—"Let freedom ring"—as a repeating trope for his own memorable peroration. Through these multiple layers of signification, King's performance demonstrated the unfinished nature of the business of emancipation, and capped a decades-long process of transforming the Lincoln Memorial, which had been "conceived in a quest for white consensus," and dedicated as such in a racially segregated ceremony in 1922, into a symbol of the emancipatory promise of the movement for civil rights.[11]

Pax Americana

Viewed within the framework of the progressive historiography of liberalism, the performative black "politics of memory" alters the white monumental landscape in such a way as to reflect the true diversity of the United States. Yet from the critical perspective I have been tracing thus far—that of black writers "in plain sight" of or, as King said, in the "shadow" of national monuments to freedom that ultimately reinforce structures of inequity and enslavement—it appears less that the protest has fundamentally transformed the meaning of the memorial, than that these iconic figures of resistance have themselves been effectively assimilated to the white hegemonic narrative such white monuments invariably advance. And though the performances of Anderson and King have undoubtedly become monumental in their own right, the notion that such performances of black protest could substantially alter the underlying meaning of the monumental landscape of Washington is to some extent belied by subsequent history.

In his lifetime King was a radical and disruptive figure, challenging the nation's commitments to both unfettered capitalism and the projection of imperial power. "Had he lived," as the political columnist Gary Younge has observed, "he would most certainly have been loathed," but in the years since his assassination, King's legacy has been widely embraced by both the Left and the Right, and his "symbolic likeness . . . effortlessly incorporated into America's self-image as the land of relentless progress."[12] While in many respects King had been assimilated to this progress narrative much earlier, in 2011 the assimilation was made official in the form his own white marble monument. As with the other national monuments we have encountered thus far, the primary function of the King statue is a whitewashing that is both figurative (in terms of its strategic elisions) and literal (in the choice of white marble for the construction). As Philip Kennicott, art and architecture critic for the *Washington Post*, wrote in his review of the monument: "from beginning to end" the design and construction was "about a sanitized, feel-good fiction," one determined to render King solely "a saintly hero of civil rights," not the wide-ranging "anti-war goad to the national conscience" that he actually was, a radical critic not only of the legacy of slavery, but also of the ongoing project of American empire.[13]

King's assimilation to the monumental landscape followed on the heels of Barack Obama's considerably more ironic appropriation of King's words for his Nobel Prize acceptance speech, which offered up an apologia for ongoing US military action in the "War on Terror." Obama even suggested that his moral justification for America's perpetual state of war was somehow "mindful" of King's unequivocal assertion that "Violence never brings permanent peace," nor does it solve any "social problem: it merely creates new and more complicated ones." Obama's speech, in concert with the new white marble monument, in many respects concludes a transformation diametrically opposite to the one King had supposedly effected through his performative protest of 1963. Whereas King's appearance in Lincoln's shadow had drawn the Memorial into a narrative of black liberation and racial justice, Obama's speech and the marble monument to King replicated the process by which Lincoln had previously been co-opted as a symbol of white reconciliation and rededication to the unifying projects of imperial expansion and economic growth. Eliding King's vehement condemnation of "the racism, materialism and violence that has characterized Western civilization," Obama's speech and the marble monument effectively appropriated King's words and image for the enabling rhetoric of empire and the celebratory public historiography of American exceptionalism.[14]

While King has been thus assimilated to a narrative of progressive liberalization with respect to civil rights in the United States, that narrative has been consistently opposed by a countercurrent of African American writing in the twentieth century, one that shares with its nineteenth-century antecedents a deep skepticism of the capacity for monumental imagery to do anything but replicate and reinforce these enabling and celebratory discourses of nationalism and empire. As I have argued in the previous chapters, African American writers like Brown, Chesnutt, Douglass, and Du Bois have articulated a view of American monumental architecture, especially in its neoclassical form, as less emblematic of the principles of freedom and democracy than expressive of the ideology of white supremacy and the project of empire. This apprehension of the imperial dimensions of both American policy and its representation in public art and architecture has persisted throughout the twentieth century and into the twenty-first; and in light of this continuing apprehension, African American writers and artists have persisted in reframing monuments to American freedom and progress as signs of imperial excess and harbingers of ruin.

This kind of prophetic reframing is clearly evident in the essays Amiri Baraka (then LeRoi Jones) was writing simultaneously to King's rise to national prominence. While King's oration on the steps of the Lincoln Memorial represented for some the highest achievement to date in the ongoing progress narrative of American liberalization, Baraka rather presciently imagined—in the prophetically titled essay "The Last Days of the American Empire"—that King's successes would be ultimately put in the service of "a truly democratic defense" of the American "cancer." As if anticipating Obama's appropriation of King for a defense of the War on Terror, Baraka argued that the upshot of this assimilation would be that the "black man" would be "equally culpable for the evil done to the rest of the world" by the projection of American power.[15]

Contrary to the liberal optimism inspired and embodied by King's performance at the Lincoln Memorial, in Baraka's view the stage was set for a far more "revolutionary theatre." Countering not only the legal regimes of slavery and Jim Crow, but also the cultural white supremacy manifested in the affiliation of American culture with the Western classical tradition, Baraka suggested that this theater would be peopled no longer with "victims," but with "new kinds of heroes—not the weak Hamlets debating whether or not they are ready to die for what's on their minds, but men and women (and minds) digging out from under a thousand years of 'high art' and weak-faced dalliance." This theater—which would be the theater of history playing itself out in the streets—recognized that "AN EPIC [WAS] CRUMBLING," and would "give it the space and hugeness of its actual demise."[16] The "play" this theater would produce would "be called THE DESTRUCTION OF AMERICA"— a play that would merely affirm in dramatic style what he had described in "The Last Days of the American Empire," which immediately preceded "The Revolutionary Theatre" in the collection *Home: Social Essays* (1965). In "The Last Days" Baraka echoes the layered and transnational historical consciousness of the antebellum writings of Walker, Garnet, and Brown, as well as the more recent works of Charles Chesnutt, Claude McKay, and Richard Wright. Like these other writers, Baraka linked the United States to the larger story of imperialism since Columbus, and drew this larger history of New World empire back to its precedents in the ancient world.

In his "Blueprint for Negro Writing," Wright had encouraged black writers to draw these kinds of connections across space and time. Wright wanted to situate American racial inequity in the context of the history of capitalism and Euro-American imperialism, arguing that the black writer "must learn to view the life of a Negro living in New York's Harlem or Chicago's South Side with the consciousness that one-sixth of the earth surface belongs to the working class." This consciousness would "create in his readers' minds a relationship between a Negro woman hoeing cotton in the South and the men who loll in swivel chairs in Wall Street." Expanding this perspective in time as well as space, the revolutionary "theme" of black writing would "emerge" when its practitioners could "feel the meaning of the history of their race as though they in one life time had lived it themselves throughout all the long centuries."[17]

Similarly, Baraka invited the "black man" to consider his situation from within the perspective of his "three-hundred year residency in the West," from which the United States would appear as nothing exceptional, but rather a reiteration of both European "New World" empires and the ancient precedent of a "crumbling Rome."[18] Having evoked this traditional analogy, he concludes with a dark prophecy that recalls, quite explicitly, both William Wells Brown's lecture on Haiti—which had observed an alliance between "nature and the oppressed"—and T. Thomas Fortune's post-Reconstruction prediction of a proletarian revolution in the American South. Just as Fortune had looked to the fate of the city of Pompeii as a model for the American future, Baraka exhorted his fellow black Americans to "remember all of their lives . . . what they are witness to just by being alive and black in America," in order to assemble a body of knowledge that could be used "scientifically" to inform a revolution that would "erupt like Mt. Vesuvius."[19]

Nikki Giovanni expressed a similarly wide-ranging historical consciousness in response to the assassinations of both King and Malcolm X, which she set against a backdrop of escalating conflict in Vietnam and a longer history of American imperial activity. Following the logic both King and Baraka had previously articulated, Giovanni's poem "The Great Pax Whitie" links foreign and domestic violence as part and parcel of a history of empire, bolstered by what Alain Locke had called the "root-idea" of white supremacy.[20] Picking up the tradition that goes back at least to Phillis Wheatley's famous letter to Samson Occom in 1774, Giovanni's poem challenges both the biblical and the classical underpinnings of the American "mission."

The poem opens with a dark revision of the Gospel according to John— "In the beginning was the word / And the word was / Death / And the word was nigger / And the word was death to all niggers"—before moving on to a condensed history of the West:

> Cause they killed the Carthaginians
> in the great appian way
> And they killed the Moors
> "to civilize a nation"
> And they just killed the earth
> And blew out the sun
> In the name of a god
> Whose genesis was white
> And war wooed god
> And america was born
> Where war became peace
> And genocide patriotism
> And honor is a happy slave

Like Baraka, Giovanni analogizes the United States to imperial Rome, and the Pax Americana she describes is in fact an ongoing act of war, traceable from Vietnam, back through antebellum America to the ancient world. In opposition, Giovanni invites black readers to identify with the Carthaginians as an African people subjected to Roman belligerence. This identification recalls David Walker's similarly condensed history of white people as a history of violent territorial acquisition and economic enrichment. From this historical perspective, as Walker would put it, the "sufferings of *Carthage* and of *Hayti*" were part of the same story.[21] Walker's telling of this story exemplified the "Historiography of Decline" Wilson Jeremiah Moses has described, in that it constructed a history of black people that preceded not only the age of New World slavery but also the classical civilizations that were considered the foundations of the West, while at the same time envisioning a future in which "the wheel of events" could turn again, restoring Africa and its diasporic subjects to freedom and reducing white Western empires to ruins.[22]

Like Walker's *Appeal*, Garnet's "The Past and the Present," and Wright's "Blueprint for Negro Writing," Giovanni's poem invites readers to consider disparate spatiotemporal coordinates all at once, in order to replace the progress narrative that has predominated in the American historical imagination with a conception of time as accretive rather than linear, one that figures history, as Walter Benjamin has evocatively phrased it, as "one single catastrophe which keeps piling wreckage upon wreckage" at our feet.[23] This alternative spatiotemporal perspective allows writers like Giovanni and Baraka to draw together Cold War interventions in Vietnam and the Congo with the domestic violence of slavery and its post-Reconstruction reiterations all under the signs of "American empire" and Pax Americana.

In alignment with the tradition from Walker and Garnet to Chesnutt and McKay, Baraka and Giovanni both employ ancient examples to prophesy the eventual ruination of the American empire. Both also include explicit calls to black readers to bear witness, as Baraka puts it, to what they have learned by "being alive and black in America." This call for testimony aims not only toward the development of what the literary historian John Ernest has called a "Liberation Historiography," through which African American writers could counter the systematic erasure of black lives from public memory with an empowering history written from their perspective, but also toward the related end of portraying Western culture as fundamentally and insatiably exploitative, and therefore as unsustainable and ultimately self-destructive.[24]

While this apprehension of the unsustainability of such an exploitative economy has informed an apocalyptic strain within African American writing over the course of two American centuries, with the rise of the Cold War this apocalypticism took on a particular urgency. In "The Great Pax Whitie," Giovanni writes that "america was born" from the unholy union of atavistic "war" with "a god / Whose genesis was white." And if some early iteration of this idea of "america" can be discovered in the killing of "Carthaginians" and "Moors," it is more clearly implicated in the destructive potential of the nuclear age. At the center of Giovanni's brief history, which draws the present back into the deep past, we find a past-tense articulation of an apocalyptic future: having "killed the Moors / 'to civilize a nation,'" they went on and "killed the earth / and blew out the sun."

Baraka shared this sense that white Western culture had become an existential threat not only to blacks in the United States but to the planet as a whole, insisting that there was "no reason why we should allow the white man to destroy the world, just because he will not share it."[25] Martin Luther King Jr. expressed a similar sentiment in the 1967 speech "Beyond Vietnam." Moving seamlessly between the geopolitical conflict in Vietnam and the racial conflict at home, King discerned the root causes of both in the "triplets of racism, extreme materialism, and militarism." The United States, King suggested, faced a critical choice with respect to both of these theaters of discord, between "nonviolent coexistence or violent coannihilation," and his implication was that inaction amounted to choosing annihilation. The nation was currently on a "self-defeating path of hate"—a path that had already left history "cluttered with the wreckage of nations." King concludes "Beyond Vietnam" with a hopeful return to one of his favorite passages from scripture, as he imagines a "day, all over America and all over the world, when justice will roll down like waters, and righteousness like a mighty stream." But as opposed to the soaring incantation that ended his speech on the steps of the Lincoln Memorial, which has been remembered largely at the expense of the critique the March on Washington was intended to convey, the hopeful closing of the later speech has never been able to obscure the haunting evocation of "the wreckage of nations." And while the image of King at the memorial, merged with the abstract idealism of the dream itself, would provide the ideological content for the official monument that would eventually be erected in his name, the image with which the late King actually leaves us is of "the bleached bones and jumbled residues of numerous civilizations"—the "wreckage upon wreckage" that has continued to constitute what Garnet called "the empire of ruin."[26]

The Residue of Time

In 2014, the multimedia artist Kara Walker constructed a monumental installation from what could have been quite accurately described as "the bleached
bones and jumbled residues" of the history of slavery. Entitled *A Subtlety*—a
term referring to a type of elaborate decorative confection—the installation's
central feature was a massive sculpture of an African American woman in the
form of a sphinx, fashioned out of refined white sugar, and situated within
the ruins of the Domino Sugar Factory in Williamsburg, Brooklyn. This
arrangement of a black woman made of white sugar, set inside an abandoned
site of sugar's industrial processing, was clearly calculated to conjure up the
long history of empire and slavery that drove that commodity's production
and distribution.

In brainstorming a plan for the commissioned installation Walker began
with the viscous materiality of molasses and ended with the ominous specter
of imperial ruin. This train of thought emerged from two suggestive parame-
ters of the commission: first, the interior of the building—which Walker has
called a "cathedral to industry" and "to this one commodity"—was marked
all over with the material residue of sugar production. "There was," as Walker
said in an interview with *Art21*, "molasses on the walls, molasses on the rafters,
globs of sugar fifty feet up in the air, just left over from this refining process."[27]
The second parameter was that the building itself was scheduled for demolition not long after the closing of the installation, in order to make way for a
multi-million-dollar residential development—part of the ongoing "gentrifi-
cation" of Williamsburg. Thus the site was not only materially marked with
the black byproduct of white sugar's production, it also stood as a symbol
of the transformation of the United States from an industrial to a financial
economy, and an example of the kind of wreckage the progress of capital has
historically left in its wake.[28]

Walker has said that her work does not so much "deal with" history as it is
"subsumed . . . or consumed by" it, and her monumental installation—which
takes the form of a ruin within a ruin, a giant sphinx within the empty husk of
the industrial warehouse—reveals a layered historical vision that aligns with
many of the writers we have encountered over the course of this study. Given
this alignment, it should not be surprising that the installation's centerpiece—
though referring to a specifically American history of slavery and capital—was
modeled on an iconic figure from the ancient world. The sphinx at the center
of *A Subtlety*, which Walker dubbed "The Marvelous Sugar Baby," was a three-
dimensional rendering of one of the minstrel characters she typically figures

as black-on-white silhouettes in the iconic two-dimensional works for which she has become internationally famous.[29] While the form of the sphinx draws Walker's sculpture into alignment with a long tradition of Egyptian appropriation and allusion in African American literature and culture, Walker's choice of materials—white polystyrene blocks coated with a hardened layer of Domino white sugar—reinforces her assertion that the "Sugar Baby" must be understood not as some "Egyptophile relic," but as "someone from the New World."[30] In its layering of an ancient monumental form, a white supremacist minstrel aesthetic rooted in the American nineteenth century, and the very material substance of primitive accumulation in the economy of New World slavery, Walker's sculpture constitutes a three-dimensional rendering not only of her typical two-dimensional characters, but also of an accretive sense of historical time that opposes the linear temporality of the historiography of progress.

To step into the Domino warehouse in the summer of 2014 was to enter into this kind of alternative temporality and be confronted with layer upon layer of historical time. The building itself evoked multiple time frames: its original construction in the 1850s, as part of an emergent industrial capitalism still fueled by enslaved labor; its reconstruction in the 1880s after a fire, which resonates symbolically with post-Reconstruction reunification—after the conflagration of the war—around the twin projects of imperial expansion and economic growth; and finally the triumph of American industrialization in the twentieth century.[31]

In this last time frame both the building and the particular industrial process it contained recall a critical setting for the awakening and transformation of the unnamed protagonist of Ralph Ellison's *Invisible Man*. Like the Domino refinery, Ellison's Liberty Paint Factory is in the business of manufacturing whiteness; but while sugar refining works by removing the blackness of molasses to produce what Solomon Northup described as "sugar of the finest kind—clear, clean, and as white as snow," Liberty Paints produces white paint by assimilating blackness so thoroughly that it disappears—a process that involves the actual introduction of a black chemical that draws out and emphasizes the paint's essential whiteness.[32] And while the sugar refinery evokes the longer economic history in which it was involved, the paint factory is implicated in the framing of that economic history in public memory. Liberty Paints prides itself both on its signature product—"If It's Optic White," their slogan announces, "It's the Right White"—and its special relationship with the US government. Optic White, as the protagonist's overseer tells him, is "white as George Washington's Sunday-go-to-meetin' wig and as sound as the all-mighty dollar!" It is "paint that'll cover just about anything," and the batch the invisible narrator is working on is "heading for a national monument!"[33] Liberty Paints is the primary government contractor for the project of writing American history as white history—from the figure of George Washington himself, to the Washington Monument and others that mark the landscape of the city that bears his name.

Liberty Paints is relevant to *A Subtlety*, then, not only in its focus on whiteness, but also in its relation to national monuments, as Walker's sculpture was striking in both its whiteness and its monumental scale and features. The *Sugar Baby*, so white as to appear to have been illuminated from within, was situated between two rows of load-bearing steel columns, and critics noted the resemblance of this colonnade to the entrances to ancient temples, describing the experience of walking "toward her" as similar to "approaching the Oracle of Delphi."[34] But the monumental form of the sculpture refers back not only to its ancient origins, but to the way such ancient monuments have figured within African American literary and cultural traditions. As we saw in the previous chapter, in *The Marrow of Tradition* Charles Chesnutt conjures up a striking image of a sphinx as a transhistorical witness, gazing out from the sands of Egypt onto the recurring history of racial violence in America.[35] Similar to Chesnutt's, the sphinx in Pauline Hopkins's *Of One Blood* serves simultaneously as a guardian of an illustrious "Ethiopian" past, witness to the "suffering of our souls" in the present, and as a prophetic sign of a future reversal of fortune.[36] In his poem "The Riddle of the Sphinx," W. E. B. Du Bois imagined the sphinx in such a way as to recall the novels of Chesnutt and Hopkins and to anticipate Walker's sculpture. Du Bois figures the Egyptian monument as what Cheryl Townsend Gilkes has called "a black woman sentinel," bearing witness to both the "soul-waking cry" that emerges from "the sad, black South" and the roots of racial oppression in the "white world's vermin and filth":

> All the dirt of London
> All the scum of New York;
> Valiant spoilers of women
> And conquerors of unarmed men;
> Shameless breeders of bastards,
> Drunk with the greed of gold,
> Baiting their blood-stained hooks
> With cant for the souls of the simple;
> Bearing the white man's burden
> Of liquor and lust and lies![37]

With its condemnation of the violence of slavery and the larger contexts of imperial conquest and capital accumulation in which it is embedded, as well as its explicit reference to the city of New York, Du Bois's sphinx offers a critical vision of white history similar to that which emerges from Walker's Williamsburg installation.

The blinding whiteness of Walker's *Sugar Baby* clearly invites consideration of the white supremacy that Charles Mills has called "the unnamed political system that has made the modern world what it is today," and "The Riddle of the Sphinx" seems all the more relevant as a precedent if we note that Du Bois places it at the end of the essay entitled "The Souls of White Folk," in which he reads white supremacy as the ideological justification for empire, "whiteness" as the basis for claims to "ownership of the earth forever and ever."[38] Walker has made it explicit in interviews that she thought of the project as being "about empire" and conceived of the *Sugar Baby* as "a New World Sphinx, something that envelops the sugar empire, the slave empire"; but the project was also "about monumentality . . . and public art, the sort of structures that people visit and reflect upon the culture that produce[s] them."[39] As the "culmination" of these distinct yet related "thought processes," the sculpture challenged whiteness as a force in shaping national policy and historical events, while at the same time inviting consideration of the whiteness of the kinds of American monuments for which the invisible man toils in the New York headquarters of Liberty Paints.

Recalling her motivation for writing *Beloved*, Toni Morrison observed that there was no "suitable memorial" to enslaved people in America, "no place you or I can go, to think about or not think about, to summon the presences of, or recollect the absences of slaves; nothing that reminds us of the ones who made the journey and of those who did not make it."[40] What we have is the Lincoln Memorial—erected in gratitude "by those for whom he saved the union"—and in its size, its whiteness, and the columns with which it was surrounded, Walker's sphinx conjured that monument more than any other.[41] Walker's sculpture is gone now, as is the building in which it was housed; but when it stood, the *Sugar Baby* not only served as a site of commemoration, but also provided what Dana Luciano has described as a "*countermonumental perspective*" on the material history of slavery and empire.[42] Such a perspective, as Luciano has argued, resists the strategic "amnesia" and "redemptionist teleology" that characterizes the narrative encoded in the types of national monuments we have considered throughout this study, and counters "the monumental erasure of certain perspectives."[43]

FIGURE 5.2 Lincoln Memorial. Note the clenched left hand. Photo courtesy Tim Brown.

The countermonumental perspective is most evident in Walker's installation in its layered and accretive temporality, which conveys the "assurance," as Luciano puts it, "that past, present, and future are linked not in a single linear narrative but in an ever-evolving array."[44] But the countermonumental critique of the Lincoln Memorial is more pointedly encapsulated in the *Sugar Baby*'s hands, between which visitors lined up—much like visitors at national monuments—to have their pictures taken for widespread sharing on social media. In his own monumental form, Lincoln's left hand is clenched in a fist that is conspicuously at odds with his otherwise slouching and unaggressive pose (fig. 5.2). The *Sugar Baby*'s left hand was similarly clenched, not in a conventional fist but in the *mano fico*—or hand shaped like a fig—an obscene and variously significant gesture with a history traceable to ancient Rome (fig. 5.3).[45] We might read this gesture either as an expression of kinship with the unhappily appropriated Lincoln—a recognition that as a monument and a tourist attraction Walker's work of resistance would be subject to a similar kind of assimilation to the very structures of power it was intended to resist—or as an obscene rebuke to the whole history of classical monumentalism as embodied in the Lincoln Memorial.

In either case the fist adds an ironic dimension that draws Walker's *Sugar Baby* into alignment not only with the skeptical eye that Chesnutt's sphinx casts across the sands of Egypt, but also with the kind of "joking" Robert

FIGURE 5.3 Kara Walker, *A Subtlety*. Note the thumb protruding between the first two fingers of the left hand. Artwork copyright Kara Walker, courtesy Sikkema Jenkins & Co., New York.

Hayden describes in his own rendering of the mythic-monumental figure. Hayden's sphinx is a woman with agency and power, expressed and exerted through an endless "riddling," which it is the "fate" of men "to endure." Through this riddling, the sphinx says, it has become "your fate to live / at the mercy of my / conundrum," and "it pleasures her to hold / him captive there— / to keep him in the reach of her blood-matted paws."[46] The viewer in Hayden's poem is figured only explicitly as male, but if we read it retrospectively from the vantage point of Walker's installation, we can apprehend a dialectic in which the hegemonically empowered *white* male subject is confronted with an existential challenge from the conventionally disempowered black woman embodied by the sphinx. The quintessentially free subject is here subjected to an unrelenting interrogation that constitutes a state of captivity. Having rendered her victim captive through the endless repetition of her unanswerable riddle, the sphinx suggests that now he is prepared to "consider . . . the view from" her perspective.

To regard the world from this countermonumental point of view is to depart from the ideology of exceptionalism and its linear-progressive view of history, and to adopt an alternative understanding of historical time. From this alternative perspective, history is hardly a thing of the past, but rather, as the historian Shannon King has described it, "an uninterrupted past-present."[47] This is the historical perspective that has characterized the entire tradition we have considered in this study, from Wheatley's apprehension of a repeating middle passage, to Chesnutt's sense that antebellum slavery had re-emerged after Reconstruction, much as ancient slavery had been revived as the economic engine of New World empire. This view of history was perhaps most powerfully encapsulated in Garnet's high promontory of the present, from which he invited his audience to survey "the vast empire of ruin that is scarcely discernible through the mists of former ages."[48] And as we have seen across this literary and cultural history, sites of ruin—or images of ruin conjured up—provide the points of entry into this alternative temporality. Kara Walker's brainstorming, which led her in a direct line from molasses—the material residue of white sugar production—to the ruins of empires, affirms and extends this tradition. The *Marvelous Sugar Baby* was essentially a ruin itself—a crumbling sugar monument slated for destruction along with the abandoned refinery in which it sat—specifically fashioned after an ancient Egyptian model, and providing a portal to a past that is anything but past.

Shannon King made his assessment of historical time as past-present in the context of preliminary remarks for an open discussion with students at the College of Wooster in Ohio, the aim of which was to address the brutal and public outbreak of state-sanctioned antiblack violence that marked the summer and fall of 2014. King walked his mostly undergraduate listeners backward in time, from the 2014 killings of Eric Garner, John Crawford, Mike Brown, and Tamir Rice, to those killed by the police or vigilantes in the 1980s, when King was growing up in New York City, and back through the routine racial terrorism of Jim Crow to the original violence of slavery. King's condensed history of antiblack violence, within which he positioned himself as both witness and historiographer, recalled many of the examples we have encountered, and made the case in stark and compelling terms for the ongoing relevance of Hortense Spillers's trenchant observation that "it is as if neither time nor history, nor historiography and its topics, shows movement, as the human subject is 'murdered' over and over again."[49]

If this unabated pattern of domestic racial violence, along with the nation's ongoing commitment—Obama's Nobel speech notwithstanding—to drone attacks and other imperial interventions, offers good evidence of repetition (or at least of continuity) within the realm of history as events, the new American monument at the World Trade Center site in lower Manhattan, which opened to the public nearly simultaneously with the opening of Walker's *A Subtlety*, reaffirms a similar continuity in the realm of historical representation.[50] As I mentioned in the opening pages of this book, the National September 11 Museum—like Walker's installation in the Domino factory—incorporates contemporary ruins into its structural design and appeals to antiquity via cultural allusion, prominently featuring a quotation from Virgil's *Aeneid* to memorialize the victims of the terrorist attacks in 2001. "No day shall erase you from the memory of time," the text declares, and, taken out of context—as it was intended and as it may well be by many visitors to the museum—it is merely a fitting collective epitaph to the dead. The context, however, generates a meaning that visitors would shudder to consider, since the passage refers to Nisus and Euryalus, a pair of Trojan soldiers who are killed by the enemy after having ambushed a number of them in their sleep. It is a scene saturated with violence, as the Trojans—like the American imperialists in Du Bois's "Riddle of the Sphinx"—go about the bloody business of being "conquerers of unarmed men." This immediate context was clearly meant to be ignored, but even so, as I argued at the outset, the choice of Virgil as the source—even if only of a "high-sounding, stand-alone" statement of remembrance—indicates the persistence of a strain of American classicism that continues to commemorate and justify the American enterprise through identification with the precedent of Rome.[51] If the unfortunate excerpt from Virgil's epic of empire demonstrates the ongoing validity of Ralph Ellison's perception that classical history and literature provide the sacred texts of Western cultural rituals of power—what he called the "myth and ritual business" lying "beneath the foundations of the West"—then Kara Walker's monument across the river attests to the ongoing relevance of a critical countertradition that aims to undermine the social and political power they have been made to serve.[52]

Notes

INTRODUCTION

1. Caroline Alexander, "Out of Context," *New York Times*, 6 April 2011. http://www.nytimes.com/2011/04/07/opinion/07alexander.html. Accessed 27 November 2016.
2. David Dunlap, "A Memorial Inscription's Grim Origins," *New York Times*, 2 April 2014. http://www.nytimes.com/2014/04/03/nyregion/an-inscription-taken-out-of-poetic-context-and-placed-on-a-9-11-memorial.html. Accessed 27 November 2016.
3. Alexander, "Out of Context."
4. Alexander, "Out of Context."
5. Seth L. Schein, "'Our Debt to Greece and Rome': Canon, Class and Ideology," in *A Companion to Classical Receptions*, ed. Lorna Hardwick and Christopher Stray (Oxford: Blackwell, 2008), 75.
6. Dana Luciano, *Arranging Grief: Sacred Time and the Body in Nineteenth-Century America* (New York: New York University Press, 2007), 172. For an extensive treatment of monumental culture in the antebellum United States, see Russ Castronovo, *Fathering the Nation: American Genealogies of Slavery and Freedom* (Berkeley: University of California Press, 1995), 106–189.
7. Thomas Jefferson, "Letter to James Madison," 27 April 1809. Library of Congress. https://www.loc.gov/exhibits/jefferson/149.html. Accessed 27 November 2016.
8. The frontispiece to Emma Willard's popular *Universal History in Perspective* (1835) perfectly illustrates the perceived historical relation between the United States and ancient Rome. Here the "Republic of America" appears in the forefront of "The Temple of Time"—"a classical temple," as Thomas Allen describes it, "with columns on each side representing centuries and 'empires' mapped out on the floor." As Allen argues, "the implications of this organization are clear: America . . . figured as a unified 'Republic,' is heir to, or will actually supersede, the greatest previous 'empire,' Rome" (*A Republic in Time: Temporality and Social Imagination in Nineteenth-Century America* [Chapel Hill: University of North Carolina Press, 2008], 32–33).

9. *A Sermon, on the Present Situation of the Affairs of America and Great-Britain. Written by a Black, and Printed at the Request of Several Persons of Distinguished Characters* (Philadelphia: T. Bradford and P. Hall, 1782), 9.

10. *Sermon*, 10.

11. On the importance of Addison's *Cato*, see Fredric M. Litto, "Addison's *Cato* in the Colonies," *William & Mary Quarterly* 23.3 (1966): 431–449; Carl J. Richard, *The Founders and the Classics: Greece, Rome, and the American Enlightenment* (Cambridge, MA: Harvard University Press, 1994), 57–60; John C. Shields, *The American Aeneas: Classical Origins of the American Self* (Knoxville: University of Tennessee Press, 2001), 174–193; Eran Shalev, *Rome Reborn on Western Shores: Historical Imagination and the Creation of the American Republic* (Charlottesville: University of Virginia Press, 2009), 99–100; and Margaret Malamud, *Ancient Rome and Modern America* (Oxford: Wiley-Blackwell, 2009), 10–13.

12. Jonathan M. Sewall, "A New Epilogue to *Cato*, Spoken at a Late Performance of That Tragedy" (Portsmouth, NH: Daniel Fowle, 1778), Early American Imprints, Series 1, No. 43372.

13. *Sermon*, 8. Phillis Wheatley employs a similarly imperial rhetoric in "Liberty and Peace," her poem celebrating the American victory in the Revolutionary War. On the memory of war within African American arguments for emancipation and racial unification in the new nation, see Sarah J. Purcell, *Sealed with Blood: War, Sacrifice, and Memory in Revolutionary America* (Philadelphia: University of Pennsylvania Press, 2002), 76–77.

14. "Declaration of Independence," America's Founding Documents, National Archives. https://www.archives.gov/founding-docs/declaration-transcript. Accessed 27 November 2016.

15. *Sermon*, 9.

16. *Sermon*, 9. For more on black abolitionist writing at the time of the Revolution, see Manisha Sinha, *The Slave's Cause: A History of Abolition* (New Haven: Yale University Press, 2016), 46–47.

17. Phillis Wheatley, "Liberty and Peace," in *Complete Writings*, ed. Vincent Carretta (New York: Penguin, 2001), 101–102.

18. The usefulness of the term "black classicism" remains an open question. In *Toni Morrison and the Classical Tradition: Transforming American Culture* (Oxford: Oxford University Press, 2013), Tessa Roynon has argued that the term is "in the final analysis misleading and unhelpful," in that it "ultimately reinforce[s] the notion of a pre-existing 'classicism' that is (somehow and nonsensically) at once universal, European, and white" (185). Cognizant as I am of these potential implications, I would only suggest that recognizing the "whiteness" of a dominant "classicism" is not to acquiesce to the claims of that cultural practice to universality. With this in mind, I have retained the term as a shorthand for a set of critical practices within African American cultural production that challenge not the value

of the classics per se, but the hegemonic function of classical tradition—i.e., the ways it links the ideas of whiteness and civilization—within a dominant (and predominantly white) American culture. Put more simply, black classicism is not set against an unmarked or "universal" cultural category called "classicism," but rather against a cultural *practice* of classical appropriation that is quite clearly associated with "whiteness" as a racial category.

19. Jared Hickman has recently called Bernal "the dean of black classicism" (*Black Prometheus: Race and Radicalism in the Age of Atlantic Slavery* [New York: Oxford University Press, 2016], 18).

20. Martin Bernal, *Black Athena: The Afroasiatic Roots of Classical Civilization*, vol. 1: *The Fabrication of Ancient Greece, 1785–1985* (New Brunswick, NJ: Rutgers University Press, 1987), 1–2.

21. Daniel Orrells, Gurminder Bhambra, and Tessa Roynon, introduction to *African Athena: New Agendas*, ed. Orrells, Bhambra, and Roynon (Oxford: Oxford University Press, 2011), 8. This volume explores the "ongoing relevance of the issues" *Black Athena* raised (8).

22. Orrells, Bhambra, and Roynon, 8.

23. Henry Highland Garnet, *The Past and the Present Condition, and the Destiny, of the Colored Race: A Discourse* (Troy: J. C. Kneeland and Co., 1848), 7–8; Pauline Hopkins, *Of One Blood; or, The Hidden Self* (New York: Washington Square Press, 2004), 98–100.

24. In Rankine's view, although "European classicists of the eighteenth and nineteenth centuries were oftentimes racist . . . and the classics did at times become a way of promoting a Eurocentric worldview," Bernal overstates his case through his use of "models" (the "Aryan Model" displacing the "Ancient Model") for "viewing the reception of the classics," and in figuring "the classics" as a fixed and monolithic "Eurocentric and racist ideology" (Patrice Rankine, *Ulysses in Black: Ralph Ellison, Classicism, and African American Literature* [Madison: University of Wisconsin Press, 2006], 67).

25. Toni Morrison, "Unspeakable Things Unspoken," in *Within the Circle: An Anthology of African American Literary Criticism from the Harlem Renaissance to the Present*, ed. Angelyn Mitchell (Durham, NC: Duke University Press, 1994), 374.

26. Bernal, *Black Athena*, 2.

27. As Emily Greenwood has argued in *Afro-Greeks: Dialogues between Anglophone Caribbean Literature and Classics in the Twentieth Century* (Oxford: Oxford University Press, 2010): "European colonizers appropriated the civilizational authority of Greece and Rome, and aligned these civilizations with modern European colonialism" (3). Orrells, Bhambra, and Roynon similarly suggest that "European powers" appealed to "classical cultures" as "an alibi for their imperialist and colonialist projects" (*African Athena*, 8).

28. *Black Athena* prompted a major controversy within classical studies, spearheaded by the reactionary response of Mary Lefkowitz, who derided and condemned Bernal's

work for its affiliation with what she deemed a fallacious Afrocentrism. For the controversy, see Lefkowitz's *Not Out of Africa: How Afrocentrism Became an Excuse to Teach Myth as History* (New York: New Republic and Basic Books, 1996); Bernal's review of the book in the *Bryn Mawr Classical Review*, 5 April 1996, http://bmcr. brynmawr.edu/1996/96.04.05.html; and Lefkowitz's response to the review, *Bryn Mawr Classical Review*, 19 April 1996, http://bmcr.brynmawr.edu/1996/96.04.19. html. Accessed 21 October 2016. As Rankine has argued, whatever the flaws and merits of *Black Athena* may have been, Lefkowitz's "race-infused" rejection of "Afrocentric fantasies" inadvertently did much to prove Bernal's thesis regarding the ideological commitments of academic classicism (*Ulysses in Black*, 67, 76). In a similar vein, as Tessa Roynon has observed, Lefkowitz's suggestion that Bernal's undermining of Greek "authenticity" somehow also undermined American identity and presented "a threat to American ideals" was, at the very least, "revealing" (*Toni Morrison and the Classical Tradition: Transforming American Culture* [Oxford: Oxford University Press, 2013], 183). My purpose here is not to adjudicate any of the specific claims advanced in the *Black Athena* debate, but rather to cite it as the source of a vitalized sense, within the fields of classical receptions and African American literary studies, of ancient histories and classical cultures as sites of contestation.

29. William Cook and James Tatum, *African American Writers and Classical Tradition* (Chicago: University of Chicago Press, 2010); Rankine, *Ulysses in Black*; Tracey L. Walters, *African American Literature and Classicist Tradition: Black Women Writers from Wheatley to Morrison* (New York: Palgrave Macmillan, 2007); Michele Valerie Ronnick, "William Sanders Scarborough and the Politics of Classical Education for African Americans," in *Classical Antiquity and the Politics of America: From George Washington to George W. Bush*, ed. Michael Meckler (Waco, TX: Baylor University Press, 2006); Ronnick, ed., *The Autobiography of William Sanders Scarborough: An American Journey from Slavery to Scholarship* (Detroit: Wayne State University Press, 2005). All of these writers to some extent position "black classicism"—or what Ronnick has termed *Classica Africana*—within or as an extension of the earlier field of *Classica Americana*, "the well-researched area of the role that the classics have played in American life" (Rankine, *Ulysses in Black*, 25). Major works in that field include Meyer Reinhold, *Classica Americana: The Greek and Roman Heritage in the United States* (Detroit: Wayne State University Press, 1984); Carl J. Richard, *Founders and Classics*, and *The Golden Age of the Classics in America: Greece, Rome, and the Antebellum United States* (Cambridge, MA: Harvard University Press, 2009); Caroline Winterer, *The Culture of Classicism: Ancient Greece and Rome in American Intellectual Life, 1780–1910* (Baltimore: Johns Hopkins University Press, 2002); as well as those works already mentioned: Shields, *American Aeneas*; Shalev, *Rome Reborn*; and Malamud, *Ancient Rome*. As Tessa Roynon has observed, while the various works in *Classica Americana* (and, I would add, in *Classica Africana*) "inevitably" vary "in focus and approach, all . . . agree on the pivotal role of the classical world in the political struggles that have defined American histories and identities" (*Toni Morrison*, 8).

30. Eric Ashley Hairston, *The Ebony Column: Classics, Civilization, and the African American Reclamation of the West* (Knoxville: University of Tennessee Press, 2013). In its thorough attention to the varieties of classical education black writers attained in the nineteenth century, Hairston's book provides a valuable counterpart to Winterer's *The Culture of Classicism*, which focuses on classics within nineteenth-century university curricula and professional scholarship.

31. Hairston, *Ebony Column*, 12.

32. Kenneth W. Warren, *What Was African American Literature?* (Cambridge, MA: Harvard University Press, 2011), 10.

33. A 2011 edited collection, *Ancient Slavery and Abolition: From Hobbes to Hollywood*, has further illuminated the instrumental approach to the classics on both sides of the issue of slavery in the eighteenth- and nineteenth-century Atlantic world, demonstrating that both pro- and antislavery arguments looked to classical precedents for authorization. In that collection Sara Monoson usefully explicates the ways proslavery southerners appealed to classical models—especially Aristotle's theory of the "natural slave"—to marshal affirmative arguments for slavery as a "positive good," while Margaret Malamud details abolitionist appeals to figures of resistance from classical mythology (such as Medea) and history (such as Hannibal). See S. Sara Monoson, "Recollecting Aristotle: Pro-slavery Thought in Antebellum America and the Argument of *Politics* Book I" and Margaret Malamud, "The Auctoritas of Antiquity: Debating Slavery through Classical Exempla in the Antebellum USA," in *Ancient Slavery and Abolition: From Hobbes to Hollywood*, ed. Richard Alston, Edith Hall, and Justine McConnell (New York: Oxford University Press, 2011), 247–311.

34. Though perhaps it should go without saying, what these complicated relations to the classics also clarify is that the classical tradition is itself hardly a monolithic body of work. To take just the most salient example from this introduction, though Virgil's *Aeneid* can be closely associated with the project of empire, it is by no means an unambiguous endorsement of imperialism. As classical scholars have noted, there is a "tragic movement" to the latter part of the epic, one that has informed readings of the text as "a pessimistic, even subversive and anti-Augustan epic." See Adam Parry, "The Two Voices of Virgil's 'Aeneid,'" *Arion* 2.4 (1963), 68; and Philip Hardie, "Virgil and Tragedy," in *The Cambridge Companion to Virgil*, ed. Charles Martindale (Cambridge: Cambridge University Press, 1997), 312. Hardie argues that the tensions between the epic and tragic modes within the poem make the *Aeneid* "a problematic text" (313). My argument throughout this book pertains primarily to a critique of a mode of classical reception in the United States, not to the classical texts and artifacts themselves.

35. Roynon, *Toni Morrison*, 3.

36. Roynon, *Toni Morrison*, 1, 7. For readings of Morrison's engagement with classical myth and literature, see, for example, Rankine, *Ulysses in Black*; and Walters, *African American Literature*.

37. Roynon, *Toni Morrison*, 3.

38. See, for example, Barbara Goff, ed., *Classics and Colonialism* (London: Duckworth, 2005); Barbara Goff and Michael Simpson, *Crossroads in the Black Aegean: Oedipus, Antigone and the Dramas of the African Diaspora* (Oxford: Oxford University Press, 2007); Emily Greenwood, "Re-rooting the Classical Tradition: New Directions in Black Classicism," *Classical Receptions Journal* 1.1 (2009): 87–103; Greenwood, *Afro-Greeks*; and Justine McConnell, *Black Odysseys: The Homeric Odyssey in the African Diaspora since 1939* (Oxford: Oxford University Press, 2013). Though Roynon concentrates on a single US author, she also considers Morrison within transnational contexts, situating her work within "a tradition of diasporic classically-allusive writing," while also "emphasizing" the "diasporic" nature of "the classical tradition itself" (*Toni Morrison*, 7).

39. Susan A. Stephens and Phiroze Vasunia, introduction to *Classics and National Cultures*, ed. Stephens and Vasunia (Oxford: Oxford University Press, 2010), 2. On the classics as the basis of a "school of empire," see Greenwood, *Afro-Greeks*, 69–111.

40. Barbara Goff, introduction to *Classics and Colonialism*, ed. Goff (London: Duckworth, 2005), 8, 11.

41. Goff and Simpson, *Crossroads*, 1; Greenwood, *Afro-Greeks*, 141.

42. Goff and Simpson, *Crossroads*, 20.

43. Thomas Jefferson, "First Inaugural Address," in *The Papers of Thomas Jefferson* (Princeton, NJ: Princeton University Press, 2006), https://jeffersonpapers.princeton.edu/selected-documents/first-inaugural-address. Accessed 4 December 2016.

44. On the idea of the United States as Rome in the context of the "War on Terror," see Niall Ferguson, *Colossus: The Rise and Fall of the American Empire* (New York: Penguin, 2004).

45. Walter Benjamin, "Theses on the Philosophy of History," in *Illuminations*, trans. Harry Zohn, ed. Hannah Arendt (New York: Schocken, 1968), 257.

46. Benjamin, "Theses," 262.

47. Benjamin, "Theses," 255.

48. Garnet, *Past and Present Condition*, 5.

49. Benjamin, "Theses," 257.

50. Saidiya Hartman, *Lose Your Mother: A Journey along the Atlantic Slave Route* (New York: Farrar, Straus and Giroux, 2007), 6. As Hartman has argued, "If slavery persists in the political life of black America, it is not because of an antiquarian obsession with bygone days or the burden of a too-long memory, but because black lives are still imperiled and devalued by a racial calculus and a political arithmetic that were entrenched centuries ago" (6).

51. Warren, *African American Literature*, 84.

52. As part of his rejection of the notion of an African American literature existing prior to the Jim Crow era, Warren argues "that the mere existence of literary texts does not necessarily indicate the existence of a literature" (*African American Literature*, 6).

53. In his contribution to the *PMLA* forum ("What Is Jim Crow?," *PMLA* 128.2 [2013]: 388–390), Gene Andrew Jarrett has made the case in both directions, arguing for a view of African American literature "across a *longue durée*" (390). With respect to earlier African American writing, Jarrett aligns himself with scholars such as Hartman and Ivy Wilson in asserting a much stronger continuity, in terms of both cultural production and the conditions from which it emerges, between the antebellum period, the decades of Reconstruction and its aftermath, and the eventual rise of the era of Jim Crow. And with respect to more recent works, Jarrett joins others in the *PMLA* segment in citing Michelle Alexander's *The New Jim Crow: Mass Incarceration in the Age of Colorblindness* (New York: New Press, 2010) as evidence that just as Jim Crow represented a "second slavery," the rise of the carceral state—which is inextricably bound up with the persistence of many other indicators of political, social, and economic inequality along the lines of race—essentially constitutes a new Jim Crow. As the range of reactions within the *PMLA* forum indicates, Warren has posed an open and generative question to scholars of African American literature. In contrast to some of the more antagonistic responses, Glenda Carpio, for example, while criticizing Warren for what she takes to be a somewhat limited and reductive conception of African American *literature*, finds in Warren's book a "much-needed challenge" to certain "ahistorical" trends in African American *literary studies* ("What Does Fiction Have to Do with It?," *PMLA* 128.2 [2013]: 386–387). Similarly, Xiomara Santamarina reads Warren's book as "a salutary historicizing of the field of African American literary studies," one that "reveals the discipline's continuing investments in cultural 'blackness' as nostalgic, transhistorical, and exceptionalist" ("The Future of the Present," *PMLA* 128.2 [2013]: 398–399).

54. R. Baxter Miller, "When African American Literature Exists," *PMLA* 128.2 (2013): 392.

55. Morrison, "Unspeakable Things Unspoken," 375.

56. As John Ernest has said of David Walker's *Appeal*: that text, like others in the period, participates in a "textual struggle of and for history" (*Liberation Historiography: African American Writers and the Challenge of History, 1794–1861* [Chapel Hill: University of North Carolina Press, 2004], 48).

57. Benjamin, "Theses," 256.

58. Emily Greenwood elaborates the ways these linked processes unfolded in the anglophone Caribbean, and shows how postcolonial authors effect interruptions to these processes of imperial transmission. See Greenwood, *Afro-Greeks*, 112–185.

59. Goff and Simpson, *Crossroads*, 3.

60. Wilson, *Specters of Democracy*, 7. In *Representing the Race: A New Political History of African American Literature* (New York: New York University Press, 2011), Gene Andrew Jarrett has similarly aimed to "distinguish *formal* from *informal* types of politics," with the latter referring "to the context of cultural media, representation, and subjectivity" (25).

61. This dialectic might also be described in terms of the contestation between hegemonic and resistant cultures over what Pierre Nora has called *lieux de mémoire*. Typically translated as "sites of memory," *lieux de mémoire* could be library archives, works of national historiography, commemorative celebrations, or national monuments, but "the broad categories of the genre" might include "anything pertaining to the cult of the dead, anything relating to the patrimony, anything administering the presence of the past within the present" ("Between Memory and History: *Les Lieux de Mémoire*," *Representations* 26 [1989]: 20).

62. Henry Highland Garnet, "Address to the Slaves of the United States of America," in *Walker's Appeal, With a Brief Sketch of His Life. And Also Garnet's Address to the Slaves of the United States of America* (New York: J. H. Tobitt, 1848), 95; Garnet, *Past and Present Condition*, 5.

63. As Stephens and Vasunia have suggested, identification with classical civilization affords a sense "of historic rootedness that anchors the nation in the present and promises the people a continued and unending existence into the future" (*Classics and National Cultures*, 7).

CHAPTER 1

1. Yusef Komunyakaa, "Séance," *Callaloo* 24.4 (2001): 1061–1079. The poems were reprinted in a different sequence in *Taboo* (New York: Farrar, Straus and Giroux, 2004).

2. Henry Louis Gates, Jr., *The Trials of Phillis Wheatley: America's First Black Poet and Her Encounters with the Founding Fathers* (New York: Basic Civitas, 2003), 6.

3. See Henry Louis Gates Jr., introduction to *The Norton Anthology of African American Literature*, ed. Gates and Nellie Y. McKay (New York: Norton, 2004), xli; "Mister Jefferson and the Trials of Phillis Wheatley," Jefferson Lecture in the Humanities (2002), National Endowment for the Humanities (http://www. neh.gov/about/awards/jefferson-lecture/henry-louis-gates-jr-lecture); and *Trials of Phillis Wheatley*, 5. For refutations of Gates's story, see Phillip Richards, *Black Heart: The Moral Life of Recent African American Letters* (New York: Peter Lang, 2006), 72; Joanna Brooks, "Our Phillis, Ourselves," *American Literature* 82.1 (2010): 1–28; and David Waldstreicher, "The Wheatleyan Moment," *Early American Studies* 9.3 (2011): 529, 529–530 n. 13.

4. Waldstreicher, "The Wheatleyan Moment," 530.

5. Waldstreicher, "The Wheatleyan Moment," 531.

6. Brooks's key evidence is "a letter from the Boston merchant John Andrews to his brother-in-law William Barrell in Philadelphia dated 24 February 1773," in which he states the following: "she [Wheatley] has had a paper drawn up & signd by the Gov. Council, Ministers, & most of ye people of note in this place, certifying the authenticity of it" ("Our Phillis, Ourselves," 4–5).

7. Gates, *Trials of Phillis Wheatley*, 6.

8. Gates, *Trials of Phillis Wheatley*, 5.

9. On the role of classical tradition in the revolutionary and early national period, see Meyer Reinhold, *Classica Americana: The Greek and Roman Heritage in the United States* (Detroit: Wayne State University Press, 1984); Carl J. Richard, *The Founders and the Classics: Greece, Rome, and the American Enlightenment* (Cambridge, MA: Harvard University Press, 1994) and *The Golden Age of the Classics in America: Greece, Rome, and the Antebellum United States* (Cambridge, MA: Harvard University Press, 2009); John C. Shields, *The American Aeneas: Classical Origins of the American Self* (Knoxville: University of Tennessee Press, 2001); Caroline Winterer, *The Culture of Classicism: Ancient Greece and Rome in American Intellectual Life, 1780–1910* (Baltimore: Johns Hopkins University Press, 2002); and Eran Shalev, *Rome Reborn on Western Shores: Historical Imagination and the Creation of the American Republic* (Charlottesville: University of Virginia Press, 2009).

10. Waldstreicher, "The Wheatleyan Moment," 531.

11. For extended treatments of Wheatley's classicism, see John C. Shields, "Phillis Wheatley's Use of Classicism," *American Literature* 52.1 (1980): 97–111; Marsha Watson, "A Classic Case: Phillis Wheatley and Her Poetry," *American Literature* 31.2 (1996): 103–132; Shields, *American Aeneas*, 216–251; Tracey L. Walters, *African American Literature and the Classicist Tradition: Black Women Writers from Wheatley to Morrison* (New York: Palgrave Macmillan, 2007), 39–50; William W. Cook and James Tatum, *African American Writers and Classical Tradition* (Chicago: University of Chicago Press, 2010), 7–47; Emily Greenwood, "The Politics of Classicism in the Poetry of Phillis Wheatley," in Edith Hall, Richard Alston, and Justine McConnell, eds., *Ancient Slavery and Abolition: From Hobbes to Hollywood* (New York: Oxford University Press, 2011), 153–179; Eric Ashley Hairston, *The Ebony Column: Classics, Civilization, and the African American Reclamation of the West* (Knoxville: University of Tennessee Press, 2013), 25–63; and the entire first section of John C. Shields and Eric D. Lamore, eds., *New Essays on Phillis Wheatley* (Knoxville: University of Tennessee Press, 2011).

12. Walters, *African American Literature*, 44; Jennifer Thorn, "'All Beautiful in Woe': Gender, Nation, and Phillis Wheatley's 'Niobe,'" *Studies in Eighteenth-Century Culture* 37 (2008): 246.

13. John C. Shields, "Phillis Wheatley's Subversion of Classical Stylistics," *Style* 27.2 (Summer 1993): 252; see also Shields, *Phillis Wheatley's Poetics of Liberation: Backgrounds and Contexts* (Knoxville: University of Tennessee Press, 2008), 18–19.

14. For other readings that attend specifically to Wheatley's engagement with revolutionary political discourse, see Betsy Erkkila, *Mixed Bloods and Other Crosses: Rethinking American Literature from the Revolution to the Culture Wars* (Philadelphia: University of Pennsylvania Press, 2005), 77–88; Eric Slauter, *The State as a Work of Art: The Cultural Origins of the Constitution* (Chicago: University

of Chicago Press, 2009), 179–203; and Karen Lerner Dovell, "The Interaction of the Classical Traditions of Literature and Politics in the Work of Phillis Wheatley," in Shields and Lamore, *New Essays*, 35–55.

15. Waldstreicher, "The Wheatleyan Moment," 527.

16. For classicism in earlier "American" literature (e.g., the writings of Edward Taylor and Cotton Mather), see Shields, *American Aeneas*, 38–71.

17. Richard, *Founders and Classics*, 8.

18. Joseph Warren, "Oration, Delivered at Boston, March 5, 1772," in *Orations Delivered at the Request of the Inhabitants of the Town of Boston, to Commemorate the Evening of the Fifth of March, 1770; when a Number of Citizens Were Killed by a Party of British Troops, Quartered among Them, in a Time of Peace* (Boston: Wm. T. Clap, 1807), 14. Warren's speech was reprinted widely both before and after the Revolution. In the early republican period it was often included in edifying volumes such as Hezekiah Niles's *Principles and Acts of the Revolution in America* (Baltimore, 1822) and Noah Webster's *An American Selection of Lessons in Reading and Speaking, Calculated To Improve the Minds and Refine the Taste of Youth* (New York: George Bunce, 1794).

19. Shalev, *Rome Reborn*, 121–123.

20. Shalev, *Rome Reborn*, 131–132.

21. Bernard Bailyn, *The Ideological Origins of the American Revolution* (Cambridge, MA: Harvard University Press, 1967), 35–36.

22. Bailyn, *Ideological Origins*, 44.

23. Addison claimed that he "never in the least designed it as a party play." Though it is true, as Maynard Mack affirms in his biography of Alexander Pope, that "both parties claimed its patriotic sentiments for their own," the play leans in the Whig direction. At the time of the first performance, Pope was being careful to avoid identification with either party, as he was soliciting subscriptions for his translation of Homer's *Iliad*. When his prefatory lines were read aloud in the theater, however, Pope was indeed rather irked to find himself "hissed" by the Tories in the crowd. As George Berkeley noted, "Some parts of the prologue, which were written by Mr. Pope, a Tory and even a Papist," were "thought to savour of whiggism." See Maynard Mack, *Alexander Pope: A Life* (New York: Norton, 1985), 220–221.

24. Fredric M. Litto, "Addison's *Cato* in the Colonies," *William & Mary Quarterly* 23.3 (1966): 449.

25. Julie Ellison, *Cato's Tears and the Making of Anglo-American Emotion* (Chicago: University of Chicago Press, 1999), 68.

26. Ellison, *Cato's Tears*, 68.

27. On the importance of Addison's *Cato*, see Litto, "Addison's *Cato* in the Colonies"; Shalev, *Rome Reborn*, 99–100; Shields, *American Aeneas*, 174–193; Richard, *Founders and Classics*, 57–60. While Gates's examination may not have taken place, there is a record of an interview with Wheatley, entitled "A Conversation between a New York Gentleman & Phillis," in which the "Gentleman" asks Wheatley about

her reading. Among his questions was whether she had "ever read Cato a play," to which Wheatley responded that she had, and that she did indeed "like it very well." See Vincent Carretta, *Phillis Wheatley: Biography of a Genius in Bondage* (Athens: University of Georgia Press, 2011), 51.

28. George Berkeley, "Verses on the Prospect of Planting Arts and Learning in America," in *The Works of George Berkeley*, vol. 3 (London: Richard Priestly, 1820), 234.

29. John Adams, Letter to Nathan Webb, 12 October 1755. Papers of John Adams, vol. 1, Adams Papers Digital Editions, Massachusetts Historical Society. http://www.masshist.org/publications/apde/portia.php?id=ADMS-06-01-02-0003. Accessed 30 November 2016. On *translatio imperii* in the American context, see Shalev, *Rome Reborn*, 28–35; and Margaret Malamud, "*Translatio Imperii*: America as the New Rome c.1900," in *Classics and Imperialism in the British Empire* (Oxford: Oxford University Press, 2010), 249–283. *Translatio imperii* was generally linked to the concept of *translatio studii* or *translatio cultus*, which is to say, the transfer of knowledge or culture. This linkage provides us with the well-known correlation between knowledge and power. On these related ideas, see Shields, *American Aeneas*, 3–37; and Emily Greenwood, *Afro-Greeks: Dialogues between Anglophone Caribbean Literature and Classics in the Twentieth Century* (Oxford: Oxford University Press, 2010), 112–185. For *translatio imperii* and the important linkage (which informs most notably Joel Barlow's *Columbiad*) between the *Aeneid* and the voyages of Columbus, see Elise Bartosik-Vélez, "*Translatio Imperii*: Virgil and Peter Martyr's Columbus," *Comparative Literature Studies* 46.4 (2009): 560–566.

30. Philip Freneau, "A Poem, On the Rising Glory of America," Early Americas Digital Archive, University of Maryland. http://eada.lib.umd.edu/text-entries/a-poem-on-the-rising-glory-of-america/. Accessed 30 November 2016.

31. In opening with the declaration "I Sing," *The Columbiad* (1807) is even more self-consciously Virgilian than the original version, which had been published as *The Vision of Columbus* in 1787. *The Vision* opens as follows: "Long had the Sage, the first who dared to brave / The unknown dangers of the western wave, / Who taught mankind where future empires lay / In these fair confines of descending day . . ."

32. Jonathan M. Sewall, "A New Epilogue to *Cato*, Spoken at a Late Performance of That Tragedy" (Portsmouth, NH: Daniel Fowle, 1778), Early American Imprints, Series 1, No. 43372.

33. Thomas Jefferson, "Letter to James Madison," 27 April 1809. Founders Online. National Archives. https://founders.archives.gov/documents/Jefferson/03-01-02-0140. Accessed 1 April 2017.

34. Elizabeth Alexander, "Praise Song for the Day," Poetry Foundation. https://www.poetryfoundation.org/poems-and-poets/poems/detail/52141. Accessed 30 November 2016.

35. Phillis Wheatley, "Letter to Samson Occom," in *Complete Writings*, ed. Vincent Carretta (New York: Penguin, 2001), 153.

36. Shields, *American Aeneas*, 207.

37. Bailyn, *Ideological Origins*, 232. On the structural opposition between freedom and slavery in Anglo-American thinking, see David Brion Davis, *The Problem of Slavery in the Age of Revolution* (Ithaca, NY: Cornell University Press, 1975), 275; Edmund Morgan, *American Slavery, American Freedom: The Ordeal of Colonial Virginia* (New York: Norton, 1975), 4; John Phillip Reid, *The Concept of Liberty in the Age of the American Revolution* (Chicago: Chicago University Press, 1988), 38–54; and also François Furstenburg, "Beyond Freedom and Slavery: Autonomy, Virtue, and Resistance in Early American Political Discourse," *Journal of American History* 89.4 (March 2003): 1295–1330.

38. Bailyn, *Ideological Origins*, 235.

39. Wheatley, "Letter to Samson Occom," 153.

40. Nell Irvin Painter, *Creating Black Americans: African-American History and Its Meanings, 1619 to the Present* (Oxford: Oxford University Press, 2006), 66.

41. Peter Bestes et al., "Petition," in *Voices of a People's History of the United States*, ed. Howard Zinn and Anthony Arnove (New York: Seven Stories Press, 2004), 55.

42. Brooks, "Our Phillis, Ourselves," 8.

43. George deF. Lord, introduction to *Poems on Affairs of State: Augustan Satirical Verse, 1660–1714*, vol. 1, ed. Lord (New Haven: Yale University Press, 1963), xxvii.

44. James D. Garrison, *Dryden and the Tradition of Panegyric* (Berkeley: University of California Press, 1975), 5.

45. The phrase is from Erasmus's letter to Joannes Paludanus, orator of the University of Louvain, in which he lays out his defense of panegyric. The necessity for such a defense arose from the fact that Erasmus himself had been engaged to write a panegyric to Philip of Burgundy. See Erasmus, "Epistle 177," in *The Epistles of Erasmus*, trans. Francis Morgan Nichols, 3 vols. (London: Longmans, Green, 1901), 1:366. For an elaboration of Erasmus's theory as background for Dryden's practice, see Garrison, *Dryden*, 20–22.

46. John Dryden, "Dedication," in *The Works of Virgil: Translated into English Verse*, vol. 2 (London, 1721), 362. On Dryden's identification with Virgil, with respect to both his role under the Stuarts and his career as a translator of Virgil's works, see James Anderson Winn, *John Dryden and His World* (New Haven: Yale University Press, 1987), 487; and Paul Hammond, *Dryden and the Traces of Classical Rome* (Oxford: Oxford University Press, 1999), 218–282. Hammond writes: "For Dryden the translation of Virgil was in part the translation of his contemporary cares into an imagined world, a textual space which enabled a reappraisal of them" (231).

47. John F. Kennedy, "Poetry and Power," *Atlantic Monthly*, 1 February 1964. http://www.theatlantic.com/magazine/archive/1964/02/poetry-and-power/306325/. Accessed 30 November 2016.

48. John Dryden, "To His Sacred Majesty, a Panegyric on His Coronation," in *John Dryden: The Major Works*, ed. Keith Walker (Oxford: Oxford University Press, 2003), 17–20.

49. Wheatley, *Complete Writings*, 143.

50. Freedom is thus also linked to Aurora, a goddess who frequently appears in Wheatley's poems, and whom she seems to have linked with her memory of her mother. On Wheatley's memory of her mother, see Margaretta Odell's "Memoir of Phillis Wheatley," which prefaces an 1838 edition of Wheatley's poems: *Memoir and Poems of Phillis Wheatley, A Native African and a Slave* (Boston: Knapp, 1838), 13. See also April C. E. Langley, *The Black Aesthetic Unbound: Theorizing the Dilemma of Eighteenth-Century African American Literature* (Columbus: Ohio State University Press, 2008), 75. In classical mythology, the original golden age was presided over by Saturn, the primal father; therefore, the return of justice and the new golden age is linked imaginatively to benevolent fatherhood.

51. The lines also echo Pope's *Dunciad*, Book IV:

> *Wit* shoots in vain its momentary fires,
> The meteor drops, and in a flash expires.
> As one by one at dread Medea's strain,
> The sick'ning stars fade off th' ethereal plain. (633–636)

And a bit further down, we see both religion and morality depart the scene: "*Religion* blushing veils her sacred fires, / And unawares *Morality* expires" (649–650). Wheatley's language is similar, though she describes in her poem the *return* of what had been lost, and the "expiration" of tyranny and faction.

52. Paul Davis, "Dryden and the Invention of Augustan Culture," in *The Cambridge Companion to John Dryden*, ed. Steven Zwicker (Cambridge: Cambridge University Press, 2004), 78.

53. Winn, *John Dryden*, 390. Dryden had translated the poem earlier, probably as a compliment to Princess Anne when she was pregnant. It was published in the *Miscellany Poems* (1684) and again in *The Works of Virgil* (1697).

54. On classical typology see Shalev, *Rome Reborn*, 87–113.

55. On the language of family and loss, Peter Coviello has observed that the impending split between England and the colonies was often figured as a familial split or domestic disaster. He goes on to suggest that Jefferson and Wheatley in fact shared a sense that national cohesion could (and perhaps must) be produced around a communal "intensity of bereavement," such as Wheatley evinces in her poem to Dartmouth (464). See Coviello's "Agonizing Affection: Affect and Nation in Early America," *Early American Literature* 37.3 (2002): 439–468, as well as the introduction and conclusion to his book *Intimacy in America: Dreams of Affiliation in Antebellum Literature* (Minneapolis: University of Minnesota Press, 2005).

56. Shields, *American Aeneas*, 222–223; Walters, *African American Literature*, 44.

57. Shields, *American Aeneas*, 223.

58. For many fathers—including, quite notoriously, the Founding Father Thomas Jefferson—this was no matter of figuration or allegory, but biological fact.

59. The poet Honorée Fanonne Jeffers has aptly paraphrased Wheatley's poem to Dartmouth as a clear statement to the white men in power within the slave economy

of the North American colonies: "'You white men did this to me,' Wheatley essentially says in these two poems. 'You made me a slave when I was free.'" See Jeffers, "Phillis Wheatley's Word," *Common Place* 11.1. http://www.common-place-archives.org/vol-11/no-01/poetry/statement.shtml. Accessed 2 December 2016.

60. *Boston Gazette*, 13 July 1761.

61. Odell, "Memoir of Phillis Wheatley," 9.

62. Timothy Fitch, "Letter to Captain Peter Gwinn," 4 September 1761, Slave Trade Letters, Medford Historical Society & Museum. http://www.medfordhistorical.org/collections/slave-trade-letters/voyage-capt-peter-gwinn-senegal/. Accessed 2 December 2016.

63. For example, in a letter of 1 November 1761, Fitch discusses strategies for keeping the "cargo" healthy and dealing with the sick on board. Fitch even suggests that "Keeping thare Spirretts up & Exercise is good by all means." But later in the same letter, Fitch warns Gwinn of the downside of trafficking in healthy and spirited human beings—namely that they are likely to rebel. This fate had recently befallen one "Capt. Day," who "had Like to have been Cutt off by his Own Slaves Rising." Slave Trade Letters, Medford Historical Society & Museum. http://www.medfordhistorical.org/collections/slave-trade-letters/letter-peter-gwinn-mid-voyage/. Accessed 2 December 2016.

64. Anthony Paul Farley, "The Apogee of the Commodity," *DePaul Law Review* 53 (2003–2004): 1229–1246.

65. As Betsy Erkkila has noted: "Although Wheatley criticism has tended to divide between those who criticize her for writing wholly within white culture and those who have sought to identify an authentic black voice outside whiteness, it is important to bear in mind that it was only through her traumatic experience of the transatlantic slave trade and the institutions of slavery that Wheatley assumed an identity as 'African' and 'American'" (80). I would only extend this to suggest that Wheatley assumes these identities only insofar as they are *useful*. For more on a pragmatic theory of identity with respect to eighteenth-century Black Atlantic writers, see G. Michelle Collins-Sibley, "Who Can Speak? Authority and Authenticity in Olaudah Equiano and Phillis Wheatley," *Journal of Colonialism and Colonial History* 5.3 (2004). Project Muse. http://muse.jhu.edu/article/182590. Accessed 1 April 2017.

66. Slauter argues that Wheatley had "all but excised" her "patriotic verse" from her published volume, "in what seems to have been a conscious attempt to disconnect the fate of her poetry from the fate of the Whig campaign for political liberty." See Slauter, *State as Work of Art*, 184.

67. Wheatley, "To His Excellency General Washington," in *Complete Writings*, 88–90.

68. John Dryden, "Astraea Redux," in *Major Works*, 9–17.

69. Wheatley, "On the Death of David Wooster," in *Complete Writings*, 92–94.

70. Wheatley, "An Elegy, Sacred to the Memory of that Great Divine, the Reverend and Learned Dr. Samuel Cooper," in *Complete Writings*, 100.

71. Marc Egnal, *A Mighty Empire: The Origins of the American Revolution* (Ithaca, NY: Cornell University Press, 1988–2010), xiii, 1 *et passim*.

72. Thomas Hutchinson, *The History of the Province of Massachusetts Bay, from 1749 to 1774, Comprising a Detailed Narrative of the Origin and Early Stages of the American Revolution* (London: John Murray, 1828), 85–86; Egnal, *Mighty Empire*, 12–13.

73. It is worth noting that they also derived the names of their slaves from the classics. John Hancock, for example, owned slaves named "Hannibal" and, quite ironically, "Cato." Sven Beckert, Katherine Stevens, et al., *Harvard and Slavery: Seeking a Forgotten History* (2011), 8. The Harvard report is available online at http://www. harvardandslavery.com/wp-content/uploads/2011/11/Harvard-Slavery-Book-111110.pdf.

74. William Appleman Williams, *Empire as a Way of Life: An Essay on the Causes and Character of America's Present Predicament, Along with a Few Thoughts about an Alternative* (New York: Oxford University Press, 1980), viii.

75. Andy Doolen, *Fugitive Empire: Locating Early American Imperialism* (Minneapolis: University of Minnesota Press, 2005), xv. Egnal claims that the most common eighteenth-century meaning of "empire" was simply "a country embracing an extended area" (12).

76. Olaudah Equiano, *"The Interesting Narrative" and Other Writings*, ed. Vincent Carretta (New York: Penguin, 2003), 58.

77. Vincent Carretta, *Phillis Wheatley: Biography of a Genius in Bondage* (Athens: University of Georgia Press, 2011), 10.

78. Wheatley, "NIOBE in distress for her children slain by APOLLO, from *Ovid's* Metamorphoses, Book VI. and from a view of the Painting of Mr. *Richard Wilson*," in *Complete Writings*, 53–59.

79. Slauter, *State as Work of Art*, 202.

80. Thorn, "All Beautiful in Woe," 245–246.

81. On slave petitions as a salient context for Wheatley's "Niobe," see Slauter, *State as Work of Art*, 197–199.

82. Douglas R. Egerton, *Death or Liberty: African Americans and Revolutionary America* (Oxford: Oxford University Press, 2009), 58.

83. For the timing of the poem's composition, see Carretta, *Phillis Wheatley*, 218 n. 53.

84. Thomas Jefferson, *Notes on the State of Virginia* (Boston, 1801), 240.

85. Shalev, *Rome Reborn*, 117.

86. Katherine Clay Bassard, *Spiritual Interrogations: Culture, Gender, and Community in Early African American Women's Writing* (Princeton, NJ: Princeton University Press, 1999), 42.

87. Bassard, *Spiritual Interrogations*, 47.

88. Wheatley, "A Farewel to America," in *Complete Writings*, 62.

89. On Wheatley and the Somerset Case, see Carretta, *Phillis Wheatley*, 128, 133–136.

90. Carretta, *Phillis Wheatley*, 137.

91. Wheatley, *Complete Writings*, 41–42.

92. As both Shields and Shalev have shown, the trope of Aeneas's journey was at least as operative in the American self-conception as the biblical stories of exile and return. The "city upon a hill" John Winthrop envisioned was as much a New Rome as a New Jerusalem. Wheatley also draws here from other sources, including Ovid's account of the creation in book 1 of the *Metamorphoses*, as well as Pope's *Iliad*, which she had purchased while in England as part of an eighteen-volume set. But the situation of traveling westward to America, along with the clear parallel to Neptune subduing Eolus's winds, suggests she also has the *Aeneid* in mind. A textual echo may confirm this: she uses the phrase "finny sov'reign" to refer to what she earlier calls a "proud Courser," which paws the blue abode. She is presumably describing dolphins or whales she had actually seen from the deck of the ship, but this phrasing recalls Dryden's translation of *Aeneid* I, where Neptune "guides / His finny coursers and in triumph rides" (I.211).

93. W. E. B. Du Bois, *The Souls of Black Folk* (Chicago: McClurg, 1903), 32.

94. Wheatley, "Ocean," in *Complete Writings*, 78–80.

95. George Shelvocke, *A Voyage Round the World by Way of the Great South Sea* (London, 1726), 72–73. On Shelvocke as a source for Coleridge—and one that facilitates a reading of "Rime of the Ancient Mariner" as critical of slavery—see Patrick J. Keane, *Coleridge's Submerged Politics: The Ancient Mariner and Robinson Crusoe* (Columbia: University of Missouri Press, 1994), 149–150.

96. In his notes to the poem, Carretta suggests the name "Iscarius," as Wheatley has written it, may be a conflation of Icarus with Judas Iscariot, but it is difficult to make sense out of such a reading (*Compete Writings*, 185). From the surrounding context, it is clear that she is referring to Icarus, and the alteration is probably either a mistake or for the sake of the meter in the draft.

97. As Frances Smith Foster has observed, "in 'Ocean' Wheatley uses the occasion of the ship's captain casually killing an eagle who flew too close to reflect upon the meaning of seemingly random destruction of weaker humans and animals" ("Creative Collaboration: As African American as Sweet Potato Pie," in *Post-Bellum, Pre-Harlem: African American Literature and Culture, 1877–1919*, ed. Barbara McCaskill and Caroline Gebhard [New York: New York University Press, 2006], 24).

98. Doolen, *Fugitive Empire*, 15.

CHAPTER 2

1. Douglas Egerton, "Gabriel's Conspiracy and the Election of 1800," in *Rebels, Reformers, and Revolutionaries: Collected Essays and Second Thoughts* (New York: Routledge, 2002), 48.

2. Egerton, *Death or Liberty: African Americans and Revolutionary America* (Oxford: Oxford University Press, 2009), 279; "Gabriel's Conspiracy," 56.

3. Egerton, *Death or Liberty*, 272, 279.

4. Bernard Bailyn, *The Ideological Origins of the American Revolution* (Cambridge, MA: Harvard University Press, 1967), 44.

5. William Wells Brown, *Clotel; or, The President's Daughter: A Narrative of Slave Life in the United States* (London: Partridge & Oakey, 1853), 225. All further references to *Clotel* will be parenthetical in the main text.

6. Henry Highland Garnet, "Address to the Slaves of the United States of America," in *Walker's Appeal, With a Brief Sketch of His Life. And Also Garnet's Address to the Slaves of the United States of America* (New York: J. H. Tobitt, 1848), 92.

7. Garnet, "Address to the Slaves," 92.

8. Garnet, "Address to the Slaves," 95.

9. William Wells Brown, *Narrative of William W. Brown, an American Slave* (London: Charles Gilpin, 1849), 134.

10. *North Star*, 12 May 1848.

11. Douglass, *The Heroic Slave*, in *Autographs for Freedom* (Boston: Jewett, 1853), 175.

12. Garnet, "Address to the Slaves," 95.

13. *Freedom's Journal*, 14 September 1827.

14. *North Star*, 26 January 1849.

15. William W. Cook and James Tatum, *African American Writers and Classical Tradition* (Chicago: University of Chicago Press, 2011), 49–92. See also Eric Ashley Hairston, *The Ebony Column: Classics, Civilization, and the African American Reclamation of the West* (Knoxville: University of Tennessee Press, 2013), 86–99.

16. "Scene from the Tragedy of Cato," in *The Columbian Orator*, ed. Caleb Bingham (Baltimore: Philip H. Nicklin & Co., 1811), 265–267. The Sempronius speech is the same one cited in the revolutionary-era sermon I have referred to in the introduction, in which the author—self-identified as a "Black Whig" from South Carolina—calls on his "American" countrymen to "rise and revenge your slaughtered citizens or share their fate" (*A Sermon, On the Present Situation of the Affairs of America and Great-Britain. Written by a Black, and Printed at the Request of Several Persons of Distinguished Characters* [Philadelphia: T. Bradford and P. Hall, 1782], 10).

17. François Furstenberg, "Beyond Freedom and Slavery: Autonomy, Virtue, and Resistance in Early American Political Discourse," *Journal of American History* 89.4 (2003): 1312; *Columbian Orator*, 240–242. In the *Narrative* (Boston, 1845), Douglass relates that the "moral" he "gained from the dialogue" between master and slave "was the power of truth over the conscience of even a slaveholder" (40).

18. William S. McFeely, *Frederick Douglass* (New York: Norton, 1991), 35.

19. John Ernest, "The Reconstruction of Whiteness: William Wells Brown's *The Escape; or, A Leap for Freedom*," *PMLA* 113.5 (October 1998): 1110.

20. Glenda Carpio, *Laughing Fit to Kill: Black Humor in the Fictions of Slavery* (Oxford: Oxford University Press, 2008), 43.

21. William Wells Brown, *The Escape; or, A Leap for Freedom*, in *William Wells Brown: A Reader*, ed. Ezra Greenspan (Athens: University of Georgia Press, 2008), 248.

22. Brown, *The Escape*, 269.

23. Carpio, *Laughing Fit to Kill*, 44.

24. Brown, *The Escape*, 268.

25. Jonathan M. Sewall, "A New Epilogue to *Cato*, Spoken at a Late Performance of That Tragedy" (Portsmouth, NH: Daniel Fowle, 1778), Early American Imprints, Series 1, No. 43372.

26. Eran Shalev, *Rome Reborn on Western Shores: Historical Imagination and the Creation of the American Republic* (Charlottesville: University of Virginia Press, 2009), 40–72. The idea that England had replicated the errors of Rome while the United States would avoid them was widely held, informing major popular histories such as George Bancroft's *History of the United States* as well as Willard's history of the same title. See Thomas M. Allen, *A Republic in Time: Temporality and Social Imagination in Nineteenth-Century America* (Chapel Hill: University of North Carolina Press, 2008), 42–46.

27. Alexander Ramsey, "Speech of Mr. Ramsey, of Pennsylvania, On the Bill for the Reduction of the Tariff," *Daily National Intelligencer*, 1 September 1846. While Sewall's original is in the second person, throughout the nineteenth century the lines appeared in the first-person plural.

28. John L. O'Sullivan, "More! More! More!," *New York Morning News*, 7 February 1845; Robert D. Sampson, *John L. O'Sullivan and His Times* (Kent, OH: Kent State University Press, 2003), 201.

29. Thomas Jefferson, "Letter to James Madison," 27 April 1809, Library of Congress. http://www.loc.gov/exhibits/jefferson/149.html. Accessed 4 December 2016.

30. Thomas Jefferson, "First Inaugural Address," *The Papers of Thomas Jefferson* online (Princeton, NJ: Princeton University Press, 2006). https://jeffersonpapers.princeton.edu/selected-documents/first-inaugural-address. Accessed 4 December 2016. Interestingly, Jefferson's first draft only foresaw room enough for "the thousandth generation." He added the emphatic repetition ("the thousandth and thousandth generation") to the second draft.

31. Richard Guy Wilson, "Thomas Jefferson's Classical Architecture: An American Agenda," in *Thomas Jefferson, the Classical World, and Early America*, ed. Peter S. Onuf and Nicholas P. Cole (Charlottesville: University of Virginia Press, 2011), 102–103.

32. James H. S. McGregor, *Washington from the Ground Up* (Cambridge, MA: Harvard University Press, 2007), 38.

33. McGregor, *Washington*, 38.

34. McGregor, *Washington*, 4.

35. Lawrence J. Vale, *Architecture, Power, and National Identity* (New Haven: Yale University Press, 1992), 66.

36. Vale, *Architecture*, 10.

37. On the role of slaves in the construction of the Capitol and other major buildings in Washington, see Jesse J. Holland, *Black Men Built the Capitol: Discovering*

African-American History in and around Washington, D.C. (Guilford, CT: Globe Pequot, 2007). In 2012, Congress unveiled a marker that "commemorates" the "important role" played by "laborers, including enslaved African Americans . . . in building the Capitol." The marker can be seen in Emancipation Hall at the Capitol, or online: http://www.aoc.gov/capitol-hill/other/slave-labor-commemorative-marker. Last accessed 24 April 2015.

38. Garnet, "Address to the Slaves," 95.

39. *Weekly Advocate*, 7 January 1837.

40. Benjamin Fagan, "'Americans as They Really Are': The *Colored American* and the Illustration of National Identity," *American Periodicals* 21.2 (2011): 97.

41. *Weekly Advocate*, 14 January 1837.

42. Thomas Hamilton, *Men and Manners in America*, vol. 2 (London: Blackwood, 1833), 142–143. For Mansfield's decision, see "The Somerset Case," Howell's State Trials, vol. 20, cols. 1–6, 79–82, UK National Archives. http://www.nationalarchives.gov.uk/pathways/blackhistory/rights/transcripts/somerset_case.htm. Accessed 5 December 2016. As the art historian Kirk Savage has observed, any antebellum viewer who stood "at the Seventh Street crossing of the Mall near a well-known slave pen . . . gazing east at the domed Capitol on the hill . . . could visibly connect the private commerce in human flesh to the political bargaining in Congress that sustained the trade" (46). For Savage's analysis of the problem of slavery within the monumental landscape of Washington, see *Monument Wars: Washington D.C., the National Mall, and the Transformation of the Memorial Landscape* (Berkeley: University of California Press, 2009), 44–52.

43. *Liberator*, 5 February 1831.

44. *Liberator*, 23 April 1831.

45. *Liberator*, 30 August 1834.

46. "Speech of Solomon P. Chase," *Colored American*, 15 July 1837.

47. Solomon Northup, *Twelve Years a Slave* (London, 1853), 42–43.

48. William Wells Brown, *Narrative of William W. Brown, An American Slave, Written by Himself* (London: Charles Gilpin, 1849), 129.

49. Brown, *Narrative*, 136.

50. William Wells Brown, *A Description of William Wells Brown's Original Panoramic Views of the Scenes in the Life of an American Slave, from His Birth in Slavery to His Death, or His Escape to His First Home of Freedom on British Soil*, in *The Black Abolitionist Papers*, vol. 1: *The British Isles, 1830–1865*, ed. C. Peter Ripley (Chapel Hill: University of North Carolina Press, 1985), 191.

51. Brown, *Description*, 196.

52. Thomas Jefferson, "Letter to Benjamin Latrobe," 12 July 1812, "Founders Online," National Archives. http://founders.archives.gov/documents/Jefferson/03-05-02-0188. Accessed 9 September 2016. See also Vale, *Architecture*, 64.

53. A number of scholars have noted that this "performative" element is central to the counterhegemonic historiography in which African American writers

engaged in the nineteenth century. See, for example, John Ernest, *Liberation Historiography: African American Writers and the Challenge of History, 1794– 1861* (Chapel Hill: University of North Carolina Press, 2004); Daphne Brooks, *Bodies in Dissent: Spectacular Performances of Race and Freedom, 1850–1910* (Durham, NC: Duke University Press, 2006); and Sergio Costola, "The Limits of Representation: William Wells Brown's Panoramic Views," *Journal of American Drama* 24.2 (2012): 13–31.

54. Charles Baraw, "William Wells Brown, *Three Years in Europe*, and Fugitive Tourism," *African American Review* 44.3 (Fall 2011): 453.

55. Timothy Flint, *The History and Geography of the Mississippi Valley* (Cincinnati, 1833), 163.

56. For Banvard and the panorama form in relation to national expansion and the discourse of empire, see Thomas Ruys Smith, *River of Dreams: Imagining the Mississippi before Mark Twain* (Baton Rouge: Louisiana State University Press, 2007), 111–140.

57. Brown, *A Description*, 213.

58. Costola, "The Limits of Representation," 14. As the emphasis on "*dialectical images*" (in the original) suggests, Costola discerns similarities between Brown's "approach to history" and Walter Benjamin's historical materialism (14). For more on Benjamin, see the introduction above.

59. John L. O'Sullivan, "The Great Nation of Futurity," *United States Magazine and Democratic Review*, November 1839, 426.

60. Brown, *Narrative*, 136.

61. *Colored American*, 13 June 1837; Benjamin Fagan, *The Black Newspaper and the Chosen Nation* (Athens: University of Georgia Press, 2016), 60–61.

62. Fagan, "Americans," 105.

63. Fagan, *Black Newspaper*, 62. See also Allen, *A Republic in Time*, 48–50.

64. Fredric Jameson, *The Political Unconscious: Narrative as a Socially Symbolic Act* (Ithaca, NY: Cornell University Press, 1981), 20.

65. Karl Marx and Friedrich Engels, *The Communist Manifesto*, trans. Samuel Moore (Oxford: Oxford University Press, 2008), 3.

66. William Appleman Williams, *Empire as a Way of Life: An Essay on the Causes and Character of America's Present Predicament, along with a Few Thoughts about an Alternative* (New York: Oxford University Press, 1980).

67. A popular historical account attributing the fall of Rome specifically to slavery was George Bancroft's 1834 essay "The Decline of the Roman People," in which he claimed that slavery "had destroyed the democracy, had destroyed the aristocracy, [and] had destroyed the empire" (*Literary & Historical Miscellanies* [New York: Harper & Brothers, 1855], 317). Like the similar statements in the black press, Bancroft's essay, as Thomas Allen has suggested, "is really a warning to his fellow citizens, veiled in a Roman allegory" (*A Republic in Time*, 48).

68. "The Mutability of Human Affairs," *Freedom's Journal*, 6 April 1827.

69. "Mutability of Human Affairs."

70. Wilson Jeremiah Moses, *Afrotopia: The Roots of African American Popular History* (Cambridge: Cambridge University Press, 1998), 44–95.

71. Moses, *Afrotopia*, 6, 55–56.

72. Frankenstein's monster learns history from Volney's *Ruins*, and Volney clearly informs Melville's "Frankensteinian" allegory of slavery, "The Bell-Tower." Chesnutt lists *The Ruins* among the texts to be found in the Walden home in *The House behind the Cedars* (Boston: Houghton, Mifflin, 1901), 161.

73. C. F. Volney, *A New Translation of Volney's Ruins; or Meditations on the Revolution of Empires* (Paris: Levrault, 1802), 34–35. Both Volney and his African American readers considered Herodotus to be the classical authority on the African roots of civilization, and specifically on the racial identification of the Egyptians as black. The essay in *Freedom's Journal* cites the relevant passage from the *Histories* in making its own case for African origins: "Mankind generally allow that all nations are indebted to the Egyptians for the introduction of the arts and sciences; but they are not willing to acknowledge that the Egyptians bore any resemblance to the present race of Africans; though Herodotus, 'the father of history,' expressly declares that the 'Egyptians had black skins and frizzled hair.'" On the importance of Herodotus to "The Egyptocentric Mode" of African American historiography, see Moses, *Afrotopia*, 23–24.

74. Volney, *Ruins*, 73.

75. Volney, *Ruins*, 91.

76. Olaudah Equiano, *The Interesting Narrative of the Life of Olaudah Equiano, or Gustavus Vassa, the African*, vol. 1 (London, 1789), 79.

77. Volney, *Ruins*, ix–x.

78. "Mutability of Human Affairs," *Freedom's Journal*, 20 April 1827.

79. "On the Mutability of Human Things," *Colored American*, 25 March 1837.

80. "Catiline" was an epithet routinely applied to Calhoun by his adversaries. For slavery as "a positive good," see John C. Calhoun, "Speech on the Reception of Abolition Petitions, February, 1837," in *Speeches of John C. Calhoun* (New York: Harper & Brothers, 1843), 225.

81. Thomas R. R. Cobb, *An Historical Sketch of Slavery, from the Earliest Periods* (Philadelphia: T. & J. W. Johnson & Co., 1858), ccxxix. See also John Cairns, "The Definition of Slavery in Eighteenth-Century Thinking: Not the True Roman Slavery," in *The Legal Understanding of Slavery: From the Historical to the Contemporary*, ed. Jean Allain (Oxford: Oxford University Press, 2012), 65.

82. Thomas R. R. Cobb, *An Inquiry into the Law of Negro Slavery in the United States of America* (Philadelphia: Johnson & Co., 1858), lxi.

83. George Fitzhugh, *Sociology for the South, or The Failure of Free Society* (Richmond: A. Morris, 1854), 244. For more on proslavery classicism, see Margaret Malamud, *Ancient Rome and Modern America* (Oxford: Wiley-Blackwell, 2009), 76–89, and Carl J. Richard, *The Golden Age of the Classics in America: Greece, Rome, and*

the Antebellum United States (Cambridge, MA: Harvard University Press, 2009), 181–192.

84. On Jefferson's translation, see his letter to Volney, 17 March 1801, "Founders Online," National Archives. http://founders.archives.gov/documents/Jefferson/01-33-02-0289. Accessed 7 December 2016.

85. Thomas Jefferson, *Notes on the State of Virginia* (Philadelphia, 1788), 173. Jefferson suggested that slavery was "an unhappy influence on the manners of our people." It was "a perpetual exercise of the most boisterous passions, the most unremitting despotism on the one part, and degrading submissions on the other." This was especially bad—as Jefferson would know—for young white men growing up in such a society: "The parent storms, the child looks on, catches the lineaments of wrath, puts on the same airs in the circle of smaller slaves, gives a loose to his worst of passions, and thus nursed, educated, and daily exercised in tyranny, cannot but be stamped by it with odious peculiarities" (172–173).

86. For the basics of the "Aryan model" and its wider implications for European and American classicism and historiography, see Martin Bernal, *Black Athena: The Afroasiatic Roots of Classical Civilization*, vol. 1: *The Fabrication of Ancient Greece 1785–1985* (New Brunswick, NJ: Rutgers University Press, 1987), 1–2.

87. David Walker, *Walker's Appeal, in Four Articles; Together with a Preamble, to the Coloured Citizens of the World, but in Particular, and Very Expressly, to Those of the United States of America* (Boston, 1830), 20.

88. Walker, *Walker's Appeal*, 6–7.

89. Walker, *Walker's Appeal*, 7.

90. Henry Highland Garnet, *The Past and the Present Condition, and the Destiny, of the Colored Race: A Discourse* (Troy: J. C. Kneeland & Co., 1848), 5.

91. "The Mexican War—Its Origins Its Justice and Its Consequences," *United States Magazine and Democratic Review*, January 1848, 1.

92. John Keats, "On First Looking into Chapman's Homer," *Poetry Foundation*, http://www.poetryfoundation.org/poem/173746. As a matter of fact, Keats confused Cortés with Balboa. It remains unclear whether this was out of ignorance of history or respect for the meter of the line.

93. "The Mexican War—Its Origins, Its Justice and Its Consequences (Concluded)," *United States Magazine and Democratic Review*, February 1848, 119–120.

94. Readers of Walter Benjamin will quickly apprehend the ways in which Garnet's view anticipates Benjamin's ninth thesis in "On the Philosophy of History." Imagining "the angel of history" as hurtled by a "storm from Paradise" from the past into the future, to which his back is always turned, Benjamin suggests that "where we perceive a chain of events," this angel "sees one single catastrophe which keeps piling wreckage upon wreckage and hurls it in front of his feet. The angel would like to stay, awaken the dead, and make whole what has been smashed," but "the storm irresistibly propels him into the future to which his back is turned, while the pile of debris before him grows skyward. This storm is what we call

progress." See Benjamin, "Theses on the Philosophy of History," in *Illuminations*, trans. Harry Zohn, ed. Hannah Arendt (New York: Schocken, 1969), 257–258. On Benjamin in relation to current debates on African American literary history, see the introduction above.

95. Garnet, *Past and Present Condition*, 25.

96. Garnet, *Past and Present Condition*, 5. In his attention to what Saidiya Hartman and Tina Campt have described as the "weight of dead generations upon the present," we might read Garnet as an example of "the child of empire," who "suffers . . . greatly the knowledge that the past is not past" and "yearns . . . fervently for a future beyond empire" ("A Future Beyond Empire: An Introduction," *Small Axe* 13.1 [2009], 20).

97. On African American print culture in relation to the events of 1848, see Cody Marrs, "Frederick Douglass in 1848," *American Literature* 85.3 (September 2013): 447–473; and Fagan, *Black Newspaper*, 71–94.

98. Edward Bulwer-Lytton, *Athens: Its Rise and Fall*, vol. 1 (Paris, 1837), 97–98.

99. William Wells Brown, *St. Domingo: Its Revolutions and Its Patriots* (Boston, 1855), 32.

100. Brown, *St. Domingo*, 33.

101. Brown, *St. Domingo*, 32–33.

102. Brown, *St. Domingo*, 37.

103. On Brown and the Bunker Hill Monument, see Russ Castronovo, *Fathering the Nation: American Genealogies of Slavery and Freedom* (Berkeley: University of California Press, 1995), 170–171.

104. Brown, *Narrative*, 103.

105. William Wells Brown, *Three Years in Europe; Or, Places I Have Seen and People I Have Met* (London: Charles Gilpin, 1852), 141.

106. Brown, *Narrative*, 103.

107. As Dana Luciano has argued with respect to the works of Frederick Douglass, Frances Harper, and Herman Melville, Brown's writing about the Capitol and the Bunker Hill Monument counters both "the monumental erasure of certain perspectives on the nation" and "the public monument's refusal to concede the ambivalence of the national past" (*Arranging Grief: Sacred Time and the Body in Nineteenth-Century America* [New York: New York University Press, 2007], 171).

108. Brown, *Three Years*, 36.

109. A. Pugin and C. Heath, *Paris and Its Environs, Displayed in a Series of Two Hundred Picturesque Views* (London: Jennings & Chaplin, 1831), 33.

110. Brown, *Three Years*, 60–61.

111. Fekri A. Hassan, "Imperialist Appropriations of Egyptian Obelisks," in *Views of Ancient Egypt since Napoleon Bonaparte: Imperialism, Colonialism, and Modern Appropriations*, ed. David Jeffreys (London: University College London Press, 2003), 61.

112. Brown, *Three Years*, 61–62.

113. Ivy G. Wilson, *Specters of Democracy: Blackness and the Aesthetics of Politics in the Antebellum U.S.* (New York: Oxford University Press, 2011), 38.

114. Brown makes minor alterations to the syntax of Jefferson's original. Cf. Jefferson, *Notes*, 272.

115. Wilson, *Specters of Democracy*, 50.

116. For the original text, see Charles C. Shackford, *A Citizen's Appeal in Regard to the War with Mexico. A Lecture Delivered at Lyceum Hall, Lynn, January 16, 1848* (Boston: Andrews & Prentiss, 1848). In his typical fashion, Brown lifts the text without attribution. On Brown's appropriation of sources, see Lara Langer Cohen, "Notes from the State of Saint Domingue: The Practice of Citation in *Clotel*," in *Early African American Print Culture*, ed. Lara Langer Cohen and Jordan Alexander Stein (Philadelphia: University of Pennsylvania Press, 2012), 161–177; and Geoffrey Sanborn, *Plagiarama! William Wells Brown and the Aesthetic of Attractions* (New York: Columbia University Press, 2016).

117. Daniel Webster, "The Bunker Hill Monument," in *The Works of Daniel Webster*, vol. 1 (Boston: Little, Brown, 1853), 59.

118. Matthew 23:3.

119. Matthew 23:27.

120. For the original text, see John Relly Beard, *The Life of Toussaint L'Ouverture: The Negro Patriot of Hayti* (London: Ingram, Cooke, & Co., 1853): "The French . . . gave no attention to the religious duty of burial, so that the dead bodies became food for dogs, vultures, and crocodiles; and their bones, partly calcined by the sun, remained scattered about, as if to mark the mournful fury of servitude and lust of power" (193). As Cohen has noted, Beard's *Toussaint* "is *Clotel*'s most frequently cited text" ("Notes from Saint Domingue," 169).

121. Matthew 23:37.

122. In typical fashion, Brown drew this scene almost verbatim from an account by the Congressman Seth Gates of an actual occurrence. Gates's account was originally published in the *New York Evangelist*, 8 September 1842, but was widely reprinted. See Geoffrey Sanborn, "'People Will Pay to Hear the Drama': Plagiarism in *Clotel*," *African American Review* 45.1–2 (2012): 66; and Cohen, "Notes from Saint Domingue," 176.

123. Walker, *Walker's Appeal*, 9.

124. This is the transformation, as the legal theorist Anthony Farley has argued, of "the black" into the "apogee of the commodity." See his essay "The Apogee of the Commodity," *DePaul Law Review* 53 (2003–2004): 1229–1246.

125. *North Star*, 12 May 1848.

126. In this regard Clotel's burial site might be understood as what Luciano has called a "countermonument." As Luciano writes, "in response to the sacralizing appeal of the monumental," as well as the linear temporality of the historiography of progress encoded within it, the "untimely countermonument marks out spaces in which damaged time becomes visible" (*Arranging Grief*, 170).

127. In *Walden* (Princeton, NJ: Princeton University Press, 2004), Thoreau similarly links present construction to ancient ruins: "Nations," he observes, "are possessed with an insane ambition to perpetuate the memory of themselves by the amount of hammered stone they leave" (57).

CHAPTER 3

1. Pierre Nora, "Between Memory and History: *Les Lieux de Mémoire*," *Representations* 26 (1989): 12.
2. Ferzina Banaji, "Rethinking Memory: The Violation of a 'lieu de mémoire' in Marcel Ophuls's *Le Chagrin et la pitié*," in *Anamnesia: Private and Public Memory in Modern French Culture*, ed. Peter Collier, Anna Magdalena Elsner, and Olga Smith (Bern: Peter Lang, 2009), 132.
3. Nora, "Between Memory and History," 23.
4. In this regard, *Clotel* affirms Carla Peterson's argument that "the writing of historical fiction as artistic invention and imaginative remembrance constitutes an act of commemoration" (37). On African American commemorative practices during the "Post-Bellum, Pre-Harlem" era, see Peterson's essay "Commemorative Ceremonies and Invented Traditions: History, Memory, and Modernity in the 'New Negro' Novel of the Nadir," in *Post-bellum, Pre-Harlem: African American Literature and Culture, 1877–1919*, ed. Barbara McCaskill and Caroline Gebhard (New York: New York University Press, 2006), 34–56.
5. Pauline Hopkins, "Some Literary Workers," in *Daughter of the Revolution: The Major Nonfiction Works of Pauline E. Hopkins*, ed. Ira Dworkin (New Brunswick, NJ: Rutgers University Press, 2007), 140. For a comprehensive view of African American literature in relation to US empire during this period, see John Cullen Gruesser, *The Empire Abroad and the Empire at Home: African American Literature and the Era of Overseas Expansion* (Athens: University of Georgia Press, 2012). As Greusser notes, the period from 1890 to 1910 saw the beginnings of "an aggressive pursuit to establish a U.S. overseas empire," an agenda that coincided with the rise of Jim Crow as a legal and extralegal system (4).
6. As Dana Luciano has argued with respect to nationalist celebrations prior to the Civil War, these forms of "national-public memorial . . . sacralize foundational virtues—the freedoms of the nation, the affections of the family—to legitimate the forward movement of national history" (*Arranging Grief: Sacred Time and the Body in Nineteenth-Century America* [New York: New York University Press, 2007], 170).
7. Charles Chesnutt, *The Journals of Charles W. Chesnutt*, ed. Richard Brodhead (Durham, NC: Duke University Press, 1993), 111.
8. Chesnutt, *Journals*, 108.
9. Vivien Green Fryd, *Art and Empire: The Politics of Ethnicity in the United States Capitol, 1815–1860* (Athens: Ohio University Press, 2001), 211.

10. Jonathan M. Sewall, "A New Epilogue to *Cato*, Spoken at a Late Performance of That Tragedy" (Portsmouth, NH: Daniel Fowle, 1778), Early American Imprints, Series 1, No. 43372. Sewall's original uses the second person (i.e., "the whole boundless continent is *yours*"), but the switch to first-person plural was typical of nineteenth-century reiterations of the passage.

11. Fryd, *Art and Empire*, 142; Guy Gugliotta, *Freedom's Cap: The United States Capitol and the Coming of the Civil War* (New York: Hill and Wang, 2012), 407–408.

12. Chesnutt, *Journals*, 114.

13. Chesnutt, *Journals*, 90.

14. Chesnutt, *Journals*, 114.

15. Chesnutt, *Journals*, 114.

16. Chesnutt, *Journals*, 114.

17. Martha J. Lamb, "The Story of the Washington Centennial," *Magazine of American History* 22.1 (1889): 3, 20.

18. Charles Hedges, ed., *Speeches of Benjamin Harrison* (New York: US Book, 1892), 206–208.

19. Barry Schwartz, *George Washington: The Making of an American Symbol* (Ithaca, NY: Cornell University Press, 1987), 176–177; Robert P. Hay, "George Washington: American Moses," *American Quarterly* 21.4 (1969): 780–791.

20. On the importance of Cato to the revolutionary imagination, see Fredric M. Litto, "Addison's *Cato* in the Colonies," *William and Mary Quarterly* 23.3 (1966): 431–449; Eran Shalev, *Rome Reborn on Western Shores: Historical Imagination and the Creation of the American Republic* (Charlottesville: University of Virginia Press, 2009), 99–100; John Shields, *The American Aeneas: Classical Origins of the American Self* (Knoxville: University of Tennessee Press, 2001), 191–192; Carl J. Richard, *The Founders and the Classics: Greece, Rome, and the American Enlightenment* (Cambridge, MA: Harvard University Press, 1994), 57–60; and Gordon S. Wood, "Prologue," in *Thomas Jefferson, the Classical World, and Early America*, ed. Peter Onuf and Nicholas Cole (Charlottesville: University of Virginia Press, 2011), 11–32.

21. Schwartz, *George Washington*, 8; Schwartz, *Abraham Lincoln and the Forge of National Memory* (Chicago: University of Chicago Press, 2000), 99.

22. Benjamin Harrison, "The Inaugural Address," in *Speeches*, 195–203.

23. Ellen J. Goldner, "(Re)staging Colonial Encounters: Chesnutt's Critique of Imperialism in *The Conjure Woman*," *Studies in American Fiction* 28.1 (2000): 39–64. As Christopher Connery has pointed out, the naval review is an imperial practice that also derives from ancient Rome. The practice of staging "*naumachiae*, reenactments of naval battles and other naval scenes from history and mythology" was inaugurated "in 46 BCE" as "part of Julius Caesar's triumph in that year" (Connery, "Sea Power," *PMLA* 125.3 [2010]: 688). Queen Victoria, President Harrison's contemporary, was a great lover of such naval reviews, and had staged an impressive one only two years earlier to celebrate her own fiftieth anniversary as monarch (Connery, 690).

24. The original arch at Washington Square was a temporary plaster and wood construction, which was replaced between 1890 and 1892 with the marble arch that stands there today. See Committee on Erection of the Washington Arch, at Washington Square, *The History of the Washington Arch, in Washington Square, New York* (New York: Ford & Garnett, 1896).

25. Russ Castronovo, *Fathering the Nation: American Genealogies of Slavery and Freedom* (Berkeley: University of California Press, 1995), 109. Luciano calls this "the public monument's pedagogy of awe" (*Arranging Grief*, 174).

26. Caroline Winterer, *The Culture of Classicism: Ancient Greece and Rome in American Intellectual Life, 1780–1910* (Baltimore: Johns Hopkins University Press, 2002), 133–134.

27. Lamb, "Story of Washington Centennial," 4.

28. Chesnutt, *Journals*, 140; "The Race Problem," in *Charles W. Chesnutt: Essays & Speeches*, ed. Jospeh R. McElrath Jr., Robert C. Leitz III, and Jesse S. Crisler (Stanford, CA: Stanford University Press, 1999), 196.

29. While many scholars have written about Chesnutt's critique of slavery, the politics of race, and the failure of Reconstruction, and others have taken note of classical influences in Chesnutt's stories, the connection between Chesnutt's classics and his politics has yet to be fully explored. For readings of Chesnutt focusing on the politics of race and representation, see, for example, Eric Sundquist, *To Wake the Nations: Race in the Making of American Literature* (Cambridge, MA: Harvard University Press, 1993); Robert Nowatzki, "'Passing' in a White Genre: Charles W. Chesnutt's Negotiations of the Plantation Tradition in *The Conjure Woman*," *American Literary Realism* 27.2 (1995): 20–36; Henry Wonham, "What Is a Black Author? A Review of Recent Chesnutt Studies," *American Literary History* 18.4 (2006): 829–835; and Neill Matheson, "History and Survival: Charles Chesnutt and the Time of Conjure," *American Literary Realism* 43.1 (2010): 1–22. On Chesnutt's classicism, see Karen Magee Myers, "Mythic Patterns in Charles Waddell Chesnutt's *The Conjure Woman* and Ovid's *Metamorphoses*," *Black American Literature Forum* 13.1 (1979): 13–17; Werner Sollors, "The Goopher in Charles Chesnutt's Conjure Tales: Superstition, Ethnicity, and Modern Metamorphoses," *Letterature d'America: Rivista Trimestrale* 6 (1985): 107–129; and Erik Redling, *"Speaking of Dialect": Translating Charles W. Chesnutt's Conjure Tales into Postmodern Systems of Signification* (Würzburg: Königshausen, 2006). Sarah Wagner-McCoy has done the most so far to read Chesnutt's classicism politically, suggesting that Chesnutt draws on Virgilian georgic and pastoral and emphasizes the presence of slavery within these classical sources; in doing so, Wagner-McCoy argues, Chesnutt critiques both genres for the ways they obscure antebellum slavery and its postbellum reiterations. See her essay "Virgilian Chesnutt: Eclogues of Slavery and Georgics of Reconstruction in the *Conjure Tales*," *ELH* 80.1 (2013): 199–220.

30. Stephanie Smallwood, "Slavery's Past Lives and Afterlives," American Studies Association Annual Meeting, San Juan, Puerto Rico, 17 November 2012.

31. Henry Highland Garnet, "Address to the Slaves of the United States of America," in *Walker's Appeal, With a Brief Sketch of His Life. And Also Garnet's Address to the Slaves of the United States of America* (New York: J. H. Tobitt, 1848), 95; Matthew Frye Jacobson, "Where We Stand: US Empire at Street Level and in the Archive," *American Quarterly* 65.2 (June 2013): 265.

32. Winterer, *Culture of Classicism*, 99–102.

33. Winterer, *Culture of Classicism*, 142.

34. Michele Valerie Ronnick, "William Sanders Scarborough and the Politics of Classical Education for African Americans," in *Classical Antiquity and the Politics of America: From George Washington to George W. Bush*, ed. Michael Meckler (Waco, TX: Baylor University Press, 2006), 60; Atticus G. Haygood, "The South and the School Problem," *Harper's*, July 1889, 230.

35. Seth L. Schein, "'Our Debt to Greece and Rome': Canon, Class, and Ideology," in *A Companion to Classical Receptions*, ed. Lorna Hardwick and Christopher Stray (Oxford: Blackwell, 2011), 75.

36. George Fitzhugh, *Sociology for the South; or, The Failure of Free Society* (Richmond: A. Morris, 1854), 241–244; John C. Calhoun, "Speech on the Reception of Abolition Petitions, February, 1837," in *Speeches of John C. Calhoun* (New York: Harper & Brothers, 1843), 225; Ronnick, "William Sanders Scarborough," 61–62.

37. Chesnutt, *Journals*, 93.

38. Ralph Ellison, *Invisible Man* (New York: Vintage, 1995), 581.

39. Ronnick's introduction to Scarborough's *Autobiography* and her essay "William Sanders Scarborough and the Politics of Classical Education" provide useful social and political context for both Scarborough and Chesnutt. In 1881, Chesnutt bought a copy of Scarborough's textbook, *First Lessons in Greek*. See Joseph R. McElrath, Jr., "Charles W. Chesnutt's Library," *Analytical & Enumerative Bibliography* 8.2 (1994): 114.

40. Eric Ashley Hairston, *The Ebony Column: Classics, Civilization, and the African American Reclamation of the West* (Knoxville: University of Tennessee Press, 2013), 136–140.

41. Chesnutt, *Journals*, 139–140.

42. Christopher Francese, *Ancient Rome in So Many Words* (New York: Hippocrene, 2007), 169.

43. Acts 20:4–10; Romans 16:22–23.

44. John Edgar Wideman, "Charles Chesnutt and the WPA Narratives: The Oral and Literate Roots of Afro-American Literature," in *The Slave's Narrative*, ed. Charles T. Davis and Henry Louis Gates Jr. (New York: Oxford University Press, 1985), 68. Christopher Koy has similarly noted that "when rendered into African American vernacular," the Latin language becomes "inimitable and therefore opaque to whites" ("African American Vernacular Latin and Ovidian Figures in Charles Chesnutt's Conjure Stories," *Litteraria Pragensia* 21.41 [2011]: 55–56).

45. Wideman, "Charles Chesnutt," 59–60; Chesnutt, *Journals*, 85–93, 159; Goldner, "(Re)staging Colonial Encounters," 40.

46. W. E. B. Du Bois, *The Souls of Black Folk* (Chicago: A. C. McClurg, 1903), 7.

47. Nora, "Between Memory and History," 23.

48. Chesnutt, *Journals*, 139–140.

49. Lamb, "Story of Washington Centennial," 12.

50. Frederick Douglass, "The Need for Continuing Anti-slavery Work," in *Selected Speeches and Writings*, ed. Philip S. Foner and Yuval Taylor (Chicago: Hill, 1999), 579.

51. Chesnutt, "A Roman Antique," *Puck*, 17 July 1889, 351.

52. For Chesnutt and the plantation tradition, see Sundquist, *To Wake the Nations*; Nowatzki, "Passing"; Heather Tirado Gilligan, "Reading, Race, and Charles Chesnutt's 'Uncle Julius' Tales," *ELH* 74.1 (2007): 195–215; and Glenda Carpio, *Laughing Fit to Kill: Black Humor in the Fictions of Slavery* (New York: Oxford University Press, 2008), 29–71.

53. Thomas Nelson Page, "Marse Chan," *Century Magazine* 27.6 (April 1884): 932–942. The narrator of "Marse Chan" is Sam, "Marse Channin's body-servant," who serves his ill-fated master dutifully in the Civil War (934). Sam's dialect phrase "Dem wuz good ole times" (935) is repeated verbatim by Chesnutt's storyteller in "A Roman Antique."

54. On the *roman antique*, see E. R. Truitt, "'Trei Pöete, Sages Dotors, Qui Mout Sorent di Nigromance': Knowledge and Automata in Twelfth-Century French Literature," *Configurations* 12.2 (2004): 171–172; and Catherine Sanok, "Almoravides at Thebes: Islam and European Identity in the Roman de Thèbes," *Modern Language Quarterly* 64.3 (2003): 279, 298. Sanok's essay is especially suggestive in relation to Chesnutt and black classicism. As she argues, the writers of "*romans antiques* inaugurate the genre of romance itself . . . at least in part, to define European identity in terms of classical civilization, a myth of cultural inheritance that persists into the early modern period" (279). This is essentially what Chesnutt encounters in the American context: an imagined cultural history that excludes nonwhites. Sanok argues that the classicism of the *romans antiques* allowed a similar exclusion of Muslims from the history of the Christian West. In her view, "*romans antiques* . . . contribute to the myth that European cultural identity is an inheritance from the classical past, passed on through the linear forms of *translatio imperii* and genealogical succession" (298).

55. Rachel Adams, *Sideshow U.S.A.: Freaks and the American Cultural Imagination* (Chicago: University of Chicago Press, 2001), 11.

56. Benjamin Reiss, *The Showman and the Slave: Race, Death, and Memory in Barnum's America* (Cambridge, MA: Harvard University Press, 2001), 63.

57. Reiss, *Showman and Slave*, 220; Simeon Booker, "Ticker Tape U.S.A.," *Jet*, 21 October 1976, 10.

58. Scott E. Casper, *Sarah Johnson's Mount Vernon: The Forgotten History of an American Shrine* (New York: Hill and Wang, 2008), 7.

59. "Chips from the Cherry Tree," *Puck*, 24 April 1889, 151.

60. Henry Wonham, *Playing the Races: Ethnic Caricature and American Literary Realism* (Oxford: Oxford University Press, 2004), 156.

61. Indeed, by stipulating in his will that his slaves (except his "body-servant," William Lee) not be freed until Martha's death, Washington can be seen as divesting himself of the issue of emancipation altogether. See Henry Wiencek, *An Imperfect God: George Washington, His Slaves, and the Creation of America* (New York: Farrar, Straus and Giroux, 2003), 353–357.

62. Castronovo, *Fathering the Nation*, 47; Reiss, *Showman and Slave*, 62.

63. Chesnutt, "The Origin of the Hatchet Story," *Puck*, 24 April 1889, 132.

64. Morrison Heady, *The Farmer Boy, and How He Became Commander in Chief* (New York: Thomas Y. Crowell, 1863), 45.

65. Wiencek, *Imperfect God*, 290–310.

66. Linda Allen Bryant, a descendant of Ford, has published the family's quasi-fictional oral retelling as *I Cannot Tell a Lie: The True Story of George Washington's African American Descendants* (Lincoln, NE: iUniverse, 2001).

67. Chesnutt, "Abraham Lincoln and Frederick Douglass," in *Essays and Speeches*, 506.

68. Ellison, *Invisible Man*, 439.

69. Chesnutt, *Journals*, 92 (my translation).

70. The decapitated slave's name, Abednego, links him with the mummy, who, like the biblical Abednego, is cast into a "fiery furnace," as fuel for the Nile steamer (Dan. 3:12–30, KJV).

71. Edward L. Wilson, "Finding Pharaoh," *Century* 34.1 (1887): 4–5.

72. Scott Trafton, *Egypt Land: Race and Nineteenth-Century American Egyptomania* (Durham, NC: Duke University Press, 2004), 240.

73. Pauline Hopkins, *Of One Blood; or, The Hidden Self* (New York: Washington Square Press, 2004), 96–97.

74. Hopkins, *Of One Blood*, 163.

75. Hopkins, *Of One Blood*, 193.

76. Hopkins, *Of One Blood*, 154.

77. Alan Trachtenberg, *The Incorporation of America: Culture and Society in the Gilded Age*, 25th anniversary ed. (New York: Hill and Wang, 2007), 209.

78. Stanley Applebaum, *Spectacle in the White City: The Chicago 1893 World's Fair* (Mineola, NY: Calla Editions, 2009), 15.

79. Wister qtd. in Trachtenberg, *Incorporation of America*, 218.

80. Frederick Douglass, introduction to *The Reason Why the Colored American Is Not in the World's Columbian Exposition*, ed. Ida B. Wells (Chicago, 1893), University of Pennsylvania Digital Library. http://digital.library.upenn.edu/women/wells/exposition/exposition.html. Accessed 13 December 2016.

81. William Wells Brown, *Clotel; or, The President's Daughter* (London: Partridge & Oakey, 1853), 225.

82. T. Thomas Fortune, *Black and White: Land, Labor, and Politics in the South* (New York, 1884), 104.

83. Fortune, *Black and White*, 30.

84. Fortune, *Black and White*, 221.

85. Fortune, *Black and White*, 233. For Brown's account of the Helot rebellion in Sparta, see chapter 2.

86. C. F. Volney, *A New Translation of Volney's Ruins; or Meditations on the Revolution of Empires* (Paris: Levrault, 1802). On Volney's influence, see chapter 2.

87. For Morrison the key here is the investigation of "*motive*," which is "so seldom an element brought to bear on the history of history" ("Unspeakable Things Unspoken: The Afro-American Presence in American Literature," in *Within the Circle: An Anthology of African American Literary Criticism from the Harlem Renaissance to the Present*, ed. Angelyn Mitchell [Durham, NC: Duke University Press, 1994], 374).

CHAPTER 4

1. Charles Chesnutt, *The Marrow of Tradition* (Boston: Houghton, Mifflin, 1901), 60–62.

2. Chesnutt, *The Marrow of Tradition*, 62.

3. Henry Highland Garnet, *The Past and the Present Condition, and the Destiny, of the Colored Race: A Discourse* (Troy: J. C. Kneeland & Co., 1848), 5.

4. Marx and Engels, *The Communist Manifesto*, trans. Samuel Moore (Oxford: Oxford University Press, 2008), 3.

5. John C. Calhoun, "Speech on the Reception of Abolition Petitions, February, 1837," in *Speeches of John C. Calhoun* (New York: Harper & Brothers, 1843), 225. Calhoun also anticipates Fitzhugh's argument that slavery is an ideal form of "socialism." If there is always, as Calhoun argued, "in an advanced stage of wealth and civilization, a conflict between labor and capital," the "condition of society in the South exempts us from the disorders and dangers resulting from this conflict . . . which explains why it is that the political condition of the slaveholding States has been so much more stable and quiet than that of the North."

6. C. F. Volney, *The Ruins; or, Meditations on the Ruins of Empires* (Paris: Levrault, 1802). For Volney's influence, see Wilson Jeremiah Moses, *Afrotopia: The Roots of African American Popular History* (Cambridge: Cambridge University Press, 1998), 6, 55–56, and chapter 2.

7. Thomas Jefferson, "First Inaugural Address," *The Papers of Thomas Jefferson* online (Princeton, NJ: Princeton University Press, 2006). https://jeffersonpapers.princeton.edu/selected-documents/first-inaugural-address. Accessed 16 December 2016.

8. Frederick Douglass, "The Work of the Future," in *Frederick Douglass: Selected Speeches and Writings*, ed. Philip S. Foner and Yuval Taylor (Chicago: Lawrence Hill Books, 1999), 522–523.

9. Frederick Douglass, "The Need for Continuing Anti-slavery Work," in *Selected Speeches and Writings*, 577–580.

10. W. E. B. Du Bois, *The Souls of Black Folk* (Chicago: McClurg, 1903), 11.

11. Charles Chesnutt, "The Disenfranchisement of the Negro," in *Charles W. Chesnutt: Essays and Speeches*, ed. Jospeh R. McElrath, Jr., Robert C. Leitz III, and Jesse S. Crisler (Stanford, CA: Stanford University Press, 1999), 182.

12. As Jarrett explains it, "minstrel realism" is "a term I have coined to define a post-bellum phenomenon in which audiences regarded the romance and sentimentality of black minstrelsy (performed by blacks) as racially authentic and realistic" (*Deans and Truants: Race and Realism in African American Literature* [Philadelphia: University of Pennsylvania Press, 2006], 17).

13. William Dean Howells, "Mr. Charles W. Chesnutt's Stories," *Atlantic*, 1 May 1900; Howells, "An Exemplary Citizen," *North American Review* 173.537 (1901): 284. According to Howells, Chesnutt shared this "ability" with Booker T. Washington and Paul Laurence Dunbar, other black writers who were susceptible to being read as minstrel realism.

14. Howells, "An Exemplary Citizen," 284.

15. Chesnutt would eventually win the Spingarn Medal from the Association.

16. Charles Chesnutt, "Letter to W. E. B. Du Bois," 16 September 1924, in *An Exemplary Citizen: Letters of Charles W. Chesnutt, 1906–1932*, ed. Jesse S. Crisler, Robert C. Leitz III, and Joseph R. McElrath Jr. (Stanford, CA: Stanford University Press, 2002), 207.

17. Christopher A. Thomas, *The Lincoln Memorial and American Life* (Princeton, NJ: Princeton University Press, 2002), xxiii.

18. Thomas, *Lincoln Memorial*, xxvi, 13. Lincoln's emergence as a figure of national importance rivaling Washington's was also aided by a demographic shift. As Barry Schwartz has observed, by 1900, only "20% of Americans born before the Civil War were still living . . . and most of them regarded George Washington as the nation's treasure; few could imagine Abraham Lincoln in the same light. Their children, however, had not lived through Lincoln's war and . . . conceived of him as 'a half-mythical figure, which in the haze of historic distance, grows to more and more heroic proportions'" (*Abraham Lincoln and the Forge of National Memory* [Chicago: University of Chicago Press, 2000], 107–108).

19. Du Bois, *Souls of Black Folk*, 41–42.

20. Susan Mizruchi, *The Science of Sacrifice: American Literature and Modern Social Theory* (Princeton, NJ: Princeton University Press, 1998), 272.

21. Thomas, *Lincoln Memorial*, 18–19. The original conception for this monumental landscape—with the memorial envisioned as part of a larger redesign of the Mall—would become known as the McMillan Plan. Though the plan was not enacted per se, many of its features, including the basic geography, were retained in the final design.

22. Abraham Lincoln, "Gettysburg Address," Avalon Project: Documents in Law, History and Diplomacy, Lillian Goldman Law Library, Yale Law School. http://avalon.law.yale.edu/19th_century/gettyb.asp. Accessed 16 December 2016.

23. Thomas, *Lincoln Memorial*, 70.

24. Thomas, *Lincoln Memorial*, 70.

25. Thomas, *Lincoln Memorial*, 128.

26. The *Crisis* condemned the "shameful," "discourteous," and "abusive" treatment "of our reputable colored citizens," many of whom were forcibly relegated to the "colored" seating area ("Lincoln, Harding, James Crow and Taft," *Crisis*, July 1922, 122).

27. Robert Moton, "Draft of Speech at the Lincoln Memorial," in *The Lincoln Anthology: Great Writers on His Legacy from 1860 to Now*, ed. Harold Holzer (New York: Library of America, 2009), 433.

28. Moton, "Draft of Speech," 433.

29. Frederick Douglass, introduction to *The Reason Why the Colored American Is Not in the World's Columbian Exposition: The Afro-American's Contribution to Columbian Literature*, ed. Ida B. Wells (Chicago, 1893). University of Pennsylvania Digital Library. http://digital.library.upenn.edu/women/wells/exposition/exposition.html#I. Accessed 16 December 2016. On the "White City," see Alan Trachtenberg, *The Incorporation of America: Culture and Society in the Gilded Age*, 25th anniversary ed. (New York: Hill and Wang, 2007), 208–234.

30. This refiguration of the monument as a ruin echoes the editorial practices of the *Colored American* in the 1830s and 1840s, which invited readers to compare the ruins of ancient empires with the architecture of American buildings such as the Capitol (see chapter 2).

31. "Lincoln, Harding, James Crow and Taft," 122.

32. For more on Fortune and Hopkins, see chapter 3.

33. Volney, *Ruins*, 91.

34. William Wells Brown, *St. Domingo: Its Revolutions and Its Patriots* (Boston, 1855); Garnet's "Address to the Slaves of the United States of America," in *Walker's Appeal, With a Brief Sketch of His Life. And Also Garnet's Address to the Slaves of the United States of America* (New York: J. H. Tobitt, 1848).

35. The quote appears, among other places, in Garnet's "Address to the Slaves" (93), in Douglass's *My Bondage and My Freedom* ([New York: Miller, Orton & Mulligan, 1855], 249) and "The Heroic Slave" (in *Autographs for Freedom*, ed. Julia Griffiths [Cleveland: Jewett, Proctor, and Worthington, 1853], 225), and as the motto on the masthead of the *Mystery*, a Pittsburgh newspaper established by Martin Delany in 1843 (*Martin R. Delany: A Documentary Reader*, ed. Robert Levine [Chapel Hill: University of North Carolina Press, 2003], 27). Noting these examples as a background for Du Bois's epigraph in *The Souls of Black Folk*, Robert Gooding-Williams rightly suggests that *Childe Harold's Pilgrimage* was "a text with a notable history in black political thought" (*In the Shadow of Du Bois: Afro-Modern Political Thought in America* [Cambridge, MA: Harvard University Press, 2009], 162).

36. Charles Chesnutt, "The Marked Tree, in Two Parts—Part I," *Crisis* 29.2 (December 1924): 59. Cited hereafter in the text.

37. Volney, *Ruins*, 5.

38. Volney, *Ruins*, 5.
39. Charles Chesnutt, "The Marked Tree, In Two Parts—Part II," *Crisis* 29.3 (January 1925): 110–113. Cited hereafter in the text.
40. That it is an oak also suggests an allusion to Ovid's Medea, who avenges herself on her betrayer by murdering the children of their union. Medea specifically mentions the oak she has uprooted through her own variety of "black magic." Shakespeare took Medea's incantation as the source for Prospero's soliloquy in *The Tempest*, in which he recounts the effects of his own magical "art"—a speech that served Shakespeare (as "The Marked Tree" did Chesnutt) as a valedictory comment on his own work. Prospero, following Medea and prefiguring Phillis, has "rifted Jove's stout oak / With his own bolt" (5.150–151). As a mother mourning the loss of her own child, Phillis also resembles Niobe, another Ovidian character who was— as we have seen in the opening chapter above—the subject of a Phillis Wheatley poem in 1773. Given this connection, along with Phillis's rather conspicuous name, Chesnutt may be alluding to Wheatley herself—the "founding mother" of both black classicism and African American literature.
41. The other sources are Erasmus Darwin's *The Loves of the Plants* (1789), Pushkin's "The Upas Tree" (1828), and John Greenleaf Whittier's "The Panorama" (1856).
42. In Volney's invocation, the ruins effect a leveling of hierarchy: "confounding the dust of the king and of the slave," the "solitary ruins" announce "to man the sacred dogma of Equality" (*Ruins*, ix–x).
43. John maintains what Fredric Jameson calls the "convenient working distinction between cultural texts that are social and political and those that are not" (*The Political Unconscious: Narrative as a Socially Symbolic Act* [Ithaca, NY: Cornell University Press, 1981], 20).
44. Walter Johnson, "Possible Pasts: Some Speculations on Time, Temporality, and the History of Atlantic Slavery," *Amerikastudien / American Studies* 45.4 (2000): 498.
45. John also lists Grimm and Hoffman as possible analogues, but Aesop is most apropos, given his traditional status as a slave and ethnic outsider. On Aesop's outsider status, see Leslie Kurke, *Aesopic Conversations: Popular Tradition, Cultural Dialogue, and the Invention of Greek Prose* (Princeton, NJ: Princeton University Press, 2010), 10, 25, 40, 61, 137–138, and 396–397. On the prominence of Aesop in the specifically American context, see Caroline Winterer, *The Culture of Classicism: Ancient Greece and Rome in American Intellectual Life, 1780–1910* (Baltimore: Johns Hopkins University Press, 2002), 11, and Tessa Roynon, *Toni Morrison and the Classical Tradition: Transforming American Culture* (Oxford: Oxford University Press, 2013), 180–181.
46. Aesop, *The Fables of Aesop, with a Life of the Author* (New York: Hurd and Houghton, 1865), 1–2.
47. The Aesopic tradition is the only extended "biography of a slave to survive from the ancient world," and Aesop has been widely viewed as a "culture hero of the oppressed" (Keith Hopkins, "Novel Evidence for Roman Slavery," *Past and Present*

138 [1993]: 10; Kurke, *Aesopic Conversations*, 11). Kurke explicitly links Aesop to "folktale tricksters" (like Julius) of "many different cultures" (11).

48. Chesnutt, *Journals*, 139.

49. Further subverting the force of classical tradition as an enabler of social hierarchy, Chesnutt also noted—in a sentence linking Horace and Aesop as examples of the achievements of enslaved people in antiquity—that Horace himself "was the son of a freedman" (*Essays*, 519).

50. Volney, *Ruins*, x.

51. Herman Melville, "Benito Cereno," in *The Piazza Tales* (New York: Dix & Edwards, 1856), 267.

52. Saidiya Hartman and Tina Campt, "A Future beyond Empire: An Introduction," *Small Axe* 13 (2009): 20.

53. McKay's poem draws the imagination back specifically to Egypt through the intermediary of Percy Shelley's *Ozymandias*, in which the ruined monument to the ancient "King of Kings" has become little more than a "colossal wreck" on the "lone and level sands" that "stretch far away."

54. Anthony Farley, "The Apogee of the Commodity," *DePaul Law Review* 53.1229 (2003–2004): 1244.

55. Cecil Brown, "Interview with Toni Morrison," in *Toni Morrison: Conversations*, ed. Carolyn Denard (Oxford: University Press of Mississippi, 2008), 113.

56. Houston A. Baker Jr., *Modernism and the Harlem Renaissance* (Chicago: University of Chicago Press, 1987), 47.

57. Farley, "Apogee of the Commodity," 1229.

58. Roynon has suggested that the decaying Butler mansion may recall the Chorus in Aeschylus's *Agamemnon*: "Justice shines in sooty hovels, / loves the decent life. / From proud halls crusted with gilt by filthy hands, / she turns her yes to find the pure in spirit" (*Toni Morrison*, 146).

59. On "empire as a way of life," see William Appleman Williams, *Empire as a Way of Life: An Essay on the Causes and Character of America's Present Predicament, along with a Few Thoughts about an Alternative* (New York: Oxford University Press, 1980). See also chapter 2.

60. Erik Redling reads the story as a deconstructive uprooting of the "logocentric assumptions (e.g. racism)" that "still govern the thought of white America." The "use of explosives" works "to deconstruct [these] logocentric foundations" (*"Speaking of Dialect": Translating Charles W. Chesnutt's Conjure Tales into Postmodern Systems of Signification* [Würzburg: Konigshausen and Neumann, 2006], 57–60).

61. Alain Locke, "The Contribution of Race to Culture," in *The Works of Alain Locke*, ed. Charles Molesworth (Oxford: Oxford University Press, 2012), 295.

62. Baker, *Modernism*, 46–47.

63. Johnson, "Possible Pasts," 499.

64. Locke, "Contribution of Race," 293.

65. Garnet, *Past and Present Condition*, 5.

66. Richard Wright, "Blueprint for Negro Writing," in *The New Negro: Readings on Race, Representation, and African American Culture, 1892–1938*, ed. Henry Louis GatesJr. and Gene Andrew Jarrett (Princeton, NJ: Princeton University Press, 2007), 272.

67. Wright, "Blueprint for Negro Writing," 272.

68. Wright, "Blueprint for Negro Writing," 272.

69. Wright, "Blueprint for Negro Writing," 273.

70. In another poem, simply entitled "The Negro," Hughes echoes Chesnutt's earlier sketches, constellating American, Roman, and Egyptian slavery through the figures of George Washington, Julius Caesar, and the pyramids: "I've been a slave: / Caesar told me to keep his door-steps clean. / I brushed the boots of Washington. / I've been a worker: / Under my hand the pyramids arose" (*The Collected Works of Langston Hughes*, vol. 11: *Works for Children and Young Adults: Poetry, Fiction, and Other Writing* [Columbia: University of Missouri Press, 2003], 80). Hughes's high school Latin teacher, it is worth noting, was Chesnutt's daughter Helen. Tessa Roynon cites Hughes in relation to Morrison's "potent fusion of Israelite slaves and Pharaonic culture" in *Tar Baby*—a fusion that also has an antecedent in Chesnutt's "The Origin of the Hatchet Story." See Roynon, *Toni Morrison*, 170, and chapter 3.

71. On Ellison's conception of "antagonistic cooperation," see Jerry Gafio Watts, *Heroism and the Black Intellectual: Ralph Ellison, Politics, and Afro-American Intellectual Life* (Chapel Hill: University of North Carolina Press, 2000), 22, 56–57, 107; and Walton M. Muyumba, *The Shadow and the Act: Black Intellectual Practice, Jazz Improvisation, and Philosophical Pragmatism* (Chicago: University of Chicago Press, 2009), 56. Muyumba's reading of this Ellisonian idea makes it especially applicable to the cases of "The Marked Tree" and *Song of Solomon*. For Muyumba, "antagonistic cooperation" is not only "a theory of reader-writer relations," but also "a theorization of the 'violence' that the black novelist must act out on the American imagination, the American literary tradition, and Negro stereotypes" (56).

72. Ralph Ellison, "Letter to Albert Murray," 22 October 1955, in *Trading Twelves: The Selected Letters of Ralph Ellison and Albert Murray* (New York: Random House, 2001), 98–99.

73. Morrison, "Unspeakable Things Unspoken," 374; Chesnutt, "Literature in Its Relation to Life," *Essays and Speeches*, 114.

74. Hartman and Campt, "A Future beyond Empire," 20.

75. Chesnutt, *The Conjure Woman and Other Conjure Tales*, ed. Richard Brodhead (Durham, NC: Duke University Press, 1993), 53.

CHAPTER 5

1. Christopher Thomas, *The Lincoln Memorial and American Life* (Princeton, NJ: Princeton University Press, 2002), 158.

2. Scott Sandage, "A Marble House Divided: The Lincoln Memorial, the Civil Rights Movement, and the Politics of Memory," *Journal of American History* 80.1 (1993): 137. On *lieux de mémoire*, see Pierre Nora, "Between Memory and History: *Les Lieux de Mémoire*," *Representations* 26 (1989): 7–24.

3. On dominant and resistant sites of memory, see Nora, "Between Memory and History," 23.

4. On this practice of juxtaposition, see chapter 2.

5. James M. Whitfield, *America and Other Poems* (Buffalo: James A. Leavitt, 1853), 9.

6. Whitfield, *America and Other Poems*, 15.

7. Though he described the past as an "empire of ruin," he envisioned a future in which "truth, love, and liberty are descending the heavens, bearing the charter of man's destiny to a waiting world" (Henry Highland Garnet, *The Past and the Present Condition, and the Destiny, of the Colored Race: A Discourse* [Troy: J. C. Kneeland & Co., 1848], 5).

8. Whitfield, *America and Other Poems*, 15–16.

9. Whitfield, *America and Other Poems*, 16.

10. Sandage, "A Marble House Divided," 143.

11. Sandage, "A Marble House Divided," 160. For the text of the speech, see "'I Have a Dream,' Address Delivered at the March on Washington for Jobs and Freedom," Martin Luther King, Jr. Research and Education Institute, Stanford University. https://kinginstitute.stanford.edu/king-papers/documents/i-have-dream-address-delivered-march-washington-jobs-and-freedom. Accessed 21 December 2016.

12. Gary Younge, "America Lauds Martin Luther King, but Undermines His Legacy Every Day," *Guardian*, 31 March 2008. https://www.theguardian.com/comment-isfree/2008/mar/31/usa.race. Accessed 21 December 2016.

13. Philip Kennicott, "MLK Memorial Review: Stuck between the Conceptual and Literal," *Washington Post*, 26 August 2011. https://www.washingtonpost.com/life-style/style/mlk-memorial-review-stuck-between-the-conceptual-and-literal/2011/08/05/gIQAv38JgJ_story.html. Accessed 28 December 2016. The placement of the King Memorial on the margins of the Mall—a position that might recall the description in the *Crisis* of the segregated section at the Lincoln Memorial dedication, "nearly a block away from the memorial in the grass and weeds"—is perhaps not insignificant. For the segregation of the Lincoln Memorial dedication, see "Lincoln, Harding, James Crow and Taft," 122, and chapter 4.

14. Martin Luther King Jr., "Nonviolence: The Only Road to Freedom," *Ebony* 21.12 (October 1966): 34. In "Beyond Vietnam," a speech delivered at Riverside Church on 4 April 1967, King would call these the "giant triplets of racism, extreme materialism, and militarism." See "Beyond Vietnam," Martin Luther King, Jr. Research and Education Institute, Stanford University. https://kinginstitute.stanford.edu/king-papers/documents/beyond-vietnam. Accessed 21 December 2016.

15. Amiri Baraka, "The Last Days of the American Empire (Including Some Instructions for Black People)," in *Home: Social Essays* (1965; rpt. New York: Akashic, 2009), 226.

16. Amiri Baraka, "The Revolutionary Theatre," in *Home*, 241.

17. Richard Wright, "Blueprint for Negro Writing," in *The New Negro: Readings on Race, Representation, and African American Culture, 1892–1938*, ed. Henry Louis Gates Jr. and Gene Andrew Jarrett (Princeton, NJ: Princeton University Press, 2007), 273.

18. Baraka, "Last Days," 230, 222.

19. Baraka, "Last Days," 235.

20. Alain Locke, "The Contribution of Race to Culture," in *The Works of Alain Locke*, ed. Charles Molesworth (Oxford: Oxford University Press, 2012), 295.

21. David Walker, *Appeal to the Coloured Citizens of the World* (Boston, 1830), 23.

22. Walker, *Appeal*, 22. On the "historiography of decline," see Wilson Jeremiah Moses, *Afrotopia: The Roots of African American Popular History* (Cambridge: Cambridge University Press, 1998), 44–95, as well as chapter 2.

23. Walter Benjamin, "Theses on the Philosophy of History," in *Illuminations*, trans. Harry Zohn, ed. Hannah Arendt (New York: Schocken Books, 1968), 257. Benjamin's philosophy of history has been particularly useful to Americanist scholars working on the history of slavery and its reiterations across time. For a critical response to this use of Benjamin, see Kenneth W. Warren, *What Was African American Literature?* (Cambridge, MA: Harvard University Press, 2011).

24. John Ernest, *Liberation Historiography: African American Writers and the Challenge of History, 1794–1861* (Chapel Hill: University of North Carolina Press, 2004).

25. Baraka, "Last Days," 217.

26. King, "Beyond Vietnam"; Benjamin, "Theses," 257; Garnet, *Past and Present Condition*, 5.

27. Ian Forster, "Kara Walker: 'A Subtlety, or the Marvelous Sugar Baby,'" *Art 21*, 23 May 2014. http://www.art21.org/videos/short-kara-walker-a-subtlety-or-the-marvelous-sugar-baby. Accessed 28 December 2016.

28. Nathan Kensinger, "Artist Kara Walker Says Farewell to the Domino Sugar Refinery," *Curbed: New York*, 23 May 2014. http://ny.curbed.com/2014/5/23/10096010/artist-kara-walker-says-farewell-to-the-domino-sugar-refinery. Accessed 28 December 2016.

29. Walker established herself as major figure in the world of contemporary art with her two-dimensional, black-and-white depictions of scenes of the kind of violence—especially sexual violence—that was commonplace on the plantations of the antebellum South. Both slaves and enslavers in these scenes appear as black silhouettes on white backgrounds, and all the figures are caricatures drawing on the iconography of minstrelsy. As Carol Diehl, a critic hostile to the work, described the centerpiece of *A Subtlety*, the sphinx was a conflation of "two familiar white parodies of black women: the . . . sexually available Jezebel . . . and her opposite, the maternal, large-breasted but desexualized Mammy." For Diehl's commentary, see "Dirty Sugar: Kara Walker's Dubious Alliance with Domino," *Carol Diehl's Art Vent*, 16 June 2014. http://artvent.blogspot.com/2014/06/dirty-sugar-kara-walkers-dubious.html. Accessed 28 December 2016.

30. Forster, "Kara Walker."

31. Hallie Busta, "A Look inside the Former Domino Sugar Refinery," *Architect*, 7 July 2015. http://www.architectmagazine.com/design/exhibits-books-etc/a-look-inside-the-former-domino-sugar-refinery_0; Leigh Raford and Robin J. Hayes, "Remembering the Workers of the Domino Sugar Factory," *Atlantic*, 3 July 2014. http://www.theatlantic.com/business/archive/2014/07/remembering-the-workers-of-the-domino-sugar-factory/373930/. Both accessed 28 December 2016.

32. Solomon Northup, *Twelve Years a Slave* (London, 1853), 213.

33. Ralph Ellison, *Invisible Man* (New York: Vintage, 1995), 201–202.

34. Roberta Smith, "Sugar? Sure, but Salted with Meaning: 'A Subtlety, or the Marvelous Sugar Baby' at the Domino Plant," *New York Times*, 11 May 2014. https://www.nytimes.com/2014/05/12/arts/design/a-subtlety-or-the-marvelous-sugar-baby-at-the-domino-plant.html. Accessed 28 December 2016. Kay Larson, *"A Subtlety, or the Marvelous Sugar Baby," Curator: Museum Journal* 57.4 (October 2014): 510.

35. Charles Chesnutt, *The Marrow of Tradition* (Boston: Houghton, Mifflin, 1901), 62.

36. Pauline Hopkins, *Of One Blood; Or, the Hidden Self* (New York: Washington Square Press, 2004), 126.

37. Cheryl Townsend Gilkes, "The Margin as the Center of a Theory of History: African-American Women, Social Change, and the Sociology of W. E. B. Du Bois," in *W. E. B. Du Bois on Race and Culture: Philosophy, Politics, and Poetics* (New York: Routledge, 2013), 120; W. E. B. Du Bois, *Darkwater: Voices from within the Veil* (New York: Harcourt, Brace, and Howe, 1920), 53.

38. Charles Mills, *The Racial Contract* (Ithaca, NY: Cornell University Press, 1997), 1; Du Bois, *Darkwater*, 30.

39. Marina Galperina, "The Sphinx and Kara Walker at the Domino Sugar Factory: 'Sugar Comes and Goes, Condos Come and Go,'" *Animal New York*, 9 May 2014. http://animalnewyork.com/2014/sphinx-kara-walker-domino-sugar-factory-sugar-comes-goes-condos-come-go/. Accessed 16 October 2016.

40. "A Bench by the Road: *Beloved* by Toni Morrison," in *Toni Morrison: Conversations*, ed. Carolyn Denard (Jackson: University Press of Mississippi, 2008), 44. Morrison's claim leaves to the side, of course, the problematic Freedmen's Memorial Monument in Washington's Lincoln Park.

41. Though a full discussion of the new National Museum of African American History and Culture is beyond the scope of the present work, it is worth noting that the stated aims of the museum align with the project I describe in this chapter, which subsumes black history under the exceptionalist heading of "American" history. Most obviously, the museum claims to explore "what it means to be an American," and to demonstrate "how American values like resiliency, optimism, and spirituality are reflected in African American history and culture." See the "About the Museum" section of its website. https://nmaahc.si.edu/about/museum. Accessed 29 December 2016.

42. Dana Luciano, *Arranging Grief: Sacred Time and the Body in Nineteenth-Century America* (New York: New York University Press, 2007), 170.

43. Luciano, *Arranging Grief*, 171.

44. Luciano, *Arranging Grief*, 171.

45. Leslie Adkins and Roy A. Adkins, *Handbook to Life in Ancient Rome* (Oxford: Oxford University Press, 1998), 284.

46. Robert Hayden, "Sphinx," in *Collected Poems*, ed. Frederick Glaysher (New York: Liveright, 2013), 65.

47. Shannon King, "Public Forum on the Events in Ferguson, MO," College of Wooster (2014).

48. Garnet, *Past and Present Condition*, 5.

49. Hortense Spillers, "Mama's Baby, Papa's Maybe: An American Grammar Book," *Diacritics* 17.2 (1987): 68.

50. The sense of the present past, with respect to American state violence both foreign and domestic, becomes almost uncanny if we look back again to Du Bois's *Darkwater* (1920) from the perspective of Ferguson, Missouri, in 2014: "Conceive this nation," Du Bois wrote, with an irony unrestrained, "of all human peoples, engaged in a crusade to make the 'World Safe for Democracy'! Can you imagine the United States protesting against Turkish atrocities in Armenia, while the Turks are silent about mobs in Chicago and St. Louis?" (34). For America's drones and "dirty wars," see Jeremy Scahill, *Dirty Wars: The World Is a Battlefield* (New York: Nation Books, 2013).

51. On the issues with the inscription, see Caroline Alexander, "Out of Context," *New York Times*, 6 April 2011. http://www.nytimes.com/2011/04/07/opinion/07alexander.html; and David W. Dunlap, "A Memorial Inscription's Grim Origins," *New York Times*, 2 April 2014. http://www.nytimes.com/2014/04/03/nyregion/an-inscription-taken-out-of-poetic-context-and-placed-on-a-9-11-memorial.html. Both accessed 16 October 2016.

52. Ralph Ellison, "Letter to Albert Murray," 22 October 1955, in *Trading Twelves: The Selected Letters of Ralph Ellison and Albert Murray* (New York: Random House, 2001), 98–99.

Index